RED
WINE

Also by Kevin Zraly

Kevin Zraly Windows on the World Complete Wine Course

Also by Mike De Simone and Jeff Jenssen

Wines of California: Special Deluxe Edition

Wines of the Southern Hemisphere: The Complete Guide

RED WINE

THE COMPREHENSIVE GUIDE TO THE 50 ESSENTIAL VARIETIES & STYLES

Kevin Zraly, Mike DeSimone & Jeff Jenssen

STERLING EPICURE
New York

STERLING EPICURE
New York

An Imprint of Sterling Publishing Co., Inc.
1166 Avenue of the Americas
New York, NY 10036

ISBN 978-1-4549-1823-3

Distributed in Canada by Sterling Publishing Co., Inc.
c/o Canadian Manda Group, 664 Annette Street
Toronto, Ontario, M6S 2C8, Canada
Distributed in the United Kingdom by GMC Distribution Services
Castle Place, 166 High Street, Lewes, East Sussex, BN7 1XU, United Kingdom
Distributed in Australia by NewSouth Books
45 Beach Street, Coogee, NSW 2034, Australia

For information about custom editions, special sales, and premium and corporate purchases,
please contact Sterling Special Sales at 800-805-5489 or specialsales@sterlingpublishing.com.

Manufactured in China

2 4 6 8 10 9 7 5 3 1

sterlingpublishing.com

Design by Christine Heun

A complete list of image credits appears on page 255.

NEXT PAGES Zena Crown Vineyard in Willamette Valley in Oregon.

To our friends in the world of wine and
to red wine drinkers around the world.
May your glass always be full
and your cellar never be empty.

Contents

Introduction

INTENSE, EARTHY, VOLUPTUOUS, SILKY—these are a few of the many words that describe the color, aroma, taste, and texture of red wine, one of the world's most fascinating beverages. Numerous nations advance competing claims about where exactly wine was made first, but archaeological and written evidence points to the Middle East, eastern Asia, and the Mediterranean basin. Archaeologists have discovered stone crush pads, fossilized grape seeds, and potsherds that highlight the importance of wine at religious festivals and at the tables of both royals and commoners.

Sarcophagi decorated with images of wine pitchers and drinking vessels bear witness that people have been making wine in what we know today as the nation of Georgia for at least 7,000 years. The ancient world, notably Sumeria and Egypt, ascribed medicinal properties to red wine, which the modern world happily has confirmed. Wine makes many appearances in the poetry of the ancient world, from the Minoans and Phoenicians through the Greeks and Romans and in the religious texts of Jews and Christians.

Fossilized grape seeds found in Macedonia carbon-date to 4000 BC, when clay amphorae filled with wine sailed the Mediterranean. Winemaking in Cyprus dates back at least 5,000 years, as recorded by ancient Babylonian writers, Greek poets, and the Hebrew Bible. Winemaking in ancient Thrace reaches back to the Cult of Dionysus, in which people made black wine from wild grapes, sweetened it with honey, then diluted it with water. Archaeological evidence unearthed from that period shows that 90 percent of the drinking vessels bore wine. Other relevant finds include coins, figures, and effigies featuring images of grapes and Dionysus. Evidence also shows ancient winemaking on Crete and other Greek islands as well as in Moldova, Turkey, Armenia, Lebanon, Israel, China, and elsewhere.

The "wine-dark sea" in both *The Iliad* and *The Odyssey* conjures depth and complexity. A Cypriot chalice from the sixth century BC has an inscription that reads "Be happy, and drink well." Centuries later Virgil, Horace, and Pliny also evocatively describe wine, and they weren't referring to Riesling. In the time of the Roman Empire, people drank red wines that likely gave rise, down the ages, to Pinot Noir, Syrah, and other grapes grown and made into wine around the world today. At the Last Supper, the cup of Jesus contained red wine.

Regardless of which country or civilization did it first, ancient winemaking was a relatively simple process with minimal intervention. Farmers grew grapes, which they harvested, crushed, and fermented with the naturally occurring yeast on the grapeskins. The resulting wine, stored in clay vessels, usually was mixed with water when served.

Winemaking in the Middle Ages centered around European kingdoms, where the same basic process continued. Priests and monks made it for religious purposes, with the Benedictine and Cistercian orders among the largest producers in France and Germany. Around this time, winemakers noticed differences in wines made from grapes grown in different areas or soils, and the process of charting and naming vineyard blocks began. Wine slowly began to take on a more important cultural status. Da Vinci, Michelangelo, and other artists depicted red wine in their masterpieces. Napoléon Bonaparte drank the red wines of Burgundy during his military campaigns, and while in exile he almost exclusively drank wine from Bordeaux, another famed red wine region.

Grape growing and winemaking moved from Europe to the New World in a variety of ways, much of it tied directly or indirectly to the Catholic Church. In South America and New Zealand, missionaries planted the earliest grapes for both sacramental and table wine, while in South Africa and Australia persecuted Protestants played an important role in the development of a viable winemaking industry. Winemaking in California began in the eighteenth century as missionaries moved north from Chile, Argentina, and Mexico.

The past forty years have seen many changes in how the world enjoys wine, especially as it has become a commodity on the global market. Because reds age longer than whites, the world's most valuable wines are red. Consumers have many more choices now than just a few decades ago, and winemakers the world over have learned different techniques and styles by traveling to the opposite hemisphere—Northern to Southern and vice versa—and working an off-season harvest with their geographic counterparts.

OPPOSITE *Bacchus* by Caravaggio, c. 1595.

Today countless articles and news pieces extol the cardio-vascular benefits of the antioxidants in red wine. Winemaking itself also relies on rigorous science, including weather stations, soil analysis, DNA testing, temperature-controlled fermentation, and on-site laboratories. Yet with all the technology available to agronomists and oenologists, winemaking remains an art. The many decisions about when to pick the grapes, which yeast to use, and which barrels or tanks to use for blending involve instinct, skill, and the basic senses of smell and taste. Above all, it's important to remember that wine—from vines growing in a field to the liquid in the glass you bring to your lips—is a kind of living organism.

In this book, we have decided to tell the stories of the red grapes themselves. Hundreds of varieties become wine, but we have chosen the fifty essential varieties, styles, and blends that you're most likely to encounter. You might think we've gone overboard, or you might wonder why your favorite obscure variety didn't make the cut. We've tried to strike a considered balance. You'll find the most widely known varieties, such as Cabernet Sauvignon and Pinot Noir—both natives of France but now grown all over the world—as well as lesser-known grapes, such as Mavrud and Plavac Mali. The latter two haven't traveled much beyond their native Bulgaria and Croatia as far as plantings go, but many sommeliers are fascinated with these "new" varieties and want to share them. We want to share them with you as well because the broad availability of wine by the glass allows you to experiment and find new palate pleasers, such as these, with every trip to the wine bar or tasting room.

Reading about wine is infinitely less enjoyable than drinking it, but as your knowledge of wine expands, your appreciation for what's in your glass will increase. You could read this book

beginning to end, like any other work of nonfiction, but you wouldn't open all your bottles of wine at once and taste all of them in a single sitting, would you? No, we suggest instead that you dip into and out of this volume, reading about particular grapes and blends both before and after enjoying them in order to put what you're tasting in context. You'll notice subtleties and complexities, such as how the same grape exhibits different tastes depending on where it grew and variations in terroir, climate, winemaking style, and aging. You also can use this book to plan a tasting party. Invite friends to gather for, say, a Pinot Noir party featuring wines from five different countries. Then compare and contrast how they taste. Or try several different wines from the same region. For instance, you can try Syrah and Grenache blends from the Rhône Valley in the same sitting.

We've included a checklist at the back of the book so you can keep track of the many wines you experience, hopefully with a deeper enjoyment after reading about them here. But, again, dip in and out, take your time, enjoy the adventure. Consider this a field guide, and use it as you would a travel guide to a new city: You don't have to try everything, just what appeals to you. Some of us prefer long-aged Cabernet Sauvignon, while others enjoy young Sangiovese. If something catches your eye, go for it. At a wine bar, if you try something new that you don't like, then that lesson cost you only a few dollars. If you do like it, though, you've just opened a new door in the palace of wine.

If you have the opportunity, attend tastings, seminars, and classes. Follow your favorite wine regions on social media to discover local events. Wine doesn't exist in a void. Enjoy it with friends, family, and food. Nor can wine writing exist in a void: Put down the book and pick up your glass. Savor your newfound knowledge on the subject, but most of all have a good time.

Cheers!

OPPOSITE Modern fermentation vats and equipment.

Color, Aroma, Flavor & Taste

Color

Wines come in a variety of styles, including color, which can vary from producer to producer and even year to year. Throughout this book you will see the following color bar, which gives the typical range for the given variety or style, but remember: every wine is different and may not perfectly match our color designations.

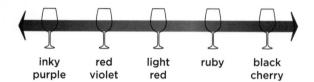

| inky purple | red violet | light red | ruby | black cherry |

Aroma

Our sense of smell represents about 80 percent of our sense of taste. (Don't believe us? Pinch your nose shut and take a bite of your favorite dessert. It likely will taste like bland mush.) Smell is so important to our brains that it never shuts off. Even while we sleep, it keeps us alert to danger, such as smoke, or pleasure, such as brewing coffee, both of which can wake us.

If you don't have a glass of wine by your side right now, open a bottle and pour yourself one. Seriously!

Swirl the wine a few times to release some of the aromas. Raise it to your nose and inhale deeply. You've just activated one of the most ancient, important regions of your brain. In your nasal cavity, a membrane known as the olfactory epithelium contains specialized receptors. When you smell something, the odor particles pass over the membrane and bind to those receptors. This bond triggers an electrical signal in your brain, which categorizes the signal with odors you've smelled before, labels it, and perhaps even assigns it an emotion or a feeling. Is it pleasant? Is it an apple or a rose? Is it dangerous, or does it make you hungry?

KEVIN'S FIRST MEMORIES OF SMELL

In some of my earliest memories, chamomile tea is brewing on the wood stove at my grandfather's farm. The smell of pine trees surrounded my childhood house, which is probably why as an adult I built my house in the middle of a pine forest. I also remember the smell of chlorine in my hair and on my skin from the local swimming pool and how much I hated the smell of rotting seeds from the ginkgo tree in our front yard.

As a young man, the smell of wine, grapes, and the earth itself enthralled me. I wanted to learn everything that I could about wines. I am pleased to remain in their thrall forty years later and still continuing to learn. The smells of fermenting grapes after harvest and the new wines they produce seduce me as much as the aromas of an old red wine with notes of damp earth, tobacco, mushrooms, and fallen leaves. I love *all* the smells that wine has, and I never forget that I am a lucky man to have made a lifelong career from wine.

MIKE'S FIRST MEMORIES OF SMELL

My grandmothers and mother, I remember at age four, all made sauce. They all contained tomatoes and meat, but Grandma Termini's kitchen had a bright, sweet smell, while Grandma DeSimone's was earthier and more herbal. At age six or seven, I sipped Chianti from Grandpa Termini's wine glass on holidays and Sundays. He never let me have much, but I loved the slightly sour taste, especially after a forkful of well-sauced pasta.

I've always loved cooking at home and eating in restaurants, so from the time I was old enough to order wine, wine and food pairings have fascinated me. Every time I pour a glass, I focus on the aroma, flavor, and texture, and my mind immediately jumps to what I would eat with it.

JEFF'S FIRST MEMORIES OF SMELL

My parents took my brother and me to the Jersey Shore when I was six years old. As we neared the beach, the salt air was intoxicating. I stuck my tongue out and smelled *and* tasted the salt at the same time. It was mind-boggling. We walked the boardwalk, and the smell of sun-baked wood planks intrigued me, but it was the aromas of Italian sausage, peppers, and onions that started my love affair with food.

Years later I was working at an Italian restaurant with a great wine list, and I remember smelling every empty glass as I carried it back to the kitchen, imagining how the wine tasted. I smelled cherries, blackberries, licorice, leather, and smoked

meats. I was hooked. I asked my manager, Bobby, where I could learn more about wine. He handed me an engraved personalized invitation to a professional wine tasting and sent me in his place. I was blown away. (Thanks, Bobby, for starting me on my lifelong journey!)

Seriously tasting wine involves creating and expanding the aroma databank in your brain. Does a wine smell like red cherry and brown baking spices, black raspberry and violet, or black plum and green bell pepper? Every time you taste and smell wine, you're building a larger databank. With practice, you can identify a grape by its aroma characteristics—a fun party trick! With a little more practice, you can suss out its country of origin, and with even more you might be able to pinpoint the region, vintage, or perhaps producer.

Flavor

Once you smell a glass of wine, your brain instantly decides whether you like it. Is it pleasant? Is that vanilla? Do I detect strawberry jam? But take a sip and see what happens next. As the wine washes over your palate, it hits your taste buds. You have about 7,500 of them on your tongue and the back of your throat. Your saliva dilutes the wine, and your taste buds convert this sensation into an electrical signal that your brain identifies, much as with smell.

Different areas of your tongue detect different characteristics in wine. Sourness, tartness, and acidity register along the sides of the tongue. The tip of your tongue is more sensitive to sweet notes, while the back identifies bitterness. Many wines feature some or all of these characteristics, making them extremely exciting to taste, and all of them derive their many flavors from the grapes used to make them, the fermentation process, and the aging process (if any).

GRAPES

The vast majority of the world's wine comes from *Vitis vinifera*, a species that encompasses hundreds of different varieties. As you saw in the table of contents, we've organized this book into two parts: grape varieties and styles and blends. As you might guess, the grape variety plays an enormous role in determining a wine's flavors. Dark, thick-skinned grapes naturally contain more tannins, which will make a young wine made from them taste highly astringent, for example.

Where the grapes grow also has a calculable effect on the final flavor. Through photosynthesis, grape vines convert sunlight into sugar. Red grapes in particular usually require more growing time than white grapes, so, in the world's two wine belts, growers tend to plant red varieties closer to the equator. Terroir—the French concept of "somewhereness" or locality—also plays a role. Geography, soil, sunlight, and weather all influence how a wine will taste. For example, Cabernet Sauvignons from Australia often contain notes of eucalyptus, which grows freely there. Nero d'Avola and Sangiovese grow in the arid landscape of the Mediterranean and taste of dried herbs.

Old vines tend to yield fewer grapes, which in turn have stronger flavors.

Growers also must pick the grapes at the optimal time for the desired sugar-to-acid ratio. Too soon in the season, and the grapes won't have enough sugar, making a wine taste overly acidic. Too late, and the wine might taste overly sweet.

The vintage of a wine indicates the year the grower harvested the grapes. In the Northern Hemisphere, this takes place at the end of the year, in the fall. The reverse holds true for the Southern Hemisphere, where the harvest happens at the beginning of the year.

FERMENTATION

Sugar + yeast = alcohol + carbon dioxide. That's the magic formula that all wines follow!

Fermentation begins as soon as yeast starts consuming sugar, usually when the winemaker crushes the grapes, and stops when the alcohol level naturally kills the yeast cells, usually around 15 percent. When yeast cells die in the winemaking process, they sink and form a sediment, called "lees." The longer a wine sits on its lees, the more yeasty—think freshly baked bread—it will taste.

Fermentation temperature (hot or cold), fermentation vessel (wooden vats or steel tanks), and final alcohol level also affect the final flavor. Red wines often go through a process called maceration, in which the must, or grape juice, soaks with the skins to intensify aromas, flavors, and body. (The longer the contact with the skins, the more color the final wine will have.) Some wines, such as some young Beaujolais (page 66), undergo a variation of this step called carbonic maceration, in which the grapes remain whole and fermentation takes place within the fruit, which explains why some Beaujolais has a lighter color and stronger, brighter fruit flavors.

AGING

Barrels, if a wine ages in them, also play an important role in a wine's flavor. If you've ever noticed that a red wine tastes of black pepper, caramel, cinnamon, pine, or toast, then you've tasted the effect that barrel aging can have. The smaller the barrel, the greater the surface-area contact with the wine and the greater the influence the aging process will have. Oak sourced from different countries can give different flavor notes. Barrels made from new wood impart more tannins and flavors than older barrels. Charring or toasting the wood also changes how a finished wine will taste. Aging in stainless steel or cement vats, for example, allows for a fruitier, lighter-tasting wine.

Taste

Taste represents the combined 80-20 sensory experience of smell and flavor.

Abbreviations

Throughout *Red Wine* you'll find many abbreviations for designations of controlled origin. The abbreviations vary from country to country, but they all guarantee a wine's place of origin and a certain level of composition and quality control. Not all designations control the same aspects of a wine, though. For example, Italy's DOC mandates aging requirements, while France's AOC doesn't.

AOC *Appellation d'Origine Contrôlée*, or controlled name of origin, used in France.

AOP Under new European Union rules, France has begun to replace AOC with AOP, or *Appellation d'Origine Protégée*, which means protected name of origin. However, AOC continues to appear on bottles, especially older vintages not yet released or resold.

AVA American Viticultural Area, used in the USA.

DAC *Districtus Austriae Controllatus*, or controlled Austrian district, used in Austria.

DO *Denominación de Origen*, or place of origin, used in Spain.

DOC *Denominazione di Origine Controllata*, or controlled designation of origin, used in Italy.

DOCa/DOQ Spain has two "qualified" DOs, which have stricter standards than other regions. Rioja is a DOCa, *Denominación de Origen Calificada*, or qualified name of origin. Priorat is a DOQ, which means the same thing but uses the Catalan word *Qualificada*.

DOCG *Denominazione di Origine Controllata e Garantita*, or controlled and guaranteed name of origin. This designation within Italy refers to wines made in a more specialized region or with a stricter set of standards than DOC wines.

GSM Not an abbreviation for a regional designation. In France: Grenache, Syrah, Mourvèdre; in Spain: Garnacha, Syrah, Monastrell.

IGT *Indicazione Geografica Tipica* stands for typical geographical indication in Italy and refers to wines from a specific area that don't follow the more stringent rules of a DOC or DOCG but are superior in quality to wine labeled VdT, *vino da tavola* or table wine.

PGI Protected Geographical Indication, used in the European Union.

Price Guide

BARGAIN	less than $20
VALUE	$21 to $40
SPECIAL OCCASION	$41 to $99
SPLURGE	$100 and up

We chose these price points after much deliberation and discussion. We all agreed that a wine costing more than $100 certainly doesn't count as an everyday wine, but we had difficulty choosing the other parameters. It's tough to find a wine for $1, but a lot of people regularly enjoy two-buck bottles. The bargain category identifies wines that overdeliver quality for their cost; in other words, they have an outstanding price-to-quality ratio. We considered capping the category at $15, but too many very good wines cost just a dollar or two more, and we didn't want to leave them out.

With the value wines, price and quality align. You get what you pay for: a good or very good wine at a fair price. The special-occasion and splurge wines are self-evident and not meant to be opened on a regular Tuesday night.

When assigning a wine to a specific price category, we always tried to use the producer's suggested retail price. In cases where we couldn't find one, we used the average price as shown on national wine websites, such as Wine-Searcher.com, Wine.com, or similar.

OPPOSITE Selecting a bottle of wine. **NEXT PAGES** Agiorgitiko grapes at Domaine Skouras in Greece.

GRAPE VARIETIES

AGIORGITIKO

(ah-yor-YEE-tee-ko)

IN THE GLASS

small Bordeaux glass, red violet to black cherry in color

TASTING PROFILE

ACIDITY

BODY

TANNIN

LOW   MEDIUM   HIGH

TASTING NOTES

PLUM   RASPBERRY   BLACK PEPPER

Characteristic fruit aromas include red plum, black plum, and raspberry. Pepper and spice notes enhance the bouquet. In the mouth, fruit flavors, such as black plum, prune, and black raspberry, come through with a hint of spice and freshly ground black pepper in the finish.

FOOD PAIRINGS

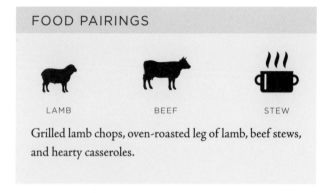

LAMB   BEEF   STEW

Grilled lamb chops, oven-roasted leg of lamb, beef stews, and hearty casseroles.

RECOMMENDED WINES

BARGAIN

KEVIN Semeli Mountain Sun
Skouras Saint George

MIKE Boutari
Domaine Spiropoulos

JEFF Ktima Tselepos
Kouros

VALUE

KEVIN Mitravelas Estate Red on Black

MIKE Vassiliou Vineyard

JEFF Gaia Wines Agiorgitiko by Gaia

YOU SHOULD KNOW

Many Greek vineyards have very old Agiorgitiko vines, but the better producers have been replacing their root-stock with new disease-resistant clones that yield higher sugar levels. Wines made from these new clones will have darker colors and potentially higher alcohol levels in the coming years.

OPPOSITE Domaine Skouras vineyard in Greece.
NEXT PAGES Red wine bottles awaiting labeling at Domaine Skouras in Greece.

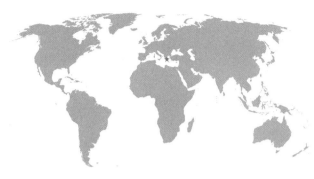

This grape grows throughout Greece but since ancient times has been planted traditionally in the Nemea region of the Peloponnese peninsula. The wine made from it there is called the Blood of Hercules. According to legend, Hercules (Herakles in Greek) drank the local wine either before or after slaying the Nemean Lion. Perhaps it was both: The wine gave him the courage to face the task, and he had a celebratory drink afterward. *Agiorgitiko* means "Saint George's grape." Some historical accounts link it to Saint George's Day to commemorate his death in the spring, while other accounts mention it in connection to autumn, closer to the harvest.

This versatile grape is one of the most important indigenous Greek varieties. In the mid-2010s it ranked as the most widely planted red grape in Greece (more than 20,000 acres). It grows primarily in the Nemea wine region but also in Macedonia and Attica. The vines tend to have very high yields, and the wine's characteristics can vary widely depending on the winemaker. It can produce reds with light to medium body as well as extremely concentrated, dark, tannic wines. If the vines are allowed to produce a lot of grapes, the wine tends to have more fruit flavors and softer tannins, but if the winemaker practices green harvesting (removal of whole grape bunches) or severe winter pruning, the wines will taste more concentrated with higher tannins and spicy characteristics. Vines planted at higher altitudes, which allow for nighttime cooling, tend to produce the most interesting wines, which have moderate acidity, good color, and a fruit-filled bouquet, while grapes grown at lower altitudes and on valley floors impart cooked or jammy fruit flavors. Agiorgitiko often is made as a single-variety wine, but it can be blended with other grapes. For instance, the area surrounding Metsovo in the north of Greece makes interesting blends of Agiorgitiko and Cabernet Sauvignon.

AGLIANICO

(ahl-YAH-nee-ko)

IN THE GLASS

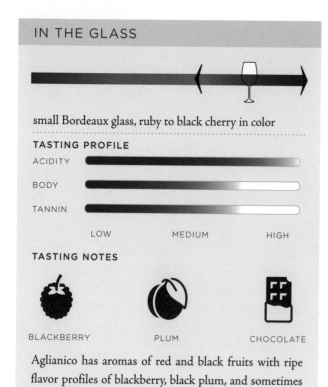

small Bordeaux glass, ruby to black cherry in color

TASTING PROFILE

ACIDITY

BODY

TANNIN

LOW   MEDIUM   HIGH

TASTING NOTES

BLACKBERRY   PLUM   CHOCOLATE

Aglianico has aromas of red and black fruits with ripe flavor profiles of blackberry, black plum, and sometimes hints of dark chocolate in the finish.

YOU SHOULD KNOW

Aglianico is bottled most often as a single varietal. Some of the best examples are 100 percent Aglianico, but it can be blended with Cabernet Sauvignon or Merlot or made into an IGT wine in certain areas.

FOOD PAIRINGS

PIZZA   PASTA   LAMB

Lighter versions call for lighter fare, such as pizza and pasta, but fuller-bodied styles call for rich meat dishes, such as roast beef or leg of lamb in a red wine sauce. Try it with Mozzarella di Bufala from Campania—but be careful: You may never want to eat another cheese in your life!

RECOMMENDED WINES

BARGAIN

KEVIN Feudi di San Gregorio Aglianico Irpinia

MIKE Grifalco Aglianico del Vulture

JEFF Bisceglia Terra di Vulcano

VALUE

KEVIN Basilisco Aglianico del Vulture Teodosio

MIKE Bisceglia Gudarrà
      San Martino Arberesko

JEFF Feudi di San Gregorio Aglianico dal Re

SPECIAL OCCASION

KEVIN Cantine del Notaio Aglianico del Vulture Il Sigillo

MIKE Paternoster Don Anselmo

JEFF Grifalco Daginestra
      Re Manfredi Vigneto Serpara

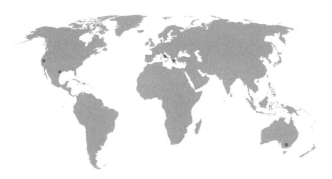

Not many grapes have been around long enough for Pliny the Elder (AD 23–79) to comment on wine made from them, but Aglianico might qualify. Some historians believe this to be the case, while others scoff at the notion. Different theories of origin have arisen over the years; perhaps the most romantic is that Aglianico originated in Greece and colonists brought it to southern Italy. If true, this hypothesis would make it one of humankind's oldest commercial wine grapes. The origin of the name could be a mispronunciation of the Greek word *Hellenika*, or *Ellenico* in Italian, both meaning "Hellenic," or Greek. It also could derive from a Spanish name from when Spain dominated Italy in the fifteenth and sixteenth centuries.

Although the birthplace of Aglianico remains fodder for discussion, today it grows mostly in the former Greek territories of southern Italy. Few if any plantings remain in Greece. It grows most widely in the provinces of Matera and Potenza in Basilicata and the provinces of Benevento and Avellino in Campania. Aglianico thrives best in volcanic soils, which may explain why it's grown on the extinct volcano Mt. Vulture in Basilicata. Some of our favorites come from the Aglianico del Vulture DOCG. In eastern Campania, some of the best come from the town of Taurasi near Avellino. Even in the hottest of Italy's climates, the grapes can reach high levels of acidity that exhibit freshness in the finished wines. It also grows in small amounts in Texas, California, and Australia.

IN HIS OWN WORDS

"I have also tasted Aglianico from Australia, the United States, and more recently from China. I was impressed by overall quality. Although Aglianico does not show the same elegance it can achieve in Irpinia, it displays strong power and richness in fruit. I'm pleased to find our native grape in these countries."

—*Antonio Capaldo, winemaker, Feudi di San Gregorio*

NEXT PAGES Aglianico vineyard at Feudi di San Gregorio in Italy.

ALICANTE BOUSCHET

(ah-lee-KAHNT boo-SHAY)

IN THE GLASS

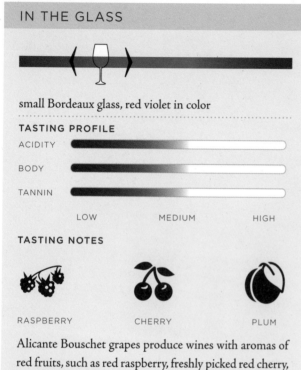

small Bordeaux glass, red violet in color

TASTING PROFILE

	LOW	MEDIUM	HIGH
ACIDITY			
BODY			
TANNIN			

TASTING NOTES

RASPBERRY   CHERRY   PLUM

Alicante Bouschet grapes produce wines with aromas of red fruits, such as red raspberry, freshly picked red cherry, and red plum. Depending on where they're produced, the wines are generally medium-bodied with a relatively short finish.

YOU SHOULD KNOW

Alicante Bouschet often is blended with other varietals to increase the color. It tends to lack complexity when bottled as a single varietal.

FOOD PAIRINGS

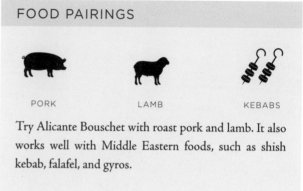

PORK   LAMB   KEBABS

Try Alicante Bouschet with roast pork and lamb. It also works well with Middle Eastern foods, such as shish kebab, falafel, and gyros.

RECOMMENDED WINES

BARGAIN
KEVIN   Herdade do Esporão, Portugal
MIKE   Herdade do Rocim, Portugal
Aluado, Portugal
JEFF   João Portugal Ramos Alentejo Ramos Reserva, Portugal

VALUE
OUR PICKS   João Portugal Ramos Vila Santa Reserva Red, Portugal
Soplo, Spain
Herdade dos Grous Moon Harvest Red, Portugal

SPECIAL OCCASION
OUR PICKS   Quinta de São Sebastião 2 Tintos Petit Verdot Alicante Bouschet Red, Portugal
Carlisle, USA: California

SPLURGE
OUR PICK   Julio Bastos Julio B. Bastos, Portugal

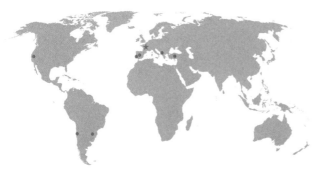

n the mid-nineteenth century in southern France's Languedoc-Roussillon region, father and son Louis and Henri Bouschet developed new cross breeds of grapes, naming them after themselves. Henri crossed Petit Bouschet—created by his father—with Grenache in 1866 and called it Alicante Henri Bouschet. Today it's known by the shorter sobriquet Alicante Bouschet. Winery owners planted his grape with great enthusiasm in the early 1890s because of its large yield, easy maintenance, and intense color.

Alicante Bouschet is one of the few "teinturier" *Vitis vinifera* grapes, meaning it has both red skin and red flesh. As such, it often goes into blends to darken the color profile. It has fallen to France's thirteenth most planted grape. Only 14,000 acres remain here, with most plantings in southern regions and the Jura and Loire valleys.

It proved popular in California during Prohibition because its large yields, high juice content, and thick skins allowed it to be shipped legally to the East Coast, where home vintners not-so-legally fermented it. Plantings are increasing in Spain and southern Portugal these days. John Reynolds receives credit for introducing Alicante Bouschet, more than a century ago, to Portugal's Alentejo region, which features more than 5,000 acres. Spain has more than 25,000 acres of it (also known as Garnacha Tintorera) in Castilla–La Mancha alone and about 55,000 acres in the country. It grows to a lesser extent in Bosnia and Herzegovina, Croatia, and Turkey. Slightly more than 1,000 acres remain in California's Central Valley. Chile has an equal number, while Argentina has about half that.

ABOVE Alicante Bouschet vineyard at J. Portugal Ramos in Portugal.

IN HIS OWN WORDS

"The Alentejo's exceptional conditions of high temperatures, low relative humidity, low rainfall during maturation, and relatively poor soils result in low yields during harvest. By allowing complete maturation on the vine, Alicante Bouschet from Alentejo offers a wine of excellent concentration and structure."

—*João Portugal Ramos, winemaker, J. Portugal Ramos*

BACO NOIR

(BAH-ko NWAHR)

IN THE GLASS

Burgundy glass; inky purple to black cherry in color

TASTING PROFILE

ACIDITY			
BODY			
TANNIN			
	LOW	MEDIUM	HIGH

TASTING NOTES

CHERRY   DRIED HERBS   CEDAR

Expect aromas and flavors of red fruits, such as tart cherry and red raspberry, as well as herbal qualities, including lavender and herbes de Provence. Darker, oaked styles have flavors of cassis, cedar, and toasted bread with a lingering finish.

YOU SHOULD KNOW

Before the phylloxera epidemic in the 1870s, Folle Blanche, one of Baco Noir's progenitors, was best known as the white grape used in the production of Armagnac and Cognac.

FOOD PAIRINGS

SAUSAGE   CHILI   STEW

All sorts of charcuterie, including jamon, prosciutto, salami, and liver paté. It also pairs well with soups, stews, and hearty fall and winter fare. Put together a make-your-own-chili bar, and pop open a few bottles of Baco Noir for friends on a cold winter's day. Fuller-bodied versions stand up nicely to the acidity of the tomato and the spiciness of the chili.

RECOMMENDED WINES

BARGAIN

KEVIN Girardet Wine Cellars Southern Oregon, USA: Oregon

Torrey Ridge, USA: New York

Bully Hill, USA: New York

MIKE Niagara Landing Wine Cellars, USA: New York

JEFF Henry of Pelham, Canada: Ontario

VALUE

KEVIN Hudson-Chatham Fieldstone Old Vines, USA: New York

MIKE Hudson-Chatham Casscles Vineyard Reserve, USA: New York

JEFF Benmarl Winery, USA: New York

Baco Noir is a cross between the French white *Vitis vinifera* Folle Blanche and a virtually unknown North American red *Vitis riparia* variety. At the turn of the twentieth century, François Baco—teacher by day, grape breeder by night—crossed the phylloxera resistance of the American species with the elegance and flavors of the Loire Valley and Burgundy found in Folle Blanche. Baco Noir enjoyed limited popularity here in the early 1900s until winemakers began grafting American *Vitis vinifera* rootstocks (also resistant to phylloxera) onto their own *Vitis vinifera* French varieties.

It rose to popularity in North America in the 1950s because of its extreme resistance to cold winters. Some grape growers say that it can withstand temperatures as low as −20° Fahrenheit. Today it grows widely in America's Northeast, Midwest, and Mid-Atlantic regions and Canada's east coast. You also can find Baco Noir planted in Nebraska, North Dakota, and other Great Plains states, with many great producers making notable wines. Oregon has some excellent producers as well.

If left on its skins for a long time, Baco Noir will appear dark and inky, but if skin contact is limited the resulting wine can be as light as a well made Pinot Noir

BARBERA

(bahr-BEHR-ah)

IN THE GLASS

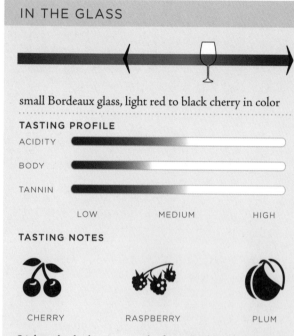

small Bordeaux glass, light red to black cherry in color

TASTING PROFILE

ACIDITY		
BODY		
TANNIN		
LOW	MEDIUM	HIGH

TASTING NOTES

CHERRY   RASPBERRY   PLUM

Lighter-bodied wines made from Barbera have bright fruit aromas and flavors—especially red cherry, tart cherry, and red raspberry—and generally see little or no oak aging. Wines with a bit more oak tend to have more body and spice in the bouquet and flavor profile.

YOU SHOULD KNOW

In Italy and elsewhere around the world, Barbera can range from light-bodied, cheap, and cheery wines to big, bold, serious reds. Some regions allow for high yields of grapes per acre, but make sure to buy from winemakers who limit their yield in order to make quality Barbera wines.

FOOD PAIRINGS

PASTA   CHICKEN   PIZZA

Enjoy Barbera with simple foods, such as antipasto and pasta, or that 1980s standby, penne with vodka sauce; the light acidic character of the wine stands up nicely to the spice and cream in the dish. It also pairs well with chicken or veal parmigiana or a simple New York–style pizza. We love it with pasta with truffles as well as risottos.

RECOMMENDED WINES

BARGAIN

KEVIN Michele Chiarlo Barbera d'Asti Le Orme
Vietti Barbera d'Asti Tre Vigne

MIKE Fontanafredda Briccotondo

JEFF Renato Ratti Barbera d'Asti
Castello del Poggio Barbera d'Asti

VALUE

KEVIN Pio Cesare Barbera d'Alba

MIKE Rivetto Zio Nando

JEFF Fontanafredda Barbera d'Alba Raimonda
Brezza Barbera d'Alba Superiore

SPECIAL OCCASION

KEVIN Giacomo Conterno Barbera d'Alba Cascina
Francia

MIKE Enzo Boglietti Vigna dei Romani
Michele Chiarlo La Court

JEFF Cascina La Barbetella Nizza La Vigna dell'Angelo

SPLURGE

OUR PICK Coppo Riserva della Famiglia Barbera d'Asti

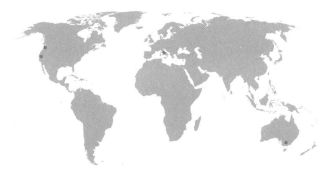

The Barbera grape first appears in writing in a 1798 document by the director of the Agricultural Society of Turin, but most researchers believe that it grew in Piedmont for centuries before this. Some even believe that it came to Piedmont by way of Lombardy in the AD 600s. Either way, it has been a staple in the region for centuries. Ampelographers think it derives from a natural cross of varieties, but researchers haven't identified the two parents yet.

It's Italy's third most planted red variety, after Sangiovese and Montepulciano, with the majority of the 70,000 acres of vines growing in Piedmont. You can find smaller plantings in Emilia-Romagna, Lombardy, and southern Italy.

Until the last few decades, it was hard to find Barbera in your local wine shop because the Italians wisely were keeping it all for themselves. They enjoy it as an everyday wine because it costs less there than wines made from Nebbiolo or Sangiovese. They drink Barbera to celebrate life's little pleasures—*dolce far niente*—and think nothing of opening a bottle to share with friends. It's a profitable grape for the region because it ripens before Nebbiolo, giving winemakers time to make wines from both varieties.

Look for wines from the Barbera d'Asti DOCG, Barbera d'Alba DOC, and Barbera di Monferrato DOC.

. . . .

IN HIS OWN WORDS

"With young Barbera, ham, salami, and pastas pair very well. When served slightly chilled, it can also be appreciated with fish dishes. Its delicate acidity balances well with fatty foods. More refined and aged Barbera is perfect for all types of meat and aged cheeses."

—*Danilo Drocco, winemaker, Fontanafredda Estate & Winery*

. . . .

NEXT PAGES Fontanafredda winery and vineyards in Italy.

Other Notable Countries

AUSTRALIA

Barbera has adapted well in Australia. Cuttings came here in the 1960s from the University of California at Davis, and a range of regions produces it now, including Mudgee, King Valley, Beechworth, Hunter Valley, Canberra District, and McLaren Vale. Although grown in relatively small amounts now, Australian Barbera is a wine to watch.

USA: CALIFORNIA AND WASHINGTON

Winemakers in California first vinified Barbera at the end of the nineteenth century, and it served as a mainstay of the Italian Swiss Colony Winery's red blends then. It fell from favor in the years after Prohibition, but a new generation of winemakers has rediscovered the variety and is making high-quality interpretations as a nod to the Golden State's winemaking history and, in many cases, to their Italian heritage as well. Plantings total just about 7,000 acres, with more than two-thirds of that in El Dorado County and another 15 percent in Madera County. When grown in California terroir, Barbera exhibits forceful flavors of blackberry, cherry, and blueberry with accents of spice and vanilla from barrel aging. It forms the backbone of many red table-wine blends, but you can find well-made single-varietal versions as well.

Because of the cooler climate, Barbera also does well in Washington State, with plantings near the Columbia River Gorge and on Alder Ridge in the Horse Heaven Hills AVA. Growers in the gorge cite westerly ocean breezes, easterly desert air, and climate-moderating effects of the Columbia River for its success in the region.

RECOMMENDED WINES

BARGAIN
KEVIN Renwood, USA: California
McManis, USA: California
MIKE Enotria, USA: California
Terra d'Oro, USA: California
JEFF Boeger, USA: California

VALUE
KEVIN Cooper's Hawk, USA: California
Woodward Canyon, USA: Washington
MIKE French Hill Grand Reserve, USA: California
JEFF Lone Madrone, USA: California
Fiddletown Cellars Reserve, USA: California

SPECIAL OCCASION
KEVIN Viansa Augusto, USA: California
MIKE Muscardini Pauli Ranch, USA: California
JEFF Portalupi, USA: California

SPLURGE
OUR PICK Borjon Complejo, USA: California

OPPOSITE Vineyard in the Barossa Valley wine region in South Australia.

BLAUFRÄNKISCH

(blahw-FRANK-eesh)

IN THE GLASS

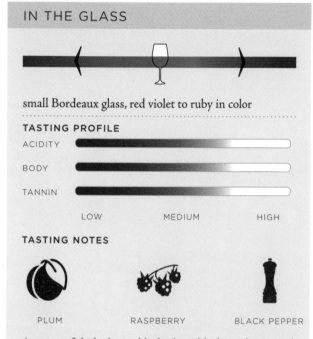

small Bordeaux glass, red violet to ruby in color

TASTING PROFILE

ACIDITY

BODY

TANNIN

LOW   MEDIUM   HIGH

TASTING NOTES

PLUM   RASPBERRY   BLACK PEPPER

Aromas of dark cherry, black plum, black raspberry, and freshly ground black pepper excite your palate for the rich, ripe fruit flavors to follow. Expect to taste juicy red plum, black cherry, red currant, blackberry, and cassis. Unoaked Blaufränkisch tastes fruity and lighter than when oak-aged, which tends to produce a fuller body.

FOOD PAIRINGS

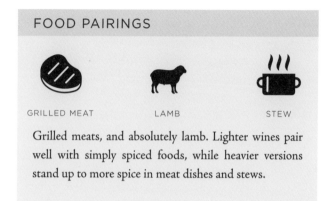

GRILLED MEAT   LAMB   STEW

Grilled meats, and absolutely lamb. Lighter wines pair well with simply spiced foods, while heavier versions stand up to more spice in meat dishes and stews.

RECOMMENDED WINES

BARGAIN

KEVIN Lenz Moser, Austria
       Burgenlander Pitti Pittnauer, Austria
MIKE   Donausonne, Hungary
       Evolucio, Austria
       Hans Igler Classic, Austria
JEFF   Glatzer, Austria
       Feravino Dika Frankovka, Croatia

VALUE

OUR PICKS Rosi Schuster, Austria
           Paul Achs, Austria

YOU SHOULD KNOW

Well-made Blaufränkisch wines have good aging potential. Sometimes aggressive when young, the tannins soften and become more velvety with oak aging. Winemakers have to be careful not to impart too much oak, however, which can overpower the fruit flavors.

The word *Blaufränkisch* means "blue Frankish" and refers to the dark, bluish-black grapes that grow in large, tight clusters. Austria takes credit as its ancestral home, and a viticultural exposition in Vienna in 1862 first documented the grape, though scientists think it's much older. It once bore the name Lemberger (or Limberger), after the town in which it originally was documented, but borders and town names have shifted in Eastern Europe over the last century and a half, so today you have to visit Maissau for a Blaufränkisch pilgrimage.

Roughly 8,000 acres grow across Austria, making it the second most important red grape variety there, behind Zweigelt (page 208). Most of the vines are planted in Burgenland and Mittelburgenland in the eastern part of the country. It also grows well in Neusiedlersee, Neusiedlersee-Hugelland, Sudburgenland, and Carnuntum. DAC regulations allow plantings in several zones, and wine styles differ from zone to zone: Some with little or no oak taste lighter and fruitier, while heavily oaked examples have more body and richness.

In Hungary, this grape is known as Kékfrankos. In the wine regions of Villany, Sopron, Szekszárd, Kunság, and Eger, it forms a major part of a red blend known as Egri Bikavér (page 218). In Germany, it grows in Franconia, Bavaria, Baden-Wurttemberg, Heilbronn-Franken, and Thuringia. It also grows in Croatia, Slovakia, Italy, Slovenia, New York's Finger Lakes, Washington State, and New Jersey.

A winemaker friend once handed us a glass of Blaufränkisch made from grapes grown in the mountains above Málaga in southern Spain, which preserved the acidity and freshness in the wine. It tasted like nothing we had had ever tried before. The quality and versatility of this grape are truly amazing.

BOĞAZKERE

(bo-AHZ-keh-reh)

IN THE GLASS

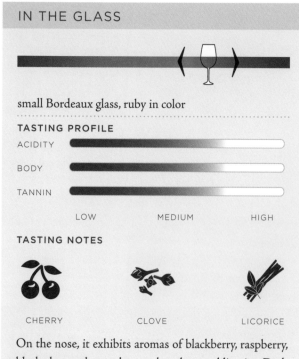

small Bordeaux glass, ruby in color

TASTING PROFILE

	LOW	MEDIUM	HIGH
ACIDITY			
BODY			
TANNIN			

TASTING NOTES

CHERRY   CLOVE   LICORICE

On the nose, it exhibits aromas of blackberry, raspberry, black cherry, clove, tobacco, chocolate, and licorice. Dark berry flavors continue on the palate along with notes of mocha, baking spices, anise, juniper berry, menthol, and pipe tobacco.

FOOD PAIRINGS

CHEESE   LAMB   STEW

Try it with double or triple crème cheeses, such as Brie, Camembert, Brillat-Savarin, and Epoisses, or with hard cheeses like Parmigiano-Reggiano and aged Gouda. Boğazkere is also at home alongside a roast leg of lamb with herbes de Provence, simply grilled lamb chops, or stew.

RECOMMENDED WINES

BARGAIN
KEVIN   Sevilen Guney
MIKE   Kavaklidere Selection Red
JEFF   Turasan

VALUE
KEVIN   Kavaklidere Pendore
MIKE   Vinkara Reserve
JEFF   Yazgan

YOU SHOULD KNOW

A strong tannic structure will mellow with age, so keep young bottles (one to two years old) for a later date. Most people aren't cellaring this variety, though, so look for bottles between three and five years old in a restaurant or wine shop. Enjoy "Reserve" bottles from well-known producers between five and ten years after harvest.

OPPOSITE Boğazkere leaves budding at Vinkara Winery in Kalecik in Turkey.

Boğazkere hails from Turkey's Diyarbakir Province near the Tigris River. Its frequent blending partner, Öküzgözü (page 120) originated closer to the Euphrates. If those two rivers ring a bell, that's because they formed the natural boundaries of Mesopotamia. Boğazkere is an ancient grape variety still cultivated in one of the oldest grape-growing regions in the world. Next time you hear a wine snob insist, "I drink *only* Old World wines," ask when he or she last enjoyed a glass of Boğazkere.

The variety has probably the least romantic name of any grape, though: It means "throat burner" in Turkish, which probably reflects early winemaking efforts. Even straight off the vine, Boğazkere grapes will make your mouth and throat feel dry. Thankfully today's vinification techniques have produced many quaffable versions.

Boğazkere grapes are small to medium in size and have thick skins, which accounts for the strong tannins. In a young bottle, harsh tannins will hit your palate and throat almost immediately, but a well made and properly aged Boğazkere can be as delicious as it is surprising. Because of its strong tannins and moderate acidity, winemakers often blend it with another popular Turkish grape, Öküzgözü, although you can find quite a few more good single-varietal examples reaching the global market each year. As its popularity has increased, so have plantings in Turkey. Today it grows in five subregions in the southwest of the country, including the Aegean coast.

IN HIS OWN WORDS

"I like Boğazkere because it is a grape that can make wine rich in tannins, with good body, and that can be aged for a long time. I can say that it is an old-style variety. I mean, it is a classical, full-body wine, with soft tannins. It reminds me of Barolo. The taste of the berries, the consistency of the skin, the kind of tannins, and the structure of the wine are very similar."

—Marco Monchiero, *winemaker, Vinkara*

CABERNET FRANC

(kab-uhr-NAY FRAHNK)

IN THE GLASS

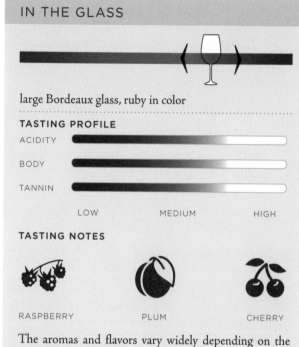

large Bordeaux glass, ruby in color

TASTING PROFILE

	LOW	MEDIUM	HIGH
ACIDITY			
BODY			
TANNIN			

TASTING NOTES

RASPBERRY   PLUM   CHERRY

The aromas and flavors vary widely depending on the terroir in which the vines grow, but expect aromas of red and black fruits with a touch of green bell pepper and graphite. On the palate, you'll taste red and black raspberries, red plums, and dark cherries.

YOU SHOULD KNOW

Cabernet Franc has relatively high levels of pyrazines, compounds that impart that green bell pepper aroma. When picked and vinified too young, the grapes can make almost undrinkable wine.

FOOD PAIRINGS

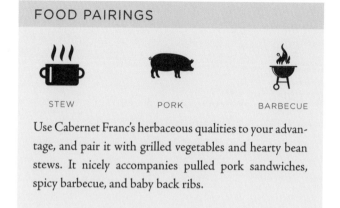

STEW   PORK   BARBECUE

Use Cabernet Franc's herbaceous qualities to your advantage, and pair it with grilled vegetables and hearty bean stews. It nicely accompanies pulled pork sandwiches, spicy barbecue, and baby back ribs.

RECOMMENDED WINES

BARGAIN
KEVIN Domaine du Petit Clocher François Thienpont
MIKE Château de Fesles la Chapelle Vieilles Vignes
JEFF Remy Pannier Chinon

VALUE
KEVIN Domaine des Roches Neuves Terres Chaudes
MIKE Charles Joguet Les Charmes
JEFF Domaine Les Pins Saint-Nicolas-de-Bourgueil

SPECIAL OCCASION
KEVIN Couly-Dutheil Clos de L'Echo
MIKE Domaine Grosbois Clos du Noyer
JEFF Vignoble de la Jarnoterie Concerto

SPLURGE
OUR PICK Château Cheval Blanc

OPPOSITE Filling a storage tank at Domaine de l'A in Bordeaux. **NEXT PAGES** Domaine de l'A in Bordeaux.

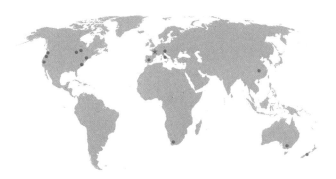

about 30,000 acres of Cabernet Franc—most at home in that region's blends, where it asserts its peppery character and finds its way into many St. Émilions—but you can find it as a stand-alone varietal as well.

France is far from its only home, though. In addition to the countries noted below, it grows in Italy, Hungary, Spain, and China.

No one knows for certain the birthplace of Cabernet Franc, but the grape got around. It's one of the parents of Cabernet Sauvignon (page 30), Carménère (page 54), Malbec (page 76), and Merlot (page 88). Some researchers claim it originated in the Basque region of Spain, while others tie it to the Loire Valley. Still others point to it as the grape and wine from ancient Burdigala (modern Bordeaux) mentioned by Pliny the Elder.

The small, blue-black, thick-skinned fruit thrives in sandy or granite-based soils, and today it's one of the most important grapes in the Loire Valley, representing about 14,000 acres there, particularly in the Bourgueil and Chinon appellations. Total plantings for France exceed 90,000 acres, making it the sixth most planted red grape in the country. Bordeaux has

IN HIS OWN WORDS

"Cabernet Franc is very demanding. The father of both Cabernet Sauvignon and Merlot, it is not a very well loved variety. You can't grow it just anywhere. I have also worked with it in California, in Morocco, and in Cappadocia in Turkey. In Bordeaux we have a rainy climate, so we have to fight against the rain. In California, Morocco, and Turkey, we have to fight against the sun, and it is easy to lose freshness."

—*Stéphane Derenoncourt, owner and winemaker, Domaine de l'A*

Other Notable Countries

AUSTRALIA

James Busby, father of the Australian wine industry, brought Cabernet Franc cuttings here and to New Zealand in the mid-1800s. On its own, Australian Cabernet Franc tastes of cherry and strawberry with strong notes of paprika and black pepper. It also can include flavors of cigar box and violet. It's most often mixed in small amounts with Cabernet Sauvignon and Merlot to form Bordeaux-style blends, so plantings aren't extensive. Its 1,700 acres comprise just 0.4 percent of the nation's grapevines.

NEW ZEALAND

Kiwi Cabernet Franc offers dark fruit flavors of cherry, plum, and blackberry; violet notes; and a strong dose of green bell pepper and earth to Bordeaux-style blends. Only about 400 acres grow here, the vast majority in the Hawke's Bay region.

SOUTH AFRICA

About 2,500 acres of Cabernet Franc grow in South Africa, where the strong smell of pepper joins flavors of cherry, cassis, and earth. It serves as a component in several Cape blends, although winemakers increasingly are making it as a single varietal.

RECOMMENDED WINES

VALUE

OUR PICKS Raats Family
Wildekrans

IN HIS OWN WORDS

"Cabernet Franc as a single variety is the best of three worlds. It has the structure of Bordeaux, the elegance of Burgundy, and the spiciness of the Rhône—all in one grape. I believe that Cabernet Franc produces the most complex wines from a single variety."

—*Bruwer Raats, owner and winemaker, Raats Family Wines*

ABOVE Cabernet Franc vines at La Jota vineyard in California.

USA

In America, Cabernet Franc finds a ready home in Bordeaux-style or Meritage blends (page 232). Noted for its assertive peppery character, American Cabernet Franc also has flavors of cherry, cassis, violet, and earth. It grows on more than 3,400 acres across California, and winemakers often blend it with high-profile—and high-priced—reds labeled Cabernet Sauvignon. Sonoma and Santa Barbara grow significant amounts. It also grows in Washington State, Oregon, New York, Virginia, Michigan, and Indiana.

IN HIS OWN WORDS

"I like Cabernet Franc as an alternate choice of planting material in places that may be cooler or more shaded and where Cabernet Sauvignon may not ripen well. Cabernet Franc, being an earlier-ripening variety, will do just fine there."

—*Chris Carpenter, winemaker, La Jota*

RECOMMENDED WINES

BARGAIN
KEVIN Osprey's Dominion, USA: New York
Owen Roe the Keeper, USA: Washington
MIKE Heron Hill, USA: New York
JEFF Anthony Road, USA: New York
Ironstone, USA: California

VALUE
KEVIN Lieu Dit, USA: California
MIKE Macari Reserve, USA: New York
Damiani, USA: New York
JEFF Columbia Winery Horse Heaven Hills, USA: Washingon

SPECIAL OCCASION
KEVIN Louis M. Martini Monte Rosso, USA: California
MIKE William Hill Estate Napa Valley, USA: California
La Jota Howell Mountain, USA: → California
JEFF Trinchero Central Park West Vineyard, USA: California
Mt. Brave Mt. Veeder, USA: California

SPLURGE
KEVIN Peju Reserve, USA: California
MIKE Ramey, USA: California
JEFF JCB Number 17, USA: California

CABERNET SAUVIGNON

(kab-uhr-NAY so-vin-YAHN)

IN THE GLASS

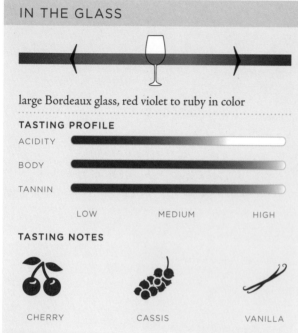

large Bordeaux glass, red violet to ruby in color

TASTING PROFILE

	LOW	MEDIUM	HIGH
ACIDITY			
BODY			
TANNIN			

TASTING NOTES

CHERRY   CASSIS   VANILLA

Aromas of black cherry and currant dominate with touches of chocolate and violet. On the palate, expect black cherry, cassis, graphite, caramel, butterscotch, and vanilla with a touch of spice. A well-made, ready-to-drink Cabernet Sauvignon will have a good balance of fruit, tannin, and acidity. Expect fruit and spice up front, a sense of chewiness through the mid-palate, and a bright, refreshing splash of acidity on the finish.

YOU SHOULD KNOW

If the grower picked the grapes before full ripeness, you may taste green bell pepper or slight "farm stand" flavors. If you open the wine while it's still young—because of strong natural tannins compounded by tannins from barrel aging—it can taste harsh or bitter, with the sensation of drying out the gums.

FOOD PAIRINGS

STEAK   TUNA   MUSHROOM

Simply prepared grilled meats are one of the best pairings for Cabernet Sauvignon, which is why it's so popular in steakhouses and at backyard barbecues alike. Well-marbled meat balances the chalky feeling that tannins leave in the mouth. Cabernet Sauvignon also matches nicely with seared tuna or mushroom risotto.

RECOMMENDED WINES

BARGAIN

KEVIN Château Larose-Trintaudon
MIKE Arrogant Frog Ribet Red Cabernet Merlot
Michel Gassier Les Piliers
JEFF Château La Freynelle Bordeaux

VALUE

KEVIN Château Cantemerle
MIKE Vignerons de Buzet Oniric
JEFF André Lurton Château de Rochemorin Red

SPECIAL OCCASION

KEVIN Château Talbot
MIKE Château Tour des Gendres Le Petit Bois
Domaine de Rochelles Les Millerits
JEFF Château de Tigné L'Insensé
Château la Varière La Chevalerie

SPLURGE

OUR PICK Château Latour

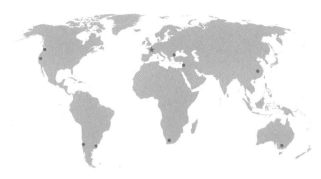

Cabernet Sauvignon is the perfect example of a full-bodied, intense red wine. It's also the most widely traveled grape in the world, growing practically everywhere that grapes do. Almost anywhere you go, winemakers are producing, trying to produce, or hoping to produce a Cabernet Sauvignon worthy of international attention. It's a naturally occurring cross between the red Cabernet Franc grape and the white Sauvignon Blanc grape. Researchers believe the field crossing occurred spontaneously in the early eighteenth century in or near the Bordeaux region. Today, it's the main grape variety used in Bordeaux wines, including all five of the first growths of the 1855 Bordeaux Classification System (page 224).

It grows predominantly on the left bank of Bordeaux in the Médoc and Graves regions and the communes of St. Estèphe, Margaux, Pauillac, and St. Julien. Today it also grows in the Pays d'Oc region, where it makes a much more accessible wine than the first-growth Bordeaux that built its reputation. It may be the most popular red grape that comes to mind when you think of French wine, but in France it actually ranks fourth, behind Merlot, Grenache, and Syrah.

The small, thick-skinned grapes make dark wines with strong tannins and high acidity. Tannins soften as wine ages, making it more drinkable, and, as wine collectors know, a well-made, oaked Cabernet Sauvignon can age for decades. In fact, many of the finest Cabs need to bottle-rest for years before they're ready to drink. That said, plenty of Cabernet Sauvignons from Bordeaux drink very well when still young.

It ripens late in the season, so, unless growers pick it at the perfect ripeness, Cabernet Sauvignon often goes into blends with other grapes to soften its overpowering, greener qualities. It counts Merlot, Cabernet Franc, Petit Verdot, Malbec, and Carménère as its blending partners in Bordeaux. In New World regions, it can blend with one or more of these plus Syrah.

ABOVE Harvesting Cabernet Sauvignon at Chateau Montelena in California. **NEXT PAGES** Lokoya Spring Mountain Villa in California.

IN HIS OWN WORDS

"Cabernet Sauvignon is considered the king of reds, and personally I think it's true. Cabernet Sauvignon wines are aromatically complex, full-bodied, with very good structure and tannic texture. Their freshness and long-lasting finish make them very pleasant to drink."

—*Jose Pepe Galante, winemaker, Bodegas Salentein*

Other Notable Countries

ARGENTINA

Cabernet Sauvignon moved to the New World with Spanish and British colonization, often transported by French viticulturists who established vineyards overseas. In Argentina, it represents slightly less than 8 percent of the country's vines. It grows in the Salta, Rioja, Catamarca, San Juan, and Mendoza regions, and flavor profiles vary with geography and climate. It typically tastes of black cherry, cassis, graphite, spice, and tobacco. Cabernet Sauvignon from Salta tends to have blackberry and green bell pepper characteristics, while Mendozan Cabernet features more cherry notes.

IN HER OWN WORDS

"Cabernet Sauvignon adapts really well to our soils, especially stony ones. It produces wonderful wines worthy of presenting as single varietals or can add great length and depth as a blend. We can obtain Cabernet with ripe fruit but not overripened, pleasant tannins, great concentration, and aging potential."

—*Susana Balbo, owner and winemaker, Susana Balbo Wines*

RECOMMENDED WINES

BARGAIN
- KEVIN Bodega Septima
  Weinert Carrascal
- MIKE Salentein →
- JEFF Terrazas de los Andes
  Alamos Winery

VALUE
- KEVIN Susana Balbo Signature
- MIKE Alta Vista
- JEFF Riglos Gran

SPECIAL OCCASION
- KEVIN Salentein PR1MUM
- MIKE Terrazas de los Andes Single Vineyard
  Los Aromos
- JEFF Viña Cobos Bramare

SPLURGE
- OUR PICKS Zuccardi Finca Los Membrillos
  Viña Cobos Volturno Marchiori Vineyard

OPPOSITE Casks in the winery at Cape Mentelle in Australia.

AUSTRALIA

Cabernet Sauvignon is the second most abundant red grape in Australia, just behind Shiraz, and the third most popular overall, right below Chardonnay. It covers about 65,000 acres, or roughly 17 percent of the country's total vine area. Depending on the region, Australian Cabernet Sauvignon can bear notes of mint and eucalyptus, green bell pepper and jalapeño, or even chocolate in addition to its standard flavors of black cherry, cassis, plum, etc. Some of the best Cabs come from Margaret River, Coonawarra, Yarra Valley, McLaren Vale, Barossa Valley, and Mudgee, where winemakers frequently blend it with Shiraz, Merlot, and Cabernet Franc, each grape adding its own special character.

ABOVE The tasting room at Cape Mentelle in Australia.

RECOMMENDED WINES

BARGAIN
KEVIN Black Opal
Jim Barry The Cover Drive
MIKE Peter Lehmann Portrait
Inkberry Mountain Estate
JEFF Château Tanunda Grand Barossa

VALUE
KEVIN Wolf Blass Gold Label
Tahbilk
MIKE Balgownie Estate
JEFF Vasse Felix

SPECIAL OCCASION
KEVIN Robert Oatley The Pennant
MIKE Moss Wood
JEFF Hickinbotham Clarendon Vineyard Trueman

SPLURGE
KEVIN Penfolds Bin 707
MIKE Cape Mentelle
JEFF Casella 1919

BULGARIA

Cabernet Sauvignon is one of Bulgaria's most cultivated grapes, covering a whopping 40,000 acres. It grows mainly in the southern wine regions of Struma Valley, Thracian Valley, and Rose Valley, although you can find plantings in the northerly Danube Plain. Bulgarian winemakers fashion it into a single-varietal or Bordeaux-style wine or blend it with Mavrud, their favorite indigenous grape. During the Cold War, Bulgaria provided bulk wine to the Soviet Union, but the industry now exports world-class, low-priced wines, including many Cabs with excellent ratios of quality to price. Expect a fresh, fruit-forward style with flavors of black cherry, blackberry, vanilla, and anise.

RECOMMENDED WINES

BARGAIN
KEVIN Todoroff Gallery
Domaine Boyar Reserve
MIKE Katarzyna Twins
Vini Veni Vidi Vici
JEFF Château Burgozone
Bulgariana
K Cellars

ABOVE Puente Alto Vineyard at Concha y Toro in Chile.

CHILE

Now preeminent, Cabernet Sauvignon played a starring role in Chile's rise to fame in the wine world. The finest examples of this variety, which accounts for more than a third of the wine grapes grown in the country, come from Colchagua, Aconcagua, Cachapoal, Maule, and Maipo.

The phylloxera epidemic that began in the 1860s wrought havoc on European vineyards, prompting French winemakers to seek other lands in which to ply their trade. They headed south to La Rioja in Spain and southwest to Santiago, where wealthy Chilean landowners already had begun importing French vines. Grape-growing here mainly took place in the Central Valley. Silvestre Ochagavía Echazarreta receives credit as the first Chilean to import and grow French *Vitis vinifera* varieties from Bordeaux, including Cabernet Franc, Cabernet Sauvignon, Malbec, Sauvignon Blanc, and Sémillon.

RECOMMENDED WINES

BARGAIN

KEVIN Cousiño Macul
Casa Lapostolle Cuvée Alexandre

MIKE Santa Rita Reserva

JEFF Emiliana Natura
The Seeker

VALUE

KEVIN François Lurton Gran Araucano

MIKE MontGras Antu

JEFF Viña Tarapacá Gran Reserva Etiqueta Negra

SPECIAL OCCASION

KEVIN Errazuriz Don Maximiano Founder's Reserve
Apaltagua Signature

MIKE Domaine Barons de Rothschild (Lafite)
Le Dix de Los Vascos

JEFF Undurraga Founder's Collection

SPLURGE

KEVIN Concha y Toro Don Melchor Puente
Alto Vineyard

MIKE Cono Sur Silencio

JEFF Errazuriz Viñedo Chadwick

"I have been fortunate and have tasted great Cabernets from France, California, Australia, and Chile. The difference lies particularly in what the French call terroir, that unique combination of climate and soil that defines the personality of a wine. If the wine is balanced, elegant, and charming, I can enjoy an opulent and very ripe black fruit–driven Californian Cab to an elegant, lighter, and skinnier Bordeaux along with everything in between."

—*Santiago Margozzini, winemaker, MontGras Winery*

Then as now, Chile's warm, dry vineyards bring out the best of Cabernet Sauvignon's notes of black cherry, cassis, tobacco, spice, and graphite. Wine made from grapes grown in cool, coastal climates show greener flavors, such as green bell pepper and olive. Wine labeled "Cabernet Sauvignon" may contain up to 25 percent of other varieties, so Carménère, Merlot, or Syrah can influence how it tastes.

"Cabernet Sauvignon has very good color and fresh fruit expression; the tannins are ripe and deliver great concentration, body, and persistence. They are very complex and expressive wines. I find in Cabernet Sauvignon the best balance between fruit, concentration, quality of tannins, and complexity."

—*Enrique Tirado, winemaker, Don Melchor*

OPPOSITE Fermentation tanks in Chile.

CHINA

China is the world's number-one consumer of red wine, and the number-one variety (60 percent) grown and vinified here is Cabernet Sauvignon. Most of China's vineyards are young, and only a handful of the wines have reached the international market. Cabernet Sauvignon grows widely in the provinces of Xinjiang, Shandong, and Hebei. In a 2011 wine competition called "Bordeaux against Ningxia," held in Beijing and reminiscent of 1976's "Judgment of Paris," a Chinese Cabernet Sauvignon from Grace Vineyard took top honors. Four of the five top-rated wines came from China. LVMH Estates and Wines recently entered the Chinese market with Ao Yun, a luxury Cabernet Sauvignon made in vineyards on Meili Mountain in Yunnan Province.

"The rainfall and temperature in North Yunnan are very similar to Bordeaux but with more UV and sun intensity. There is also a river influence; the Mekong cuts through the region very much like the Gironde."

—*Jean-Guillaume Prats, president, Moët Hennessy Estates & Wines*

ISRAEL

Extensively grown in Golan Heights, Galilee, and Jerusalem Hills, Cabernet Sauvignon is made into a wide range of styles at equally wide-ranging prices, from fresh and fruity to long-aged and expensive collector wines. Israeli Cabs tend to be very dark in color, from red violet to ruby. In addition to bold flavors of black cherry, blackberry, plum, currant, chocolate, and coffee, many of them exhibit eucalyptus, menthol, and mint flavors. These cool herb notes—attributed to eucalyptus groves growing near the vineyards—in combination with strong fruit flavors and good acidity, create a pleasing medley on the palate.

RECOMMENDED WINES

BARGAIN
KEVIN Tabor Mt. Tabor
Tishbi
MIKE Barkan Classic
JEFF Hacormim Adi 13

VALUE
KEVIN Golan Heights Winery Yarden
MIKE Recanati Cabernet Sauvignon Reserve "David's Vineyard"
JEFF Jerusalem Wineries 4990 Reserve

SPECIAL OCCASION
KEVIN Golan Heights Winery Yarden El Rom Vineyard
Barkan Vineyards Superiore
MIKE Alexander The Great
JEFF Yarden Cabernet Sauvignon El Rom Single Vineyard

SPLURGE
OUR PICK Yarden Katzrin

SOUTH AFRICA

As in China, Cabernet Sauvignon covers more vineyard area than any other red grape in South Africa, accounting for 12 percent of total plantings. It grows in every region, but it does particularly well in Durbanville, Lower Orange, Paarl, Philadelphia, Robertson, Stellenbosch, and Swartland. Its flavors of black cherry, black currant, graphite, and cedar anchor most Cape blends. South African wine labeled simply "Cabernet" will be made from this grape rather than Cabernet Franc.

RECOMMENDED WINES

BARGAIN
KEVIN Fleur du Cap
Mount Rozier
MIKE Glenelly Glass Collection
Braai
JEFF Riebeek Cellars Collection

VALUE
KEVIN Thelema
MIKE Rudi Schultz
Rustenberg Peter Barlow
JEFF Bartinney
Rust en Vrede

SPECIAL OCCASION
KEVIN Boekenhoutskloof
MIKE Kanonkop
Ernie Els Proprietor's
JEFF Glenelly Lady May

USA: CALIFORNIA

Cabernet Sauvignon is California's most populous red grape, found on more than 80,000 acres. Almost a quarter of that grows in Napa, with significant plantings in San Joaquin, Sonoma, and San Luis Obispo counties as well. "Cali Cabs" form a category unto themselves. Like Chardonnay, the state's most widely grown grape, they come in a variety of styles and prices, from entry level and easy to find to hyper-scarce and stratospherically priced. They tend to have flavors of black cherry, blackberry, purple flowers, and graphite. Many have a reputation for being high-alcohol, over-oaked fruit bombs, but just as many exhibit remarkable restraint and balance.

ABOVE The new cellar at Chateau Montelena in California. **NEXT PAGES** Mother vine at Concannon Vineyard in California.

RECOMMENDED WINES

BARGAIN

KEVIN Forest Glen
Louis M. Martini Sonoma County

MIKE Silver Totem
Edna Valley Central Coast

JEFF Josh Cellars
William Hill Estate North Coast
Bridlewood Estate Winery Paso Robles

VALUE

KEVIN Louis M. Martini Napa Valley
Buehler Vineyards Estate

MIKE Joseph Carr Coombsville
Oberon
Franciscan Estate Napa Valley

JEFF The Calling Gold
Frei Brothers Reserve Alexander Valley
Ghost Pines Napa/Sonoma

SPECIAL OCCASION

KEVIN Caymus
Louis M. Martini Monte Rosso
Oakville Ranch Napa Valley

MIKE Newton Unfiltered
Galerie Latro Knight's Valley
La Jota Howell Mountain
Bell Napa Valley Reserve

JEFF Kunde Cabernet Sauvignon Reserve Sonoma
Valley
William Hill Estate Napa Valley
Gallo Signature Series Napa Valley
Mt. Brave Mt. Veeder

SPLURGE

KEVIN Stag's Leap Cask 23
Spottswoode
Gamble Cabernet Sauvignon Cairo

MIKE M by Michael Mondavi
Clark-Claudon Eternity
Rudd Oakville Estate Samantha's Cabernet
Sauvignon

JEFF Louis M. Martini Lot No. 1 Cabernet Sauvignon
Lokoya Diamond Mountain District
Cardinale Napa Valley

"Cabernet Sauvignon was, I guess, my first love, as it was the first wine I ever tried. It was new, exotic, and spellbinding in flavor and aroma, and I just wanted to learn more and more about it."

—Joseph Carr, winemaker,
Joseph Carr Winery and Josh Cellars

"I've always appreciated the power of Cabernet but equally enjoyed when that power is met with finesse. When the tannins, acid, and fruit are all in balance, Cabernet can make such a huge statement, especially when paired with the right food."

—Glenn Hugo, winemaker, Girard Winery

"We have an 1883 Mother Vine Vineyard, one of the oldest Cabernet Sauvignon vineyards in California, that I love. Every day it speaks to the vibrant durability of its rare Cabernet vines and still produces gorgeous fruit, elegant wines, and absolute wonder every time I walk through it—if only vines could talk."

—John Concannon, vintner,
Concannon Vineyard

"Cabernet Sauvignon is considered the king of red wines. It offers a beautiful balance of dark fruit aromas, texture, structure, and suppleness and can be produced in a wide and diverse range of styles. On the palate it shows a ripe suppleness, and with all this complexity it is no wonder that it has become 'king.'"

—Rob Mondavi Jr., winemaker and cofounder,
Michael Mondavi Family Estates

"Of the Bordelaise varieties, Cabernet is the most expressive of time and place—at least in the Napa Valley. It's not uncommon to taste wines, sourced from the same vineyard across warm and cool vintages, and find something delicious but incredibly different about each. In that way it's unique."

—Matt Crafton, winemaker, Chateau Montelena

LEFT Chateau Montelena.

USA: WASHINGTON STATE

The Evergreen State also counts Cabernet Sauvignon as its number-one red variety. If you're wondering how grapes could grow in such a rainy climate, remember that Washington's wine regions lie east of the Cascade Mountains, which create hot, dry conditions ideal for growing grapes and making wine. Also note that many of the area's vineyards lie on the same latitude as Bordeaux, and they make a wide array of delicious, high-quality Cabernet Sauvignons. In years past, they had a reputation for their fruity, easy-drinking style; today they offer a delicious complexity, featuring flavors of black cherry, black plum, tobacco, flint, and violet.

RECOMMENDED WINES

BARGAIN
KEVIN Columbia Crest Grand Estates
MIKE Pendulum
Canoe Ridge The Expedition
JEFF Skyfall Vineyard ➞

VALUE
KEVIN Chateau Ste. Michelle Indian Wells
MIKE Walla Walla Vintners
JEFF 14 Hands The Reserve
Gorman Old Scratch

SPECIAL OCCASION
KEVIN Andrew Will
MIKE Va Piano DuBrul Vineyard
JEFF Woodward Canyon Old Vines

SPLURGE
KEVIN Leonetti Cellar
MIKE Quilceda Creek
JEFF Doubleback
DeLille Grand Ciel

LEFT Sunset storm passes over the Benches Vineyard and the Columbia River in Columbia Valley in Washington.

CARIÑENA

(kahr-in-YAY-nah)

IN THE GLASS

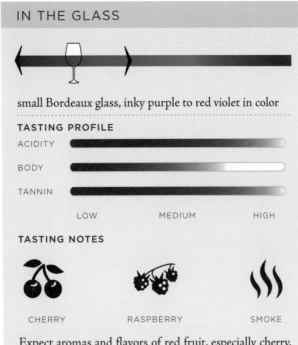

small Bordeaux glass, inky purple to red violet in color

TASTING PROFILE

	LOW	MEDIUM	HIGH
ACIDITY			
BODY			
TANNIN			

TASTING NOTES

CHERRY · RASPBERRY · SMOKE

Expect aromas and flavors of red fruit, especially cherry, raspberry, and strawberry jam, and secondary notes and tastes of violets and rose petals with whiffs of smoked meat.

YOU SHOULD KNOW

Winemakers in Spain also call this grape Cariñena or Mazuelo *(mah-THWAY-lo)* interchangeably. In Priorat, Costers del Segre, Tarragona, and other areas of Catalonia, it's known as Samso. In the 1970s, Mazuelo was made into jug wine or, worse, immediately distilled into cheap brandy, but winemakers around the world are making quality Cariñenas today. The better examples generally come from low-yielding, old bush vines rather than recent plantings.

FOOD PAIRINGS

DUCK · PORK · BEEF

Drink it with Chinese roasted duck because the red fruit, smoked meat, and brown baking spice notes of the wine pair perfectly with the Chinese five-spice powder used in the dish. The smoked meat notes complement the smoking process used to cook the duck. Also try oven-braised meats, such as pork roast or beef brisket.

RECOMMENDED WINES

BARGAIN
KEVIN Bodegas San Valero Particular
MIKE Bodegas Paniza
JEFF Grandes Vinos y Viñedos El Circo Equilibrista

VALUE
KEVIN Miguel Merino
      Gregorio Martinez
MIKE Grandes Vinos y Viñedos Anayon
JEFF Perelada Finca La Garriga Carignan

SPECIAL OCCASION
OUR PICK Vall Llach Porrera Vi de la Vila de Vall Llach

SPLURGE
KEVIN Clos Mogador Priorat
MIKE Dinastia Vivanco Colección Vivanco Parcelas de Mazuelo
JEFF Vall Llach Mas de la Rosa

OPPOSITE Crate and old bottling line at Bodega San Valero in Spain. **NEXT PAGES** Mesa and vineyard in Aragon in Spain.

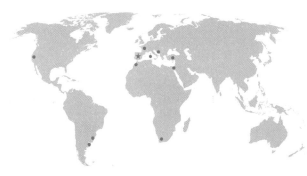

Some researchers hypothesize that Phoenician traders first brought Cariñena to Sardinia around 900 BC and then introduced it to other settlements across the Phoenician and then Roman Empires, but no written evidence confirms this assumption. Two more common theories put the place of origin in the town Mazuelo de Muño in Burgos Province or the town Cariñena in Aragon. Recent DNA investigation shows that Cariñena is identical to a Sardinian grape variety known as Bovale di Spagna, so maybe it was the Phoenicians after all!

Spain has substantial acreage of Cariñena in Catalonia and La Rioja as well as Navarre, Castilla–La Mancha, and Aragon.

Catalan vintners are making impressive wines from hundred-year-old bush vines that thrive in their soil, which is rich in quartz and schist. In the rest of Spain, however, Cariñena has a reputation for lacking in flavor, so it goes into blends—generally with Garnacha, Cabernet Sauvignon, Merlot, and Syrah, and in La Rioja with Tempranillo, Garnacha, and Graciano—that make use of its high levels of tannin and acidity and its dark color.

You can find interesting single-varietal examples from Morocco, Sardinia, and Israel and plantings in Argentina, Uruguay, Croatia, and Turkey.

IN HIS OWN WORDS

"My favorite food pairing is red meat, like a big steak. But by itself, a glass of Priorat Cariñena is a pleasure because sometimes it is too big and it gets difficult to pair with."

—*Albert Costa, winemaker, Celler Vall Llach*

Other Notable Countries

FRANCE

The French call it Carignan (*kahr-een-YAHN*) and have almost nine times as many acres as Spain, though this number will decline as a result of recent EU incentives for farmers to plant other varieties, especially Grenache, Syrah, and Mourvèdre. Much of Carignan's popularity in France comes from its workhorse yield: It produces more tons per acre than many varieties, four times the yield of Cabernet Sauvignon, for example. One good, if unintended, consequence of the EU program is that winemakers are pulling younger Carignan vines but leaving the old bush vines, which generally yield wine of a higher quality. Most of it grows in the Languedoc-Roussillon region, in the southeast, where it does extremely well in the Aude and the Herault Departments. AOC regulations call for minimum proportions of Carignan in St. Chinian, Corbières, Minervois, and Faugères wines, to name a few.

RECOMMENDED WINES

BARGAIN
KEVIN Domaine La Tour Boisée
Domaine Lafage Fortant Carignan Mountains Grand Reserve
MIKE Terre de Loups Les Terraces Royales Carignan Syrah
JEFF Paul Mas Estate Carignan Vieilles Vignes
Château Maris Le Carignan de Maris

VALUE
KEVIN Domaine D'Aupilhac Le Carignan
MIKE Domaine Bertrand-Bergé Les Mégalithes
JEFF Abbotts & Delaunay Alto Stratus

SPECIAL OCCASION
KEVIN Château Ollieux Romanis Cuvée Or Red
MIKE Gerard Bertrand La Forge Carignan-Syrah
JEFF Maxime Magnon Corbières Rozeta

SOUTH AFRICA

Cariñena made in South Africa tends to have strong acidity and tannins and a deep red color, which makes it ideal for blending, although the right combination of terroir and winemaking skill can make the best of its bright flavors of red cherry and mace. Some producers make single varietal bottlings best enjoyed when visiting South Africa because very few make it to the export market.

USA: CALIFORNIA

California has 2,500 acres of Cariñena, mostly in Madera County, but that number is falling. It often plays an anonymous role in Californian red table wine, where it adds strong acidity, healthy tannins, and a dark red color. As a single varietal, it offers bright flavors of red cherry and nutmeg.

OPPOSITE Casks at Grandes Vinos y Viñedos at Paniza in Spain. **ABOVE** Vineyard in Stellenbosch in South Africa.

CARMÉNÈRE

(kar-mehn-EHR)

IN THE GLASS

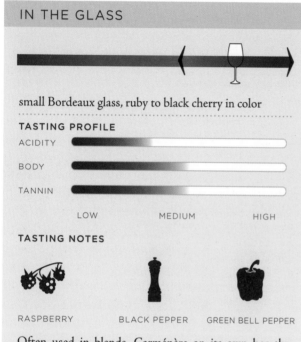

small Bordeaux glass, ruby to black cherry in color

TASTING PROFILE

	LOW	MEDIUM	HIGH
ACIDITY			
BODY			
TANNIN			

TASTING NOTES

RASPBERRY   BLACK PEPPER   GREEN BELL PEPPER

Often used in blends, Carménère on its own has the smooth flavors of fruits of the wood, freshly ground black pepper, and ripe green bell pepper. You'll also find light smoke and dried herb characteristics in the bouquet and palate.

YOU SHOULD KNOW

Carménère is a late-ripening grape. If a grower harvests too early, the resulting wine will have green aromas, such as jalapeño pepper and freshly snipped garden herbs.

FOOD PAIRINGS

BARBECUE   GRILLED VEGETABLES   CHICKEN

Carménères tend to have lower acidity than other red wines, so consider foods with a low fat content. The black pepper and smoke notes pair nicely with vegetables and low-fat meats, such as chicken, on the grill.

RECOMMENDED WINES

BARGAIN
KEVIN Santa Rita 120, Chile
Primus, Chile
MIKE San Pedro Castillo de Molina Reserva, Chile
JEFF De Martino Legado Reserva, Chile
Carmen Gran Reserva, Chile

VALUE
KEVIN De Martino Alto de Piedras, Chile
MIKE Merry Cellars Seven Hills Vineyard, USA: Washington
Elqui Wines Limited Release, Chile
JEFF Falernia Pedriscal Vineyard Reserva, Chile

SPECIAL OCCASION
KEVIN Reininger Seven Hills Vineyard, USA: Washington
MIKE Black Hills, Canada: British Columbia
JEFF Montes Purple Angel, Chile

SPLURGE
KEVIN Errazuriz Kai, Chile
MIKE Concha y Toro Carmin de Peumo, Chile
JEFF Santa Carolina Herencia, Chile

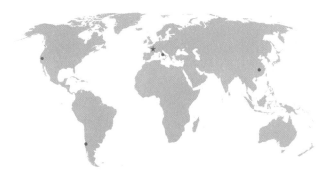

This noble grape is best known now as the lost grape of Bordeaux. A natural cross between Cabernet Franc and Gros Cabernet, Carménère grew widely in France's Gironde and Médoc before the phylloxera epidemic of the nineteenth century. Afterward, growers didn't meaningfully replant or regraft it because of its low yields and late ripening. Only fifty acres or so remain in France today, but some notable Bordeaux blends make use of it in very limited quantities. Its name derives from *carmin*, the French word for "crimson," which describes the leaves on the vine at the end of the season rather than the dark purple berries that make a deep red wine.

Carménère may have gone extinct had it not accidentally made its way to Chile in the mid-1800s, mixed in with cuttings labeled "Merlot." This happenstance helped preserve what is becoming Chile's signature grape, its answer—if you need one—to Argentina's Malbec. Chilean Carménère thrives in the alluvial soils, hot days, and cold nights there. Roughly 20,000 acres grow in Maipo, Aconcagua, Cachapoal, and Colchagua. The low acidity discourages long aging, so drink it within a few years of the vintage. De Martino produced the first varietal Carménère in 1996, and you can find many excellent versions of it as a varietal now. The addition of Cabernet Sauvignon often imparts structure and acidity.

Italy has around 100 acres of Carménère, and about 50 acres grow in California, but the wine made from them often goes into Meritage or Bordeaux-style blends rather than single-varietal bottles. In China, look for it in Gansu Province and east of Helan Mountain.

CINSAUT

(san-SO)

IN THE GLASS

small Bordeaux glass, black cherry in color

TASTING PROFILE

ACIDITY

BODY

TANNIN

LOW   MEDIUM   HIGH

TASTING NOTES

STRAWBERRY   RASPBERRY   DRIED HERBS

Cinsaut has fruit-filled, soft aromas of yellow peach, strawberry, and red raspberry, along with notes of dried Mediterranean herbs or even cardamom. It's low in tannins, so it feels smooth and silky in the mouth with a fruity finish.

FOOD PAIRINGS

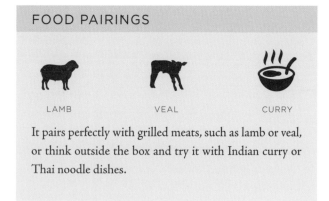

LAMB   VEAL   CURRY

It pairs perfectly with grilled meats, such as lamb or veal, or think outside the box and try it with Indian curry or Thai noodle dishes.

RECOMMENDED WINES

BARGAIN

OUR PICKS   Percheron Old Vine, France
De Martino Gallardia del Itata, Chile
Domaine des Terres Falmet, France

VALUE

OUR PICKS   Waterkloof Seriously Cool, South Africa
Onesta, USA: California
Michael David Winery Ancient Vines, USA: California
Turley Bechtoldt Vineyard, USA: California
Domaine d'Aupilhac Les Servieres, France
Badenhorst Family Wines, South Africa

YOU SHOULD KNOW

Because of the low tannin level, you should drink this wine (also spelled Cinsault) young—from release to no more than six years after the vintage.

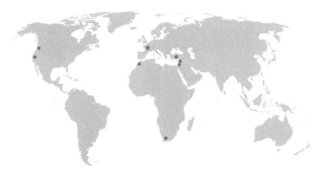

Cinsaut tolerates dry, excessively hot climates extremely well, so it thrives in other Mediterranean locations, including Morocco—where it ranks as the most planted grape—Turkey, Israel, and Lebanon. It has long-standing popularity in South Africa, especially around Paarl and Breedekloof, where it was known as Hermitage. (Fun fact for wine geeks: In 1925, it was crossed with Pinot Noir, which produced Pinotage.) Cinsaut also grows in small amounts in California and Washington State.

Cinsaut has declined in popularity since the 1970s, when France had more than 120,000 acres; today it grows there on around 50,000, mostly in the Aude, Gard, Var, and Herault regions, though it makes a good show in the Languedoc-Roussillon, Provence, and Côte d'Azur regions as well. When combined with its usual partners (Grenache, Syrah, Mourvèdre), it makes traditional, southern Rhône red blends. French regulations allow it in small doses in Châteauneuf-du-Pape blends, and it helps smooth the rough edges of Carignan.

As a straightforward single varietal, it makes a lovely, elegant, uncomplicated wine that you should chill for twenty minutes before drinking. When made as a single varietal rosé, it's worthy of sipping on the mega-yachts cruising the beaches of St. Tropez. If that's too rich for your blood, not to worry: Winemakers often blend it into simple, fruit-forward red wines that complement easygoing Provençal cuisine.

DOLCETTO

(dol-CHEH-toh)

IN THE GLASS

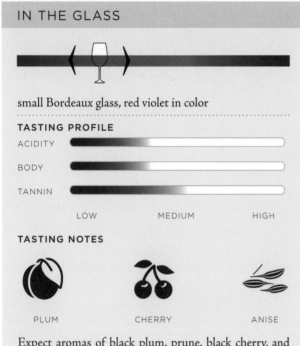

small Bordeaux glass, red violet in color

TASTING PROFILE

	LOW	MEDIUM	HIGH
ACIDITY			
BODY			
TANNIN			

TASTING NOTES

PLUM   CHERRY   ANISE

Expect aromas of black plum, prune, black cherry, and anise or licorice. On the palate you'll detect flavors of prune, fresh black cherry, licorice root, anise frond, and sometimes a touch of bitter almond in the finish.

YOU SHOULD KNOW

Because Dolcetto skins are so dark, most winemakers employ a short maceration period to produce a properly colored wine. If left to soak on the skins for too long, the resulting wine can develop an unpleasant smell.

FOOD PAIRINGS

PIZZA   PASTA   CHEESE

Because Dolcetto is light and easy-drinking, you can pair it with easy foods, such as pizza and pasta.

RECOMMENDED WINES

BARGAIN

KEVIN   Casata Monticello Dolcetto d'Asti
Domenico Clerico Langhe Visadi

MIKE   Fontantafredda Briccotondo
Paolo Scavino Dolcetto d'Alba

JEFF   Castello Banfi L'Ardi

VALUE

KEVIN   Bruno Giacosa Dolcetto d'Alba
Giuseppe Rinaldi Dolcetto d'Alba

MIKE   Mauro Sebaste Santa Rosalia Dolcetto d'Alba
Prunotto Mosesco Dolcetto d'Alba

JEFF   Elvio Cogno Vigna del Mandorlo Dolcetto d'Alba
Poderi Luigi Einaudi I Filari Dolcetto di Dogliani

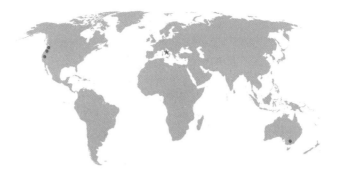

Experts believe that the name Dolcetto, which means "little sweet one" in Italian, comes from the hills where the vines originated, and documents dating back to the 1500s refer to variations of the grape's name. A 1593 ordinance in the village of Dogliani indicated when to harvest the grapes. A competing theory holds that the grape originated in France and came to Italy in the eleventh century, but hard proof has eluded ampelographers.

It grows throughout the Piedmont region of northwest Italy, where locals call it *duzet* or *duset*, and it has a long association with the villages of Ovada, Dogliani, and Diano d'Alba and the Langhe area. Many connoisseurs (ourselves included) assert that the best Dolcetto comes from Alba. These regions have minimum percentages of the grape in the bottle as well as minimum alcohol levels to achieve DOC and DOCG labeling.

This commercially important, "early to market" grape ripens up to one month before Nebbiolo, thus allowing winemakers to harvest, ferment, and transfer the Dolcetto wines from the tanks before using them for the Nebbiolo, thereby helping with cash flow. Generally not aged as long as Nebbiolo, Dolcetto wines usually should be enjoyed between one and three years after release.

The Dolcetto grape grows on more than 18,000 acres in Italy, but some winemakers in California, Washington, Oregon, and Australia are experimenting with the variety with small-scale plantings.

IN HER OWN WORDS

"Dolcetto wines are eminently drinkable; they can be simple wines that can be served slightly chilled and enjoyed on their own as an aperitivo or more complex wines that can pair so nicely with a wide range of foods. Dolcetto is the quintessential everyday wine, straightforward and unpretentious, meant to be enjoyed in its youth."

—*Cristina Mariani-May, co-CEO, Banfi Vintners*

NEXT PAGES Banfi's Piedmont vineyards and winery in Italy.

FETEASCĂ NEAGRĂ

(feh-TEH-ah-skah NEH-ah-grah)

IN THE GLASS

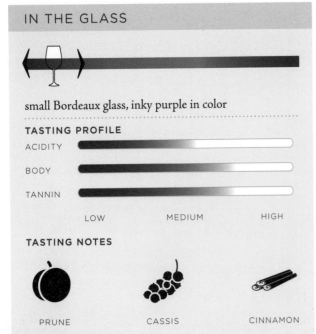

small Bordeaux glass, inky purple in color

TASTING PROFILE

ACIDITY

BODY

TANNIN

LOW   MEDIUM   HIGH

TASTING NOTES

PRUNE   CASSIS   CINNAMON

Aromas include red fruits, such as fresh strawberry and red plum, and dark fruits like cassis, black plum, and blackberry. Flavors can include fresh black plums or prunes, fresh red fruits, like strawberry and red raspberry, dried cherries, cassis, and brown baking spices, such as clove and cinnamon. In younger wines, the fruit flavors dominate, and you can experience the fruit-bomb effect, but as the wines mature some of the secondary aromas and flavors become more evident.

FOOD PAIRINGS

GRILLED MEAT   STEW   SOUP

When made with a higher alcohol level, Fetească Neagră pairs well with grilled meats and game, while lower-alcohol wines pair perfectly with stews and hearty soups.

RECOMMENDED WINES

BARGAIN

KEVIN Vinaria din Vale, Moldova
Recas La Putere, Romania
Monser, Romania

MIKE Domeniile Panciu, Romania

JEFF Murfatlar Trei Hectare, Romania

VALUE

KEVIN Cramele Halewood Hyperion, Romania

MIKE Davino Purpura Valahica, Romania

JEFF Et Cetera Serendipity Red, Moldova

SPECIAL OCCASION

OUR PICK Cramele Recas Selene, Romania

YOU SHOULD KNOW

Alcohol levels range between 12 and 14 percent. It ages well, and barrel aging produces tannins with a velvety quality.

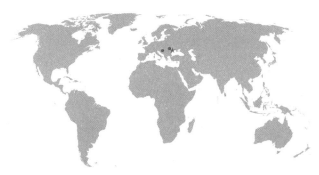

15 percent of Moldova's population, contributing 3.2 percent of the gross domestic product through more than 160 wineries. Moldova has four main PGI growing regions: Balti, Codru, Stefan Voda, and Valul lui Traian.

A new generation of producers is creating very good and highly acclaimed wines.

Some historians tie the origin of Fetească Neagră to the ancient kingdom of Dacia and tales of Dacians' domestication of wild grapevines. It makes for a romantic story, and experts have proven that pre-Christian winemaking existed in what is Moldova today, but no DNA evidence supports this claim for this specific grape variety. Wild grapes did grow here more than 7,000 years ago, though. Archaeological evidence, such as fossilized grape seeds and DNA evidence of wine on clay pots, dates back as far as 3000 BC. Early Greek colonies contributed to the rise of widespread production for home consumption and production for trade. Some very old vines exist, but Moldovan growers didn't plant Fetească Neagră widely from the 1940s until its resurgence around 2005.

We do know that Fetească Neagră is indigenous to Moldova and the Romanian region of Moldovia. It still grows in those countries and, to a lesser extent, in Ukraine and Hungary. The name means "young black girl" or "black maiden." As you might expect, the grapes are very dark, and they grow in tight bunches of relatively thick-skinned berries. The variety goes by many different names. A sampling: Coada Randunicii, Coada Rindunicu, Fetiasca Niagre, Fetjaska Neagra, Fetyaska Chernaya, Maedchentraube Schwarz, Pasareasca Neagra, Pasaryanska Chernaya, and Schwarze Madchentraube.

Moldova lies at 46 degrees latitude, similar to Bordeaux. The Black Sea influences the climate, and the nearby Dniester and Prut Rivers lay down rich sedimentary soil. It has the world's highest density of grapevines: Vineyards cover 3.8 percent of the country's total area. The winemaking industry employs

GAMAY

(GA-may)

IN THE GLASS

small Bordeaux glass, light red to black cherry in color

TASTING PROFILE

	LOW	MEDIUM	HIGH
ACIDITY			
BODY			
TANNIN			

TASTING NOTES

CHERRY · RASPBERRY · BANANA

Gamay has aromas of red fruits, such as red cherry and red raspberry, and sometimes banana. In the mouth, it features flavors of tart cherry, raspberry pie, and freshly picked red raspberries. The finish is bright and crisp.

YOU SHOULD KNOW

Most Beaujolais Nouveau and some Beaujolais Villages wines have a pronounced aroma of banana in the bouquet, which usually results from carbonic maceration, or in-fruit fermentation. This process creates fruit-bomb wine, which is ready to drink almost immediately. The downside, however, is that you really can't age these wines. You generally won't find the distinct banana smell in the better Cru appellation wines because they ferment the old-fashioned way.

FOOD PAIRINGS

CHEESE · FRUIT · SALAD

Pair these lighter-style wines with lighter foods: French cheeses, fruit plates, and salads. Gamay wines are perfect for a picnic or a day at the beach when you want something different from or more complex than a crisp white wine. Don't hesitate to chill your Gamay for twenty minutes before drinking.

RECOMMENDED WINES

BARGAIN

KEVIN Georges Duboeuf Cave Jean-Ernest Descombes
Louis Jadot Beaujolais-Villages

MIKE Château Frédignac Moulin-à-Vent
Vignerons de Bel-Air Cuvée Classique

JEFF Vaucher Père et Fils Fleurie

VALUE

KEVIN Guy Breton Morgon

MIKE Château de la Chaize Brouilly Cuvée Vielles Vignes

JEFF Château de la Chaize Brouilly
Château des Bachelards / Comtesse de Vazeilles
Pouilly-Vinzelles "Les Quarts"

SPECIAL OCCASION

KEVIN Thibault Liger-Belair Moulin-à-Vent Les Vignes
Centenaires
Louis Jadot Château des Jacques Côte
du Py Morgon

MIKE Château de Bellevue Le Clos Morgon
Château des Bachelards / Comtesse de Vazeilles
Le Grand Vin "Esprit de Finesse"

JEFF Château du Moulin-à-Vent Croix des Vérillats
Château des Jacques La Roche Moulin-à-Vent

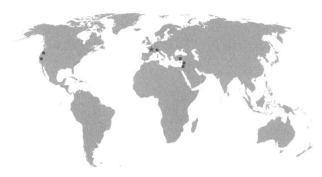

The major red grape in Beaujolais is Gamay, so the two words often are used interchangeably, but Gamay has been competing with Pinot Noir since the Middle Ages. Beaujolais technically forms part of Burgundy, but the region never had it easy. In 1395, 1455, 1567, and a few times in the 1700s the local government outlawed the growing of Gamay, and as recently as 2011 forty Beaujolais communes lost their rights to label some of their wines as "Burgundy." The 1395 ban, decreed by Philip II, duke of Burgundy, called for the destruction of all Gamay vines because wine made from the grapes reportedly infected people with serious diseases. Totally untrue!

Local Beaujolais historians say that Gamay takes its name from the village of Gamay in Saône-et-Loire, but other researchers refute this point. Gamay is native to France and covers 75,000 acres of the country. Current AOC regulations allow it for wine use in all but a few places, most notably Bordeaux. Most plantings lie in the Rhône Valley and Beaujolais, and you'll find the best wines made from Gamay in the ten Cru Beaujolais wines, listed here from north to south with some of their attributes:

JULIÉNAS Nice florality on the nose—think lilac and violet—with a bit of spice in the bouquet and on the palate.

ST. AMOUR Generally lighter and a bit more elegant, with a lot of spice on the palate.

CHÉNAS Pronounced florality, sometimes of fragrant red rose, with silky tannins.

MOULIN-À-VENT Red raspberry, blackberry, and red plum in the bouquet and nice fruit on the palate. Wines from Moulin-à-Vent tend to age well.

FLEURIE Nice floral aromas. Again, think purple flowers, such as irises or violets. Well-structured, silky tannins lead to a persistent finish.

CHIROUBLES Also floral in the nose and on the palate but a little lighter in the body.

MORGON More powerful and ageworthy, more dark fruits in the nose and mouth than other Cru wines, and persistence on the palate. More of these wines make their way to the American market because they have a flavor profile that many Americans like.

REGNIE Somewhat light bodied but lots of ripe red fruits and bright acidity.

CÔTE DE BROUILLY Medium bodied with earthy and forest-floor notes in the bouquet, good heft on the palate, and a persistent finish.

BROUILLY This largest Cru produces elegant, light-bodied wines with aromas of red plum, red raspberry, black plum, and sometimes a touch of cassis in the bouquet. Nicely weighted on the palate with a delightful acidic finish.

If the only Gamay you've tasted is a Beaujolais Nouveau, start over and pretend you've never had one. Growers harvest Gamay grapes in September or October, which winemakers quickly vinify, shipping the bottles to shops around the world in time for a coordinated sale on the third Thursday of November. The resulting wines are young and fruity at best, which makes them poor ambassadors. That eight-week window between harvest and point of sale has tarnished the reputation of this noble region. That said, if you ever visit France around the third weekend in November, head to Beaujolais for the region's harvest festivals, have one glass of the Nouveau, then graduate to the more serious Cru wines, which merit more exploration.

Other Notable Countries

Gamay also grows widely in Switzerland, where it ranks second only behind Pinot Noir. Some winemakers blend the two—which drives the French *crazy*—but it results in an interesting, tasty wine worth trying. Oregon makes a few good examples, and California, Turkey, Lebanon, and Israel have limited plantings.

IN HER OWN WORDS

"A young Gamay (aged one to five years) matches very well with poultry, vegetables, and grilled fish. If aged five to fifteen years, then the best pairing is red meat."

—*Alexandra de Vazeilles, owner and winemaker, Château des Bachelards, Comtesse de Vazeilles*

OPPOSITE Old press at Château de la Chaize in France. **ABOVE** Château de la Chaize in winter in France.

GARNACHA

(gar-NAH-cha)

IN THE GLASS

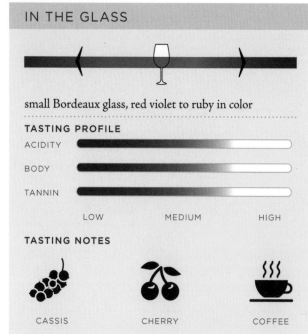

small Bordeaux glass, red violet to ruby in color

TASTING PROFILE

ACIDITY

BODY

TANNIN

LOW   MEDIUM   HIGH

TASTING NOTES

CASSIS   CHERRY   COFFEE

Aromas include cassis, black cherry, black plum, and black raspberry as well as notes of brown spices, black pepper, and espresso. Many of these continue seamlessly onto the palate with great fruit flavors and spicy secondary characteristics. Garnacha has a long ripening process, which gives it high levels of sugar that in turn can cause high levels of alcohol in the finished wine. Many Garnacha-based wines contain more than 15 percent alcohol.

YOU SHOULD KNOW

Cabernet Sauvignon–based wines can fetch a high price tag, but Garnacha-based wines can compete in the price wars. Some Châteauneuf-du-Pape wines cost $600 per bottle; 100 percent Garnacha wines from Spain can fetch from $300 to $400; and California's Sine Qua Non from Santa Barbara can set you back $500 per bottle.

FOOD PAIRINGS

GRILLED MEAT   STEW   CHEESE

When in Spain, we love to pair Gambas Pil Pil (sauteed prawns) with a full-bodied Garnacha. The high level of spice and alcohol in the wine cuts the heat of the spicy red pepper in that dish as well as grilled meat, stew, and cheese. It also pairs well with other spicy, slightly sweet food, such as Thai or Indian curries.

RECOMMENDED WINES

BARGAIN

KEVIN Viña Zorzal
Bodegas Valdemar Old Vine Grenache

MIKE Las Rocas
Scala Dei Garnatxa

JEFF Ramón Bilbao
Gran Clos Les Mines
Palacios Remondo La Montesa

VALUE

KEVIN Artadi Pasos de San Martín

MIKE Gran Clos Finca El Puig
Palacios Remondo Propiedad

JEFF Las Rocas Vinas Viejas
Embruix de Vall Llach

SPECIAL OCCASION

KEVIN Colección Vivanco Parcelas de Garnacha

MIKE Capcanes Cabrida

JEFF Gran Clos

SPLURGE

KEVIN Dominio de Pingus

MIKE Scala Dei Masdeu

JEFF Alto Moncayo Aquilon

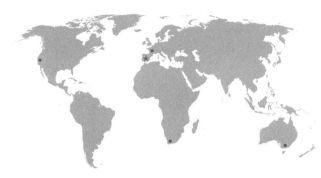

Many wine lovers know this grape by its French name, Grenache, but we use its Spanish name because it comes from Spain or possibly from Sardinia, which Spain formerly ruled. Some researchers debate whether the name derives from the Catalan word *garnaxa* used to describe the garnet color of a judge's robe, or from the Italian grape Vernaccia. Garnacha likely hails from Aragon in northeastern Spain, and some Spaniards in the region still call the variety Aragones. It grows in many wine regions, including Catalonia, Extremadura, Navarre, Valencia, and even Rioja Baja, where winemakers blend it with Tempranillo. The country has about 185,000 acres of Garnacha vineyards, mostly in Castilla–La Mancha and Aragon.

Garnacha ripens late and does best in hot, dry climates that concentrate its sugars to the fullest. It's also one of the most widely planted red grapes in the world: France has about 200,000 acres of Grenache, and about 15,000 acres grow in Sardinia, where it's known as Cannonau.

The Priorat DOQ, southwest of Barcelona, consists of eleven municipalities and has a soil composition featuring black slate and quartz. Garnacha plantations make up about 40 percent of all vines grown here. Wines traditionally made here generally consisted of 100 percent Garnacha or a Garnacha-Cariñena blend. In the 1990s, however, a group of winemakers broke the mold and added Cabernet Sauvignon and Syrah to their wines. The result? A publicity phenomenon in which collectors eagerly sought and paid high prices for these blends. The recent blend trend has been to keep Garnacha constant, decrease the Cariñena, and increase the Cabernet Sauvignon, Merlot, and Syrah. For many years, Spanish winemakers preferred to plant Tempranillo because they considered it a nobler grape, but single-varietal Garnacha wines and blends from Priorat have begun to command high prices, convincing winemakers to change their ways.

BELOW Casks at Scala Dei winery in Spain. **NEXT PAGES** Vineyard and ruins at the Scala Dei winery in Spain.

"The Garnacha clone that we had planted one hundred years ago here is so different than the clone that you can now find on the market. The blue slate of our vineyards, the deep slopes, the water stress, and the age of the plants make our Garnacha so unique, so mineral, so deep and different than others. Garnacha in Priorat is fresh and aromatic but at the same time so mineral and deep."

—*Albert Costa, winemaker, Celler Vall Llach*

Other Notable Countries

AUSTRALIA

Garnacha vines up to 150 years old still grow and fruit in South Australia. James Busby brought the first vines here in the mid-1800s, but cuttings ferried by Christopher Rawson Penfold in 1844, the year he founded his eponymous winery, proved more important. For many years, Garnacha was used to make a fortified, Port-style wine in Australia, where its flavor profile combines cherry, blackberry, and cassis with spice, tobacco, and earth but also can have a candied-fruit character. The finest examples of Australian Garnacha come from the Barossa Valley, Clare Valley, and McLaren Vale, and it often goes into GSM blends along with Syrah and Mourvèdre, its Rhône Valley cohorts.

FRANCE

Garnacha originated just south of the Franco-Spanish border, so it's easy to see how it migrated to France. Some winemakers produce Grenache (*gruh-NAHSH*) as a single varietal, but it's most well known here for its use in Châteauneuf-du-Pape blends. Grenache is France's second most planted variety, grown mostly in the southern half of the country, especially in the Vaucluse. Besides its use in Châteauneuf, Gigondas, and Côtes du Rhône blends, it also makes delicious Tavel rosés and stunning Languedoc-Roussillon GSM blends.

Châteauneuf-du-Pape takes its name from the fourteenth-century papal palace in Avignon, "the new castle of the pope" that towered over village streets. The Châteauneuf-du-Pape AOC allows for thirteen grape varieties in a blend, but Grenache generally ranks as the most prevalent or even the only variety, which makes sense when you consider that Grenache accounts for almost 75 percent of the vines in this appellation.

The name Gigondas has two possible origins: One theory claims that the name comes from the Latin phrase *gignit undas*, which means "It springs from the waves." The second theory proposes that the name derives from St. Jucunda, whose name means "joyful." In the Gigondas AOC, winemakers can use no more than 80 percent Grenache, at least 15 percent Syrah and/or Mourvèdre, and no more than 10 percent of other Rhône varietals, excluding Carignan.

For a Côtes du Rhône Village wine, 50 percent of the blend must come from Grenache, 20 percent from Syrah and/or Mourvèdre, and the balance a maximum of 20 percent of the other grape varieties.

BARGAIN

KEVIN Parallèle 45 Côtes du Rhône Jaboulet

MIKE Domaine de Gournier Grenache

JEFF Château Les Amoureuses Les Charmes Grenache
André Brunel Côtes du Roussillon Rouge

VALUE

KEVIN E. Guigal Gigondas

MIKE Louis Bernard Les Carbonnières Gigondas
Ogier Oratorio Gigondas

JEFF Château Maucoil 1895 Grenache

SPECIAL OCCASION

KEVIN Pierre-Henri Morel Lieu-dit Pignan Grenache

MIKE Château Maris Old Vine Grenache

JEFF Domaine des Saumades Châteauneuf-du-Pape
Rouge

SPLURGE

KEVIN Domaine Giraud Châteauneuf-du-Pape Grenaches
de Pierre
Domaine du Pegau Châteauneuf-du-Pape Cuvée
da Capo

MIKE Famille Perrin Château de Beaucastel Red
André Brunel Les Cailloux Châteauneuf-du-Pape
Cuvée Centenaire

JEFF Domaine de la Mordorée La Reine des Bois Red
Domaine du Pegau Cuvée Laurence Red

IN HIS OWN WORDS

"Grenache is not too serious like Cabernet Sauvignon or Pinot Noir. It gives a nice fruit, has a bright color, and makes wine that you want to share with your friends when you come back from work or for a party outside. On exceptional terroir, such as Châteauneuf-du-Pape, it gives wonderful wines that can be aged for decades. The more Grenache is aged, the more elegant it becomes."

—*Fabrice Brunel, apprentice winemaker, Domaine Les Cailloux*

SOUTH AFRICA

Garnacha also prospers in the hot, dry climate of South Africa. The common flavor profile here includes notes of red fruits, such as strawberry and raspberry, honeysuckle, and light spice.

USA: CALIFORNIA

Long used to make inexpensive, easy-drinking reds and rosés, Garnacha is most heavily planted in California, where it grows on about 6,000 acres, with more than half of those divided between Fresno and Madera Counties. Tablas Creek brought cuttings from Château de Beaucastel in Châteauneuf-du-Pape in 1989, and acreage is expanding in both San Luis Obispo and Santa Barbara, two hotbeds of Rhône-style winemaking. The Rhône Rangers, a group dedicated to the promotion of Rhône-style wines in California and the USA, are championing its cultivation and vinification.

MALBEC

(MAHL-bek)

IN THE GLASS

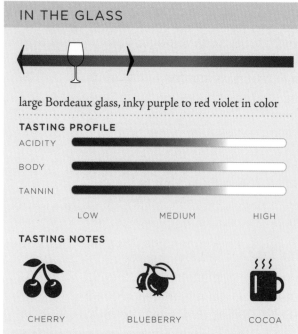

large Bordeaux glass, inky purple to red violet in color

TASTING PROFILE

	LOW	MEDIUM	HIGH
ACIDITY			
BODY			
TANNIN			

TASTING NOTES

CHERRY   BLUEBERRY   COCOA

Offering aromas of cherry, black plum, chocolate, and spice, Malbec has flavors of black cherry, raspberry, blueberry, cocoa, violet, and licorice. It comes in several styles, from fresh and fruity to up to two years of oak aging.

YOU SHOULD KNOW

Like its European counterparts, the Argentinean wine industry took steps in 2011 to define the terms "Reserva" and "Gran Reserva." A Reserva must age for at least one year prior to release. Gran Reserva wines require at least two years. A bottle labeled "Malbec" may contain 80 percent Malbec and 20 percent other varieties without listing them on the label.

FOOD PAIRINGS

STEAK   PASTA   PIZZA

Malbec pairs well with meat, but it doesn't require fatty meat to cut its tannins. Try a Malbec barrel-aged for a year with flank or skirt steak. Enjoy a longer-aged Malbec—up to two years—with well-marbled cuts, such as Porterhouse or rib eye. Argentineans often drink Malbec with tortellini with ragu or spaghetti Bolognese—both terrific pairings.

RECOMMENDED WINES

BARGAIN
KEVIN Maison Nicolas Cahors
Clos Siguier Cahors
MIKE Château Lamartine Prestige du Malbec
Château Vincens Origine
JEFF Paul Mas Estate
Château du Cèdre Héritage Cahors

VALUE
KEVIN Paul Bertrand Crocus L'Atelier Cahors
MIKE Domaine du Theron Prestige
Jean-Luc Baldes Clos Triguedina
JEFF Château Lagrézette Château Chevaliers

SPECIAL OCCASION
KEVIN Domaine de Lagrézette
MIKE Domaine de Cause Notre Dame des Champs
JEFF Château Haut-Monplaisir Pur Plaisir
Clos Troteligotte K-2

SPLURGE
KEVIN Georges Vigouroux Château de Haute-Serre
Icône Wow
MIKE Château Lagrézette Paragon
JEFF Paul Mas Estate La Violeta

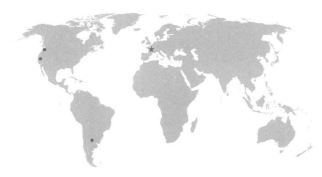

labeled Cot or Malbec, from Bordeaux or the Loire, but they're few and far between.

Like an aspiring actress who left home to be discovered, Malbec had to travel to Argentina to become the global superstar of today. A French viticulturist charged with starting Argentina's National Vine Nursery in Mendoza, Michel Pouget brought Malbec—along with cuttings of many other French varieties—to the Land of Silver. Malbec succeeded here in part because it requires more sun and heat than, say, Merlot or Cabernet Sauvignon. High-altitude vineyards in Argentina offer nighttime temperatures ideal for retaining acidity, but clear days and hot sun provide an excellent environment for Malbec to ripen to perfection. With stronger tannins than Merlot, Malbec offers the age-ability and full mouthfeel so much in demand among lovers of red wine. Its strong tannins age well, but they don't render the wine undrinkable within the first year or two after release.

Known as Cot in France, its native country, Malbec also goes by the names Auxerrois and Pressac here, where winemakers use it primarily in Bordeaux-style blends, as one of the six allowable grapes, for color and body. In the last decade or two, Malbec has exploded onto the global wine scene—more about that below—and the French wine region of Cahors now promotes itself as the birthplace of Malbec. The variety even has its own holiday: World Malbec Day, April 17, celebrates the purported day that Domingo Faustino Sarmiento, seventh president of Argentina, asked Michel Pouget to bring Malbec grapevines to Argentina. Auxerrois, one of its many synonyms, indicates that it may have grown widely around the town of Auxerre in northern Burgundy at one point.

In 1956, an infamous frost killed many Bordeaux vines, and growers replanted their vineyards with varieties other than Malbec. That same frost also devastated the Malbec vineyards of Cahors, to the east. Unlike the Bordelaise, however, Cadurcien winemakers did replant Malbec and continued vinifying it either on its own or blended with small amounts of Merlot and Tannat.

Malbec from Cahors comes in three distinct styles, described as tender and fruity, feisty and powerful, and intense and complex. Tender and fruity Malbecs generally contain 70 to 85 percent Malbec and have soft tannins and rich acidity. They pair well with fried seafood and dishes made with eggplant or tomatoes. Feisty and powerful versions contain 85 to 100 percent Malbec grapes. They make a natural accompaniment to duck and pork and hold up to spicy Chinese dishes using either of these two meats. An intense and complex Malbec from Cahors contains 100 percent of the variety, and its supple tannins and rich acidity suit roast leg of lamb and grilled venison steaks well.

Malbec also grows in other regions throughout France, but those winemakers usually give it a secondary or even tertiary role in blends. You occasionally can find a varietal version,

Other Notable Countries

ARGENTINA

Malbec put Argentina's winemaking industry on the map. Michel Pouget's cuttings arrived in 1853 and thrived in the dry soils of the Andean foothills. In the 1980s, growers ripped out a large portion of the plantings and replaced them with Criolla to make cheap, low-quality wine. A decade later, as the Argentinean economy strengthened, vintners focused their efforts on producing higher-caliber wine, and Malbec—with its intense flavor structure and opulent tannins—became the preeminent variety here. Today it sits on an international throne of popularity.

Malbec covers about 70,000 acres, or 12 percent of all vineyards in the country, the majority in the Mendoza region. Argentinean Malbec grape clusters are smaller and tighter than those in France, and they have a strikingly dark purple color—both on the vine and as a finished wine—with primary flavors of black cherry, plum, and chocolate and highlights of violet and licorice.

Argentinean Malbec often goes into blends with other grapes—mostly Bordeaux varieties, such as Cabernet Sauvignon, Merlot, Cabernet Franc, and Petit Verdot—but it thrives on its own in a variety of styles. A fresh, fruity type benefits from a short time in oak, and you can find it from multiple producers at reasonable prices. In general, as you move up the price scale, you'll see an increase in vine age and time spent in the barrel, which creates oak flavors of vanilla and spice and additional tannins. Many of these premium Malbecs spend twelve to eighteen months in the barrel and come from single vineyards. At the upper end of the spectrum, you'll find Malbec vinified into "icon" wine, meaning the finest expression of terroir, fruit, and craftsmanship. Hand-selected grapes from old vines ferment in small quantities, age at least two years in the barrel and one year in the bottle before release, and are among the most expensive—and delicious.

Malbec has DOC status in a few regions. Lujan de Cuyo came first in 1993. Wines from here, Tupungato, Tunuyan, and San Carlos in the Uco Valley rank among the country's finest. In the north, Salta has the world's highest vineyards and is making a name for itself with high-quality Malbec, mainly from small producers. Growers first planted vines here in the sixteenth century, making Salta one of Argentina's oldest successful grape-growing regions. Salta vineyards represent barely 1 percent of the nation's total acreage, but wine lovers prize the Malbec from this distinct terroir for its flavors of dark berries, roasted red pepper, and spice.

RECOMMENDED WINES

BARGAIN

KEVIN Trapiche Oak Cask
Clos de los Siete
MIKE Killka by Salentein
Alamos Selección
Monteviejo Festivo
JEFF Terrazas de los Andes Reserva
Ruta 22
Don Miguel Gascón

VALUE

KEVIN Luca
MIKE Alta Vista Classic
JEFF Don Miguel Gascón Reserva
Septima Obra

SPECIAL OCCASION

KEVIN Septima Gran
MIKE Terrazas de los Andes Single Vineyard Las Compuertas
JEFF Salentein PR1MUM

SPLURGE

KEVIN Achaval Ferrer Finca Altamira
MIKE Susana Balbo Nosotros Single Vineyard Nomade
Bodega Catena Zapata Adrianna Vineyard
JEFF Cheval des Andes

ABOVE Bodega el Esteco vineyard in Argentina. NEXT PAGES Oak barrels at Bodega El Esteco Vineyard in Argentina.

IN HER OWN WORDS

"Malbec is unique to Mendoza because it benefits from the high-altitude sites where it is planted, developing unique flavors not found anywhere else in the world. I've tried Malbec from Cahors, France, and from Chile. I can say that they are really different than the ones we produce in Argentina. Malbec from Cahors has coarser tannins, herbal characters, sharp acidity, and much more oak, while the ones that grow in Chile have hints of mint and greenish notes."

—*Susana Balbo, owner and winemaker, Susana Balbo Wines*

IN HIS OWN WORDS

"Malbec has been woven into my country's culture for decades. In many ways, Malbec is a bit of Argentina in a glass. Its flavors are full and rich, and underneath there are layers and depth. Argentina's vibrant culture has those same layers, from bold to sophisticated. Malbec also fits one of my country's passions: grilling meats. Our asado cries out for Malbec to go with the meal, and Malbec is equally ideal to enjoy while we grill and await the meal."

—*Matías Ciciani, winemaker, Don Miguel Gascón*

USA: CALIFORNIA

American winemakers aren't producing a lot of single-varietal Malbec, but about 85 percent of all the Malbec vineyards in the USA lie in the Golden State, the majority in Sonoma, Napa, and San Joaquin Counties. Malbec from California tends to have less complexity than its Argentinean counterpart, with stronger fruit flavors and fewer notes of green bell pepper, leather, and chocolate—probably because the young California vines produce wines with a simpler flavor profile. The alcohol level also trends lower in California Malbec, hovering around 14 percent, as opposed to the typical 15.5 percent from Mendoza.

In response to the Argentinean boom, plantings of Malbec in Napa County more than doubled between 2004 and 2014, and more than fifty producers here bottle it as a single varietal, although you'll be hard pressed to find a bottle beyond a winery or its wine club.

RECOMMENDED WINES

BARGAIN
KEVIN Lyeth Estate
MIKE Ironstone Reserve
JEFF Peirano The Heritage Collection
Scotto Cellars

VALUE
KEVIN Rodney Strong
MIKE Edna Valley Vineyard Winemaker Series
Napa Cellars Classic Collection Winemaker Series
JEFF Hearst Ranch Babicora

SPECIAL OCCASION
KEVIN Chappellet
Merryvale
MIKE Louis M. Martini Monte Rosso Vineyard
Trinchero Haystack Vineyard
JEFF Mt. Brave Mt. Veeder

USA: WASHINGTON STATE

The Evergreen State's first Malbec vineyard was planted in the 1980s, but most vines here are fewer than fifteen years old. Eastern Washington offers an ideal near-desert climate for the cultivation of red wine grapes, and in recent years Malbec has come into its own here. Production is relatively small, but it's making serious inroads. You'll find the highest concentration of Malbec vineyards in Walla Walla, Horse Heaven Hills, Yakima Valley, and Wahluke Slope. Expect flavors of cherry, black plum, and mocha with notes of black pepper and leather.

RECOMMENDED WINES

VALUE
KEVIN Powers
Waterbrook Reserve
MIKE Sparkman Preposterous
Walla Walla Vintners Pepper Bridge
JEFF Dusted Valley

SPECIAL OCCASION
KEVIN Columbia Crest
Hedges Family Estate Single Vineyard
MIKE K Vintners Broncho
JEFF àMaurice Cellars Amparo Estate
Milbrandt Vineyards Series Reserve

IN HER OWN WORDS

"My favorite note in Washington Malbec is the plum and Chinese five spice: star anise, red pepper, cloves, cinnamon, and ground fennel seeds. You can smell it out of the fermenter!"

—*Anna Schafer, winemaker, àMaurice Cellars*

OPPOSITE Malbec vines at àMaurice vineyard in Washington.

MARSELAN

(mahr-suh-LAHN)

IN THE GLASS

small Bordeaux glass, red violet to ruby in color

TASTING PROFILE

ACIDITY

BODY

TANNIN

LOW   MEDIUM   HIGH

TASTING NOTES

PLUM   RASPBERRY   BLACK PEPPER

Because it undergoes little or no oak aging, it has strong aromas of red fruits and berries and pleasant flavors of red plum and red raspberry with supple tannins.

YOU SHOULD KNOW

Some California winemakers, especially in the North Coast, use small amounts of Marselan to add interest and spice to their wines.

FOOD PAIRINGS

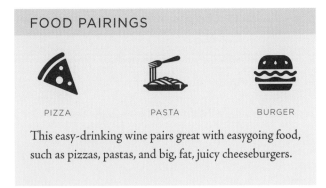

PIZZA   PASTA   BURGER

This easy-drinking wine pairs great with easygoing food, such as pizzas, pastas, and big, fat, juicy cheeseburgers.

RECOMMENDED WINES

BARGAIN

OUR PICKS Le Colombier, France
Enseduna, France
Domaine de Couron, France
Vinitrio, France
Château Camplazens, France

VALUE

OUR PICK Jerusalem Wineries Premium 3400, Israel

SPECIAL OCCASION

OUR PICK Recanati Marselan Reserve, Israel

SPLURGE

OUR PICK Grace Vineyard Tasya's Reserve, China

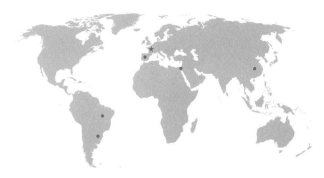

I n 1961, researcher Paul Truel was hoping that his cross of Cabernet Sauvignon and Grenache would yield large grapes that could produce a large amount of juice for wine production. Unfortunately the combination yielded small berries, and he discontinued the project. Subsequent researchers were looking for disease-resistant varieties in 1990, and Marselan got a second chance for its ability to shun molds and mildews.

The name of this lab cross comes from the town of Marseillan, on France's Mediterranean coast, where Truel bred it at the Institut National de la Recherche Agronomique. The US Alcohol and Tobacco Tax and Trade Bureau didn't recognize the variety until 2007, making it one of the newest varieties to the American market.

More than 3,000 acres grow in France, most in the Rhône Valley and Languedoc regions. You'll also find plantings in Catalonia, Spain; Mendoza, Argentina; Serra Gaucha, Brazil, and Israel. The most interesting new plantations of Marselan lie in Hebei Province and Penglai in Shandong Province, China, where Domaines Barons de Rothschild has a partnership with a Chinese investment company. The Sino-French Demonstration Vineyard in Hebei has been making a varietal Marselan for a few years now, and Domaines Barons de Rothschild will be releasing a varietal from their vineyards in Penglai soon.

MAVRUD

(mahv-ROOD)

IN THE GLASS

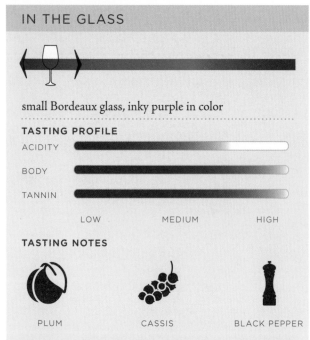

small Bordeaux glass, inky purple in color

TASTING PROFILE

ACIDITY			
BODY			
TANNIN			
	LOW	MEDIUM	HIGH

TASTING NOTES

PLUM · CASSIS · BLACK PEPPER

The nose exhibits aromas of dark fruits, such as black plum, blackberry, and cassis. Strong up-front tannins yield to luscious dark fruit flavors and secondary flavors of saddle leather and smoked meats, and you'll find quite a bit of spice in the persistent finish.

YOU SHOULD KNOW

Mavrud can be blended with other varieties, such as Cabernet Sauvignon or Merlot, but some of the best examples are single varietal. Most vintners make it in a dry style, with varying degrees of oak aging to round out the flavors and tame the tannins, but some winemakers are making delicious semisweet and sweet Mavrud dessert wines. Some winemakers also joke that a good Mavrud should have so much body that you can carry it around in a handkerchief.

FOOD PAIRINGS

LAMB · STEW · CHILI

Mavrud pairs amazingly well with charcoal grilled meats, such as lamb, beef, pork, ground meat patties, and meatballs on skewers. It also goes well with heavy stews—think Hungarian goulash and spicy Tex-Mex chilis.

RECOMMENDED WINES

BARGAIN

OUR PICKS EM
BIO Mavrud & Rubin
Villa Melnik Bergule
Manastira Ilaya Reserve
Katarzyna Mezzek
Domaine Boyar Royal Reserve
Rumelia Wine Cellar Merul Reserve
Barbarians Wealth

VALUE

OUR PICKS Edoardo Miroglio Elenovo Nova Zagora
Vinzavod Asenovgrad Version Plaisir divin
Todoroff Teres

Scholars believe that the Cult of Dionysus—which originated in ancient Thrace, today Bulgaria—held Mavrud in high esteem. Archaeologists have unearthed coins bearing images of Dionysus and figures holding grape bunches as well as silver and gold vessels for drinking wine. This history makes Bulgaria one of the world's earliest wine producers and Mavrud one of the oldest grape varieties, with more than 5,000 years of cultivation behind it. The grape takes its name from the Greek word *mavro*, meaning "black."

Mavrud grows in many places in Bulgaria, but some of the best examples come from the Thracian Lowlands PGI and the growing regions around the south-central town of Plovdiv, which have a transitional continental climate with influences from the Black and Mediterranean Seas. Here it grows at an altitude between 300 and 1,500 feet, which allows for night cooling. It grows in tight bunches of medium-sized, very dark grapes that mature late in the growing season. Some of the larger producers use mechanized equipment, but most smaller producers harvest it by hand.

IN HIS OWN WORDS

"I discovered Mavrud when I started to travel to Bulgaria almost forty years ago. It was a thin wine with a lot of green tannin but still with the capacity to age very long. In fact, at that time only long-aged bottles were a pleasure to drink."

—*Edoardo Miroglio, owner, Edoardo Miroglio Wine Cellar*

MERLOT

(muhr-LO)

IN THE GLASS

small Bordeaux glass, inky purple to red violet in color

TASTING PROFILE

	LOW	MEDIUM	HIGH
ACIDITY			
BODY			
TANNIN			

TASTING NOTES

CHERRY   BLUEBERRY   VANILLA

Flavors of black cherry, blueberry, cassis, and vanilla often give way to cooling herb notes, such as mint or eucalyptus. Soft and velvety tannins offer good mouthfeel without overpowering the palate. Aged Merlot exhibits flavors of coffee, leather, and chocolate.

YOU SHOULD KNOW

If not fully ripe when picked, Merlot can taste of green bell pepper or herbs. It tends to cost less than Cabernet Sauvignon, so flip to the Merlot section of the wine list if you want a delicious yet affordable wine with dinner.

FOOD PAIRINGS

TACO   CURRY   BURGER

Because of its soft tannins, Merlot matches well with spicy food, so try it with tacos or burritos. A well aged Merlot is delicious alongside herb-crusted rack of lamb. To experience its amazing versatility, crack open a box of mint chocolate cookies with your best friend, a good movie, and a bargain-priced bottle of Merlot.

RECOMMENDED WINES

BARGAIN

KEVIN   Château Peybonhomme Les Tours Blaye Côtes de Bordeaux

MIKE   La Forge Estate

JEFF   Château Trocard Bordeaux Supérieur

VALUE

KEVIN   Château Robin Castillon Côtes de Bordeaux

MIKE   Château Rollan de By Cru Bourgeois Médoc

JEFF   Château Lassègue Les Cadrans de Lassègue Grand Cru
Château du Moulin Rouge Haut-Médoc

SPECIAL OCCASION

KEVIN   Clos des Jacobins
Château Bel-Air
Château Le Bon Pasteur

MIKE   Clos Cantenac Saint-Emilion

JEFF   Château Haut Condissas

SPLURGE

KEVIN   Château Clinet

MIKE   Château Lafleur
Château Certan de May

JEFF   Château Petrus Pomerol

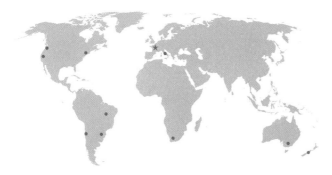

Everyone agrees that the name of this grape comes from the Old French word for blackbird, *merle*, but wine and language experts disagree about whether the name derives metaphorically from its small, almost-black grapes or the observation that blackbirds love eating them. The original spelling was Merlau, first attested in print in the late eighteenth century.

Winemakers used it as a blending grape for many years, but its early ripening and resistance to mildew made it popular with vineyard managers and winemakers starting in the nineteenth century. Today Merlot ranks as the predominant grape in France, including Bordeaux, where the bouquet features a pronounced perfume and florality that you might not find elsewhere. The Pomerol and St. Émilion appellations, on the Right Bank of the Garonne River, count it as their main grape and make some of the finest expressions of Merlot in the world. Quite a bit of Merlot also grows in the Languedoc-Roussillon region, where it makes for fairly inexpensive table wine noted for its fruit-forward flavor.

Despite a sideways dip in popularity in the early 2000s, Merlot, a descendant of Cabernet Franc, remains one of the world's most widely cultivated and enjoyed wine grapes. It grows in almost every grape-producing country and region, second in total acreage only to Cabernet Sauvignon, although the two grapes run neck-and-neck in many tallies.

Merlot's soft tannins make it an ideal blending partner for harsher grapes, but they render it highly drinkable on its own as well. Merlot enjoys a rare dual role in the wine world: Its soft tannins and fruit-forward flavors make it an ideal first red for newer wine drinkers, yet it forms the base of two of the world's most sought wines: Château Pétrus from Pomerol, France, and Tenuta dell'Ornellaia Masseto, the ultimate Super Tuscan.

ABOVE Processing Merlot grapes at Artesa Winery in Napa in California. **NEXT PAGES** Barrels at Château Rollan de By in France. **PAGES 92-93** Jean Guyon at Château Rollan de By in France.

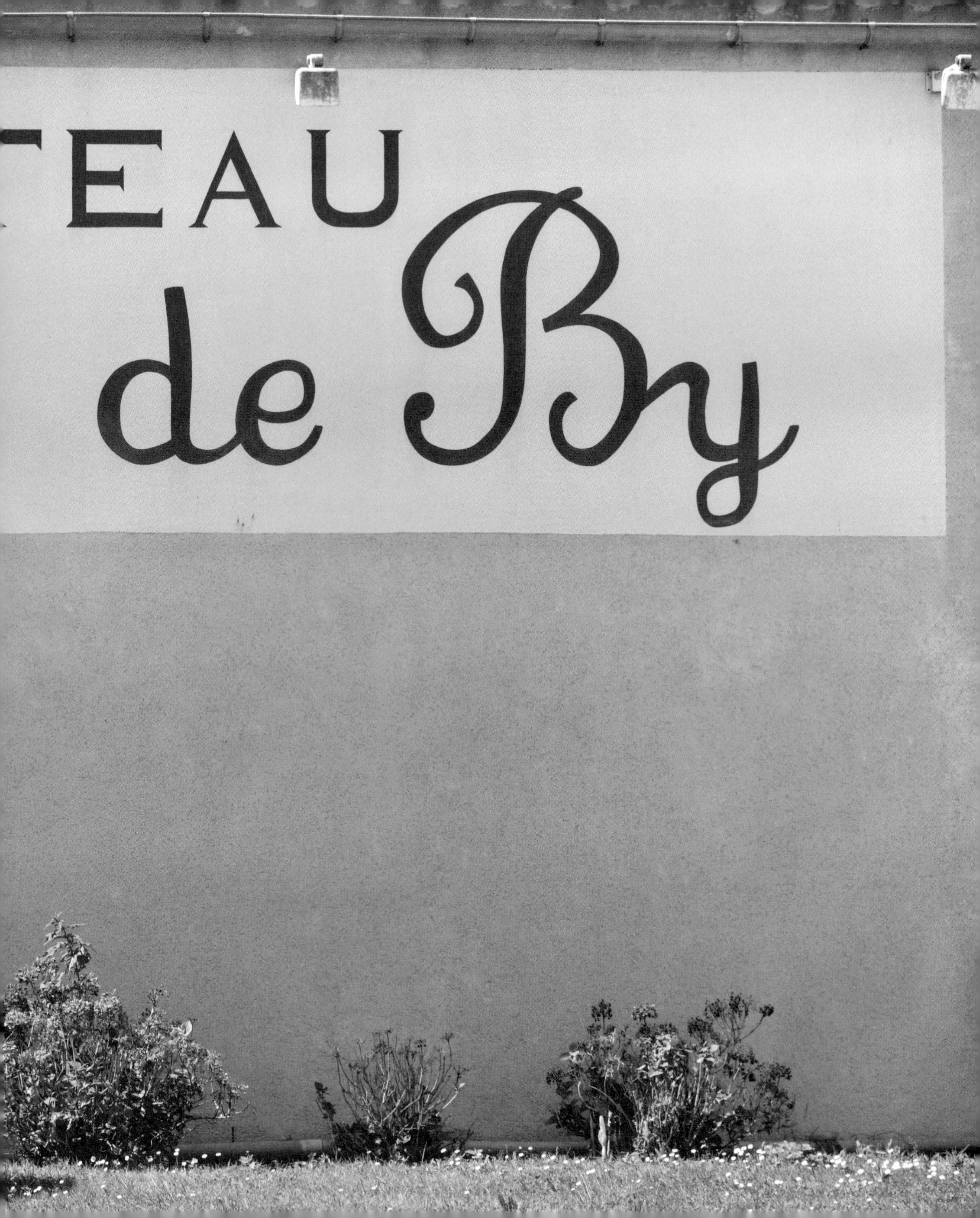
TEAU
de By

Other Notable Countries

ARGENTINA

Argentinean Merlot has a deep, inky violet color and tastes of rich cherry, blueberry, elderberry, mint, and eucalyptus. Its lower tannins bring softness when blended with Malbec or Cabernet Sauvignon. A cold-weather grape, it thrives in high-altitude vineyards, and the lion's share grows in Mendoza, especially Uco Valley. It's also perfect for the near-Antarctic vineyards in Patagonia, including the Neuquén and Río Negro regions, where it grows in small amounts.

AUSTRALIA

Covering about 25,000 acres, or 6.5 percent of Australian vineyard land, Merlot grown here has soft tannins and fresh flavors of cherry, blueberry, and mint. Australian winemakers often blend it with Cabernet Sauvignon to soften the latter's tannins and add brightness in the glass. Cab-Merlot blends typically come from warm inland areas, such as Riverland, Riverina, and Murray Darling, but, like the Barossa Valley and McLaren Vale, these regions are bottling it straight up as well. Wineries in Margaret River and the Yarra Valley, where the cool climate contributes to a stronger tannic structure and more herbal characteristics, are producing versions with an earthier style. Top-quality examples of single-varietal Merlot are still a rarity in Australia but on the rise.

RECOMMENDED WINES

BARGAIN

KEVIN Finca Flichman
Bodega Norton Reserva

MIKE Domaine Jean Bousquet Reserve
Tilia

JEFF Ferllen Reserve

VALUE

KEVIN Bodega Salentein Reserve

MIKE Weinert

JEFF Viña Cobos Felino
Rutini

SPECIAL OCCASION

KEVIN Krasia May

MIKE Trapiche Iscay

JEFF Salentein PR1MUM

RECOMMENDED WINES

BARGAIN

OUR PICKS Penfolds Rawson's Retreat
Wolf Blass Yellow Label
Mollydooker

RIGHT Merlot grapes during the harvest at Delaire Graff Wine Estate near Stellenbosch in South Africa.

BRAZIL

Merlot is the only red grape that may be labeled as a single varietal in Serra Gaucha's Vale dos Vinhedos DO, Brazil's largest and most important wine region. All dry red wines produced here must contain at least 60 percent Merlot, and to feature the grape on the label a wine must contain at least 85 percent. It also must have a minimum alcohol level of 12 percent and have aged at least one year before sale. Here, the dark purple-blue fruit bears flavors of black cherry, blueberry, cassis, and mint. Tastes run the gamut from fruity and vibrant to complex and rich, depending on winemaking technique and amount of aging.

RECOMMENDED WINES

BARGAIN
OUR PICKS Lidio Carraro Agnus
Don Guerino Reserva

VALUE
OUR PICKS Miolo Terroir
Perini Macaw

SPECIAL OCCASION
OUR PICK Pizzato Single Vineyard

CHILE

Merlot came to Chile from Bordeaux in the mid-eighteenth century but didn't gain popularity here for almost 150 years. For a long time, Chilean vintners made Merlot into an unintentional field blend: It grew alongside Carménère, and the two were mistaken for one another until 1994, when researchers discovered that "Chilean Merlot" consisted of two distinct varieties, after which growers separated the vines.

The deep color of the grape carries into the glass, where it ranges from intense black cherry to inky purple. Merlot from Chile carries black cherry, blueberry, currant, and mint flavors. It can range from young, fresh, and fruity to rich and deep, depending on where it grows, how it's made, and how long it ages. Young Chilean Merlots are one of the world's best bargains. Serious, high-end versions, alone or in blends, sell for a fraction of what their comparable counterparts from France and Italy command.

RECOMMENDED WINES

BARGAIN
KEVIN Concha y Toro Xplorador
MIKE Echeverria Reserva
JEFF Santa Rita Reserva
Cousino Macul Don Matias Reserva

VALUE
KEVIN Montes Alpha
MIKE Concha y Toro Marqués de Casa Concha
JEFF Lapostolle Cuvée Alexandre Apalta Vineyard

NEXT PAGES Santa Rita vineyards in Chile.

ITALY

Small amounts of Merlot grow all over the country, where it serves mainly as a blending grape, its relatively low acidity softening the edges of high-acid Italian varieties. One exception is Tuscany, especially around Bolgheri in the Maremma, where vintners make it into single-varietal or Merlot-dominant Super Tuscan wines. A good amount also grows in Friuli-Venezia-Giulia and Alto Adige, which both have ideally cold climates.

RECOMMENDED WINES

BARGAIN
KEVIN Folonari
Falesco
MIKE Villa Pozzi
JEFF Barone Fini Merlot Bolla
Danzante

VALUE
KEVIN Feudi del Pisciotto
MIKE Livio Felluga Vertigo Rosso
Rocca di Castagnoli Le Pratola
JEFF Le Volte dell'Ornellaia

SPECIAL OCCASION
KEVIN Avignonesi Desiderio
MIKE Arcanum Valadorna
JEFF Marchesi de'Frescobaldi Lamaione
Barone Ricasoli Casalferro

SPLURGE
KEVIN Feudi di San Gregorio Patrimo
MIKE Le Macchiole Messorio
JEFF Tenuta dell'Ornellaia Masseto

NEW ZEALAND

Merlot is the second most popular red grape in New Zealand. The majority of the vines grow in Hawke's Bay, with other notable amounts in Gisborne, Marlborough, and Auckland. New Zealand Merlot often appears as a single varietal, but it also frequently goes into Bordeaux-style blends. A Right-Bank style holds sway here, so Merlot stands in the spotlight while the more tannic Cabernet Sauvignon sings backup.

RECOMMENDED WINES

BARGAIN
OUR PICKS Mission Estate
Oyster Bay
Kim Crawford

VALUE
OUR PICKS Saint Clair Rapaura Reserve
Esk Valley

SPECIAL OCCASION
OUR PICKS Villa Maria Reserve Gimblett Gravels
Craggy Range Sophia Gimblett Gravels

SOUTH AFRICA

Merlot has thrived for many years in the cool, high-altitude vineyards of Paarl and Stellenbosch as well as in Durbanville, Klein Karoo, Lower Orange, Philadelphia, and Walker Bay. South African Merlot has a deep inky purple color on the vine and in the glass, and it offers flavors of blueberry, sweet cherry, elderberry, and cooling herbs. You can find it as an affordable, approachable single varietal with all the classic fruit notes on the palate, backed by a suggestion of chocolate and spice, as well as in more complex and higher-priced Merlot-dominant blends.

RECOMMENDED WINES

BARGAIN

KEVIN Two Oceans
Fleur du Cap
Rust en Vrede

MIKE Spier
Guardian Peak

JEFF Bellingham Mocha Java
Indaba

VALUE

OUR PICK DeTrafford

USA: CALIFORNIA

Merlot reigns strong in California, planted on more than 45,000 acres. Like its blending partner and rival, Cabernet Sauvignon, Merlot grows in every county in the state with significant plantings in San Joaquin, Napa, Sonoma, Monterey, San Luis Obispo, and Riverside Counties. Its deep blue color on the vine carries into the glass, where it can range from intense black cherry to inky purple. Its smooth tannins and bright flavors of black cherry and blueberry, often backed by a touch of mint or eucalyptus, lighten the tannins in blends and taste fresh on the palate. Because of its softer tannic structure, Merlot doesn't need as much aging as other single varietals.

RECOMMENDED WINES

BARGAIN

KEVIN Fetzer
Clos du Bois

MIKE Ghost Pines

JEFF Frei Brothers Reserve Dry Creek Valley
Spellbound

VALUE

KEVIN The Prisoner Thorn

MIKE Oberon
Matanzas Creek

JEFF Joseph Carr Rutherford

SPECIAL OCCASION

KEVIN Duckhorn Vine Hill

MIKE La Jota Howell Mountain
Cakebread Cellars

JEFF Newton Unfiltered
Saint Francis Reserve

LEFT Tractor in a vineyard in Robertson in South Africa.

USA: NEW YORK

Merlot is Long Island's most important wine grape, covering 30 percent of the region's vineyards, mainly in the North Fork and the Hamptons. Alex and Louisa Hargrave and David and Stephen Mudd planted the first commercial Merlot vines here in 1974, preceding the development of Long Island's modern wine industry by four years. Because of its cold winegrowing climate, the region has drawn frequent comparisons to Bordeaux. In 1988 and 1990, Bordeaux authorities held two symposiums, Bringing Bordeaux to Long Island, that concluded that Long Island has the potential to grow and produce the classic varieties of Bordeaux, with Merlot showing the most promise. Long Island Merlot has garnered a host of awards at national and international wine competitions, though it continues to sell mostly locally.

RECOMMENDED WINES

VALUE
KEVIN Duck Walk
Lenz
MIKE Bedel
JEFF Waters Crest Grand Vin

SPECIAL OCCASION
KEVIN Wolffer The Grapes of Roth
Shinn Estate
MIKE Clovis Point Vintner's Select
JEFF Harbes Family Vineyard Proprietor Reserve
Hallock Lane

USA: WASHINGTON STATE

When it comes to growing Merlot, Washington has it all: desert climate, huge day-to-night temperature swings, strong breezes, and volcanic soils. Merlot ranks as the second most popular red grape here, covering more than 8,000 acres. The state produces complex, supple wines at both ends of the price spectrum and everywhere in between, from regions as diverse as Yakima Valley, the Columbia Basin, Red Mountain, Horse Heaven Hills, and Walla Walla. Look to Washington for a full-bodied version with strong tannins and berry and mint flavors backed by notes of tobacco and exotic baking spices.

RECOMMENDED WINES

BARGAIN
KEVIN Canoe Ridge The Expedition
MIKE Skyfall
JEFF Columbia Winery

VALUE
KEVIN Gordon Estate Block 3
MIKE Coeur d'Alene
JEFF Coach House

SPECIAL OCCASION
KEVIN Woodward Canyon
MIKE Pedestal
JEFF Tenor

OPPOSITE Winemaker Myles Anderson punching down a tank of Merlot at Walla Walla Vintners in Washington.

MISSION

(MISH-in)

IN THE GLASS

small Bordeaux glass, light red in color

TASTING PROFILE

ACIDITY

BODY

TANNIN

LOW   MEDIUM   HIGH

TASTING NOTES

STRAWBERRY   PLUM   RASPBERRY

Aromas include red fruits and berries, and flavors include strawberry, red plum, and red raspberry. The tannins can feel slightly tart when young, but they mellow with a little time in the bottle.

FOOD PAIRINGS

CHEESE   PORK   OLIVES

Light foods, such as mild cheeses and hams, as well as a variety of tapas.

RECOMMENDED WINES

BARGAIN

OUR PICKS Sonoita Vineyards, USA: Arizona
Tularosa Vineyards, USA: New Mexico
Clos Ouvert Huasa, Chile

SPLURGE

OUR PICK Gypsy Canyon Angelica, USA: California

YOU SHOULD KNOW

Single-varietal Mission wines aren't going to win awards for their quality or age-ability any time soon, but a few Chilean winemakers are using it to make single-varietal sparkling rosés and light, easy-drinking reds. These are great, low-cost wines for a lazy summer picnic with friends.

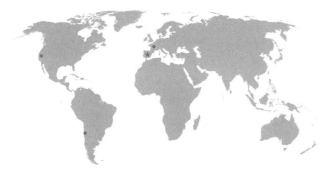

Spanish conquistadors and their priests brought this dark-skinned grape—originally from the Castilla–La Mancha region, known there as Listan Prieto—to their New World missions in the mid-1500s. Researchers consider it the first *Vitis vinifera* grown in North and South America. Hernán Cortés brought Mission vines to Mexico to produce sacramental wine for Catholic masses. From Mexico, it most likely made its way, via Peru, to Chile. Jesuit missionaries cared for these early vineyards, and cuttings eventually made their way to San Diego, California, where Junípero Serra—then a priest, now a saint—planted them at his mission in the mid-1700s. Most European Mission grapevines succumbed to phylloxera in the nineteenth century.

Mission may have originated in Spain, but the country has fewer than 100 acres of it today. Some Canary Islands DOs allow it to be grown and vinified as Listan Prieto, while others call it Moscatel Negro. California growers aren't replanting it, but about 600 acres remain in the Central Valley, where it's used for a fortified wine known as Angelica, made in an elegant fashion by a handful of producers. Chile, on the other hand, has more than 35,000 acres under vine, mostly for low-cost pink or light-red wines sold domestically. A few winemakers, especially from France, have taken a historic interest in the variety and are producing good-quality, easy-drinking reds.

MONASTRELL

(mohn-ah-STREHL)

IN THE GLASS

small Bordeaux glass, red violet to ruby in color

TASTING PROFILE

ACIDITY

BODY

TANNIN

LOW   MEDIUM   HIGH

TASTING NOTES

BLACKBERRY   RASPBERRY   VANILLA

Monastrell has rich dark berry flavors, such as blackberry, raspberry, and black currant, with notes of anise, clove, vanilla, and hints of green bell pepper. It sometimes exhibits a flavor described as earthy, green, or even feral and may have a smoked-meat quality as well.

YOU SHOULD KNOW

Monastrell has a wild side that can prove hard to control. Aside from having a high alcohol level, a lack of oxygen in the winemaking process can lead to a fault called reduction that creates sulfurous flavors. Decanting to allow this quality to blow off can solve the problem. The grape's moderate acidity and propensity for hot climates can lead to an overripe, unbalanced style that's all fruit and tannins, although once you rise above the lowest price category, the wines tend to achieve better equilibrium.

FOOD PAIRINGS

PORK   CHINESE FOOD   RIBS

Monastrell's full mouthfeel and strong tannins call for fatty cuts of meat, and its opulent fruit flavors that give the taste buds a false sense of sweetness match perfectly with foods containing a touch of sugar. Open a bottle of good Monastrell for a traditional, meat-based paella Valenciana (not one of those phony mussel-and-chorizo concoctions). For pork ribs, choose a single-varietal or Monastrell-heavy blend. A glass of Monastrell will enhance Chinese food, spareribs, and baby back ribs beyond your wildest imagination.

RECOMMENDED WINES

BARGAIN

KEVIN   Juan Gil Wrongo Dongo
        Bodegas Divus

MIKE   Bodegas Murtia
        Enrique Mendoza

JEFF   Castillo del Baron
        Bodegas Castaño

VALUE

OUR PICKS   Enrique Mendoza Estrecho
            Iberica Bruno Prats AlfYnal

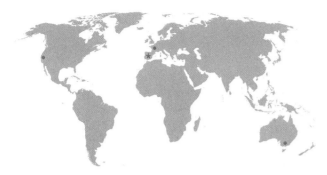

well priced and delicious Monastrells at wine shops and in restaurants at home and abroad. It's dark both on the vine and in the glass, and it has rich, juicy fruit flavors, strong tannins, and good acidity. Levante Monastrell in particular is noted for its fruit-forward berry flavors.

Grapes originating along what is now the Franco-Spanish border often have two or more common names. What the Spanish call Monastrell, the French call Mourvèdre (*moor-VEHD-ruh*). About five times as much grows in Spain as in France, but for now the two names seem to carry equal weight in the wine world. The Spanish name derives from the Latin word for monastery, suggesting that monks may have cultivated it at one time, and records indicate that it has grown in Spain since at least the middle of the fifteenth century. The French name also points to Spain. The modern Spanish town of Sagunto, near Valencia, was known in the Middle Ages as Morvedre. To confuse matters further—best not to drink while reading this section . . . just kidding, drink away!—the grape's official name in California is Mataró (*mah-tah-RO*), also a town in Spain, and for many years Mataró prevailed as the name for the variety in Australia as well.

Whichever name you use, Monastrell thrives in hot climates. The majority grows within about fifty miles of the Mediterranean coasts of Spain—particularly Murcia and Valencia, collectively the Levante—and France. You can find almost a third of Monastrell plantings farther inland, however. It's the most important grape in the Alicante, Almansa, Bullas, Jumilla, Valencia, and Yecla DOs. These hot regions provide all the sunshine it needs to ripen, while high altitudes offer nighttime coolness to help the grapes retain acidity. Here the variety may not appear on the label since locals already know that Monastrell is the main grape used in these DO wines.

Once considered a workhorse grape destined for cheap wines, it grows on almost 160,000 acres, making it one of the most widely planted grapes in Spain. The past several decades have seen a vast improvement in both vineyard management and winemaking technique, however. This rise in quality has reached critical mass, and now you can find a wide variety of

Other Notable Countries

AUSTRALIA

New South Wales and South Australia boast the highest concentrations of Australia's Monastrell plantings. Planted in 1853, the world's oldest Monastrell vines grow in the Barossa Valley. Before phylloxera devastated the vineyards of Europe, vintners used these to make sweet fortified wines. Today the grape plays an essential role in popular Rhône-style GSM blends. Winemakers have discovered, nevertheless, that it tastes great on its own, especially when produced from old bush vines. It offers rich berry flavors backed by spice and licorice with slightly wild touches of herbal notes or green bell pepper. You almost always will see it on a label as Mourvèdre, although, again, it's also known in Australia as Mataró.

FRANCE

Monastrell most likely crossed the border from Spain into France sometime in the sixteenth century. In Provence and the Rhône Valley, it took on the name Mourvèdre, while in Languedoc-Roussillon it was and still is known as Mataró. Older Mourvèdre vineyards succumbed to phylloxera in the late nineteenth and early twentieth centuries, and growers replanted other varieties. Mourvèdre is increasing in popularity both in blends and as a single variety. From the mid-twentieth century to now, plantings increased from around 1,300 acres to almost 25,000.

Mourvèdre is the primary red grape in the Bandol AOC, where it may constitute anywhere from a minimum of 50 percent up to a maximum of 95 percent. Many producers here prune, trim, and drop grapes during the growing season, maintaining a density at just over half to around three-quarters of the allowable amount in order to intensify the flavor of the finished wine. Bandol wines age in oak for at least eighteen months, which adds layers of vanilla, spice, and toast to the flavor profile. It also strengthens the wine's already-formidable tannin profile, so these wines require several years of bottle aging in order to appeal to all but the most wine-hardened palates.

Mourvèdre forms one of the pillars in GSM blends, but a handful of producers bottle single-varietal or high-composition Mourvèdre in the southern Rhône Valley and Languedoc-Roussillon. These fruit-forward wines have intense dark berry flavors joined by notes of spice and thyme and a touch of summer farm stand. Some producers within Châteauneuf-du-Pape rely on Mourvèdre for up to 30 percent of their blend.

RECOMMENDED WINES

VALUE
OUR PICKS Château Paul Mas Clos de Savignac
Bandol Tardieu-Laurent
La Bastide Blanche
Domaine Marie Bérénice
Château La Roque Pic Saint-Loup
Domaine de Terrebrune
Domaine Tempier Bandol Cuvée Spéciale

USA: CALIFORNIA

California officially calls the grape Mataró for statistical purposes, and here too it's an essential component in GSM blends. In the never-ending search for something new under the sun, quite a few California winemakers are releasing small-batch single-varietal bottlings, often available only to wine club members or at winery tasting rooms. Mataró grows on almost 1,000 acres here, with a strong showing on the Central Coast in Paso Robles and Santa Barbara. You also can find decent pockets of it in Contra Costa County near San Francisco and Oakland, and in Madera County, where traditionally it was used in fortified dessert wines. California Mataró features flavors of mixed berries, spice, and anise. It also can have some strong elements of earth or even green notes that a talented winemaker can tame.

RECOMMENDED WINES

VALUE
OUR PICKS Cline Cellars Ancient Vines
Andis
Tablas Creek

SPLURGE
OUR PICK Alban Vineyards Forsythe The Mason

MONTEPULCIANO

(MOHN-teh-pool-CHAH-no)

IN THE GLASS

small Bordeaux glass, ruby to black cherry in color

TASTING PROFILE

	LOW	MEDIUM	HIGH
ACIDITY			
BODY			
TANNIN			

TASTING NOTES

PLUM   RASPBERRY   LICORICE

Expect aromas of red fruits, especially red plum, boysenberry, and red raspberry, and flavors that can range from red fruits to plum and cassis, finishing with herbal notes of dried oregano and thyme. Wines not aged in oak tend to have more red fruit characteristics, while those that do age in oak have darker fruit flavors as well as notes of licorice, vanilla, and espresso.

YOU SHOULD KNOW

If you find a Montepulciano wine from northern Italy, put it back. These can taste very "green" because they likely didn't have the right conditions to ripen properly.

FOOD PAIRINGS

TACOS   PIZZA   PASTA

Montepulciano can stand up to fatty foods, so have a glass or two the next time you enjoy some of life's finest and guiltiest pleasures: beef or pork tacos, meatloaf, shepherd's pie, pepperoni and sausage pizza, or macaroni and cheese.

RECOMMENDED WINES

BARGAIN

KEVIN   La Quercia

MIKE   Zaccagnini Il Vino dal Tralcetto Montepulciano d'Abruzzo

JEFF   Cerulli Spinozzi Torre Migliori Montepulciano d'Abruzzo

Folonari Montepulciano d'Abruzzo

VALUE

KEVIN   Cantina Zaccagnini San Clemente

Masciarelli Villa Gemma

MIKE   Cataldi Madonna Malandrino Montepulciano d'Abruzzo

Il Feuduccio Montepulciano d'Abruzzo

JEFF   Caroso Montepulciano d'Abruzzo

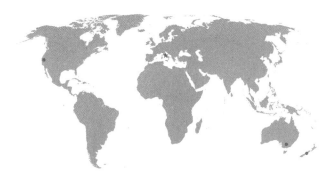

"What I love about Montepulciano is its great flexibility, its ability to get along with everybody, just like my mother did. It is perfectly in its element from when it is young, still violet-colored, intense, and sassy, a bit rough, and already deep. You can always rely on it in the course of its adult life. It is almost never unpleasant, always decisive and patient. Then it offers up pleasant surprises for those who have awaited its maturity, when all its rough edges are softened, without ever betraying its indomitable spirit."

—*Enrico Cerulli, winemaker, Cerulli Spinozzi*

Don't confuse the Montepulciano grape with Montepulciano the town in Tuscany, which specializes in wine made from Sangiovese. No Montepulciano grapevines grow in the town of Montepulciano because the grape needs a lot of southern sun and warmth to ripen. The grape originated in Abruzzo, in central Italy, where it remains important. It's often the main or only variety in the Montepulciano d'Abruzzo DOC or Montepulciano d'Abruzzo Colline Teramane DOCG. These wines must contain at least 85 percent Montepulciano, although a winemaker can blend it with Sangiovese if he or she chooses. Montepulciano is Italy's second most widely planted indigenous grape variety with about 75,000 acres growing across the country. (The first—you guessed it—is Sangiovese.) Montepulciano vines grow throughout central and southern Italy. It's also a major component (60 percent) of Controguerra Rosso DOC wines, and you can find it in some Marche DOC wines, especially Conero, Rosso Piceno, and Offida Rosso as well as the Molise DOC and Puglia DOC.

Winemakers in New Zealand and Australia's Adelaide Hills are experimenting with the variety, and you can find a good number of single varietals from Lodi, Mendocino, and Temecula in California.

NEBBIOLO

(nehb-YOH-lo)

IN THE GLASS

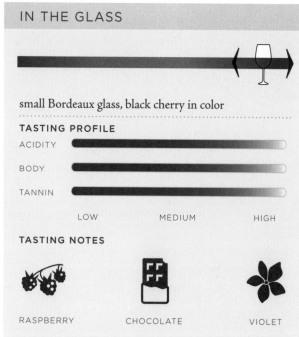

small Bordeaux glass, black cherry in color

TASTING PROFILE

ACIDITY

BODY

TANNIN

LOW   MEDIUM   HIGH

TASTING NOTES

RASPBERRY   CHOCOLATE   VIOLET

Barolos generally have a characteristic black tar and red rose scent. When young, they smell of red raspberry, red plum, violet, rose petal, and anise. As they age, aromas of licorice, brown spice, truffles, dark chocolate, and that definitive whiff of black tar develop. This powerful wine has a sturdy yet silky tannic structure and pronounced acidity, and its finish can last for days.

YOU SHOULD KNOW

In a blind tasting, the first clue that you might have a Barolo is the brick red–orange color with a touch of rust at the rim. The color gives the wine away (one of the few). Also, everyone loves Barolo and Barbaresco, but they're not inexpensive. If you like Nebbiolo, go for wines from Roero, the town just across the Tanaro River from Barolo. Great producers there are making very good wines from Nebbiolo that won't break the bank.

FOOD PAIRINGS

TRUFFLE   PASTA   MUSHROOM

The most fantastic pairing for Barolo, Barbaresco, and just about every Italian wine made from Nebbiolo is any dish with truffles from neighboring Alba. Risotto with Parmigiano-Reggiano cheese and truffles, veal loin roast studded with truffles, spaghetti with butter and truffles—you get the idea. If truffles aren't your thing, choose or make a dish with an earthy character, such as smoked duck, oven-roasted rack of lamb, or veal chop smothered in mushrooms.

RECOMMENDED WINES

BARGAIN
KEVIN Aldo Rainoldi
MIKE Pertinace Langhe
JEFF Fontanafredda Langhe
Travaglini Nebbiolo Coste della Sesia

VALUE
KEVIN Sandrone Nebbiolo d'Alba
MIKE Travaglini Gattinara
JEFF Renato Ratti Langhe
Bruno Giacosa Nebbiolo d'Alba

SPECIAL OCCASION
KEVIN Serralunga d'Alba Barolo
MIKE Travaglini Gattinara Riserva
JEFF Renato Ratti Marcenasco Barolo

SPLURGE
KEVIN Aldo Conterno Barolo Cicala
MIKE Bruno Giacosa Azienda Agricola Barbaresco
Asili Riserva
Michele Chiarlo Cannubi Barolo
JEFF Bruno Giacosa Azzienda Agricola Barolo Falletto

Nebbiolo—named for the Italian word for fog, *nebbia*—originated in Piedmont, where it continues to make the best wines. The first written mention dates to the fourteenth century, but most experts agree that it grew around the town of Alba long before that. The variety most famously makes the powerful and intense Barolo DOCG wines, but elegant Barbarescos have given them a run for their money in recent years. Winemakers worldwide have tried to reproduce the amazing styles of those two wines in their own countries with less than stellar results. Perhaps the legendary Piedmontese clouds that blanket the vines at night help ripen the grapes to perfection. Nebbiolo production centers in and on the hills of the Barolo region, where altitudes can reach 1,500 feet. Vineyards within this designation fall within the parishes of Barolo, Castiglione Falletto, and Serralunga d'Alba as well as parts of Roddi, Cherasco, Diano d'Alba, Grinzane Cavour, Verduno, La Morra, Novello, and Monforte d'Alba. Most winemakers plant their vines on the southern side of the slopes for maximum ripening. Growers historically cultivated four subvarieties of the grape, but only two, Lampia and Michet, hold any importance today.

Barolo wine must age at least thirty-eight months, with a minimum of eighteen in the barrel. Riserva Barolos must age for at least sixty-two months. Great Barolos improve in the bottle and, properly cellared, can last—and taste amazing—for forty or fifty years.

Barolo vineyards that have enamored collectors for years include Brunate, Bussia, Cannubi, Cerequio, Ginestra, Lazzarito, Monprivato, Rocche, Santo Stefano di Perno, Sarmazza, Vigna Rionda, and Villero.

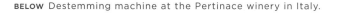

IN HIS OWN WORDS

"Barolo and Barbaresco are special wines for their extraordinary complexity, heady sensations of fruits, flowers, and surprising spicy and balsamic palate. The flavors are wide-ranging with juicy and fresh tannins, great length, and pleasantness. They are wines with extraordinary charm, due to their complex aromatics and sensations on the palate. Their taste profile and personalities differ from hill to hill within the same region, and they evolve differently over time."

—*Michele Chiarlo, owner, Michele Chiarlo*

BELOW Destemming machine at the Pertinace winery in Italy.

OPPOSITE Michele Chiarlo Vineyards in Italy. ABOVE Harvest at the Pertinace vineyards in Italy. NEXT PAGES Cellars at Michele Chiarlo vineyards in Italy.

The second most famous wine made entirely from Nebbiolo is Barbaresco, with vineyards in the Langhe and extending outward from the bank of the Tanaro River. Because of the climate difference, grapes ripen earlier here than in Barolo, which results in lower tannin levels. Barbaresco must age at least two years, one in wood, and have a minimum alcohol content of 12.5 percent. A Barbaresco Riserva must age for four years, one still in wood.

Nebbiolo plays an important role in wines produced in Roero, just across the Tanaro River from Barolo. It's the dominant variety in wines from Ghemme, Gattinara, and Valtellina as well. It grows in small quantities in the New World—America, Argentina, Australia, Brazil, Chile, New Zealand, and Uruguay, mostly by winemakers with Italian heritage—but the results don't measure up when compared to the power and elegance of the grape when it grows in its home terroir.

IN HIS OWN WORDS

"I love Nebbiolo's complexity, length, and elegance. It's a wine that you will never get bored with. After a sip you want more, after a glass you want more! It's easy to become a Nebbiolo addict."

—*Pietro Ratti, owner and winemaker, Renato Ratti*

NERO D'AVOLA

(NEHR-o DAH-vo-lah)

IN THE GLASS

small Bordeaux glass, ruby to black cherry in color

TASTING PROFILE

	LOW	MEDIUM	HIGH
ACIDITY			
BODY			
TANNIN			

TASTING NOTES

CHERRY · CHOCOLATE · DRIED HERBS

Aromas of violet, lavender, and Mediterranean herbs mingle with cherry and raspberry. Flavors range from fresh fruits, such as cherry, strawberry, and blackberry, to dried and cooked fruits, such as blackberry preserves, prunes, and cherry pie. You may detect cedar and dark chocolate along with mint and eucalyptus, oregano, anise, and thyme. These big and robust wines offer a rare softness on the palate for bold red wines, making them easy to drink on their own as well as with food.

YOU SHOULD KNOW

Nero d'Avola grows all over Sicily, in varying terroirs, creating wines that don't always have a common style. You can find many good bottles for around or less than $20. Because of these low prices, many wine bars and Italian restaurants stock it. As prices drop in the bargain range, though, the focus can shift from quality to quantity.

FOOD PAIRINGS

OLIVES · LAMB · TUNA

The strong acidity and slight tanginess of the wine nicely accompany meze platters that include caponata, Castelvetrano olives, almonds, and tomato bruschetta. It's also wonderful with lamb kebabs and gyros. Don't hesitate to drink Nero d'Avola with herb-rubbed grilled tuna or pasta tossed with olive oil and steamed salmon.

RECOMMENDED WINES

BARGAIN

KEVIN Duca di Salaparuta Corvo
Morgante

MIKE Donnafugata Sedara
Curto Eos

JEFF Villa Pozzi

VALUE

KEVIN Azienda Agricola Cos Nero di Lupo

MIKE Planeta Noto →

JEFF Mazzei Zisola Feurdo Maccari

SPECIAL OCCASION

KEVIN Tasca d'Almerita Rosso del Conte

MIKE Planeta Santa Cecilia

JEFF Donnafugata Mille e Una Notte
Morgante Don Antonio Nero d'Avola
Riserva

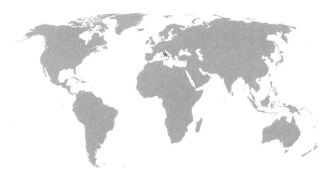

bound for export. Sicilian viticulturists and winemakers proudly tout Nero d'Avola as their signature grape—some calling it the new Malbec—but everyday Sicilians often drink local wine made from field blends of multiple varieties that grow together and think of Nero d'Avola as a marketing gimmick for the international wine market. Either way, you'll likely find a nice bottle of Nero d'Avola the next time you visit a restaurant or wine shop, and odds are good that you can buy a second for a comparison tasting.

Growers have cultivated wine grapes on Sicily since the eighth century BC, when the island and southern Italy were known collectively as Magna Graecia, or Greater Greece. The word *nero* means "black" in Italian, and Nero d'Avola first came to prominence around the town of Avola in Syracuse Province, where it has grown for at least four centuries. Over time, it has spread to every winegrowing region on the island, and, at 50,000 acres, it has become Sicily's most widely planted and well-known grape.

Long used as a blending grape throughout Italy and even France's Languedoc region, Nero d'Avola has received a lot of buzz on wine lists and in print in the last quarter century. Ten DOC regions make wine using Nero d'Avola in varying amounts, but if the DOC wine has the grape name on the label it must contain a minimum of 85 percent in the bottle. The Cerasuola di Vittoria DOCG permits up to 60 percent, and Marsala, the famous fortified wine from Trapani Province, may contain up to 70 percent. A wine labeled Nero d'Avola Sicilia IGT can be made with grapes from anywhere on the island.

Its common blending partners include local varieties Frappato and Nerello Mascalese as well as Syrah, Merlot, and Cabernet Sauvignon. Since the 1990s, winemakers have been vinifying it as a single varietal, examples of which tend toward two distinct styles, defined by both geography and winemaker preference. One producer may craft an elegant wine with restrained fruit, soft tannins, and touches of spice, while another creates fruit bombs reveling in up-front flavors of cooked cherry and blackberry and packing a wallop on the drawn-out finish.

In Sicily, it also goes by the name Calabrese (*kah-la-BRAY-say*), but you'd be hard pressed to find that on a bottle

NEXT PAGES Vineyards at the Planeta winery in Sicily.

- -

IN HIS OWN WORDS

"The Nero d'Avola vine is a symbol of Sicily—the expression of a red Mediterranean variety. It's also an aromatic wine that is easy to pair with food. From an oenological standpoint, I like that it is a variety that 'reads the terroir' and expresses different characteristics more subtly or more definitively depending on where it is grown."

—*Alessio Planeta, winemaker, Planeta Wines*

- -

ÖKÜZGÖZÜ

(o-KOOZ-go-zoo)

IN THE GLASS

small Bordeaux glass, light red in color

TASTING PROFILE

ACIDITY

BODY

TANNIN

LOW   MEDIUM   HIGH

TASTING NOTES

CHERRY   LAVENDER   GREEN BELL PEPPER

On the nose, expect cherry, blackberry, soft floral notes, and a touch of spice. This medium-bodied wine offers a combination of fruit and savory flavors, especially black cherry, lavender, brambles, chocolate, and light notes of green bell pepper. Most single-varietal versions feature soft tannins but bright acidity.

YOU SHOULD KNOW

Öküzgözü is best when oaked minimally or not at all. Drink it young: Look for the most recent vintage and nothing older than three years. You'll frequently find it in blends with Boğazkere, which often have more oak influence and can age longer.

FOOD PAIRINGS

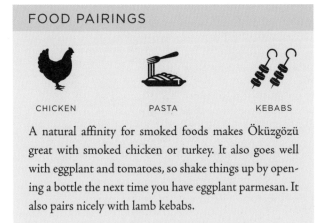

CHICKEN   PASTA   KEBABS

A natural affinity for smoked foods makes Öküzgözü great with smoked chicken or turkey. It also goes well with eggplant and tomatoes, so shake things up by opening a bottle the next time you have eggplant parmesan. It also pairs nicely with lamb kebabs.

RECOMMENDED WINES

BARGAIN

OUR PICKS   Kavaklidere Yakut Öküzgözü d'Laz
Doluca Dlc
Diren Collection
Kavaklidere Winery

VALUE

OUR PICKS   Vinkara Winehouse →
Yazgan Mahra Öküzgözü Boğazkere Red
Kayra Buzbağ Rezerv
Kavaklidere Prestige

OPPOSITE Workers harvest Öküzgözü grapes in the Pendore vineyards of Kavaklidere Wines in Kemaliye village in western Turkey.

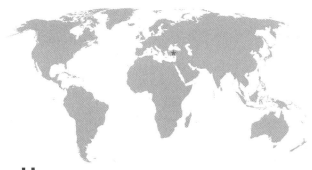

Öküzgözü means "bull's eye" in Turkish, and the wine made from these grapes is set to become Turkey's best-known variety. Native to Elâziğ Province in eastern Anatolia, today it grows throughout the country, including Malatya, Tunceli, Thrace, and Manisa Provinces and near the Aegean Sea. Many Turks also eat it as a table grape.

It does best in hot, dry summers. In Elâziğ and Malatya, vineyard elevations range from 2,800 to 3,500 feet, and this altitude, combined with the cooling effects of the Euphrates River and large reservoirs created by two dams, helps the grapes retain their acidity.

In Istanbul twenty years ago, practically every wine list featured the same two wines, both a blend of Öküzgözü and Boğazkere. (The joke at dinner every night: "Should we have the standard or the selection?") As Turkey's wine industry has grown, however, the variety of wine has increased exponentially, as has the availability of single-varietal Öküzgözü. In the past several years, the Turkish government has made it more difficult to market and sell wine domestically, so producers increasingly are looking for support from the export market.

IN HIS OWN WORDS

"Made in the modern style, Öküzgözü is harmonious and easy to drink. It is suited for short-period aging but also benefits from long aging in bottle. It has a deep color, good balance between tannins and acidity, and a rich taste of soft fruits."

—*Marco Monchiero, consulting enologist, Vinkara*

PETIT VERDOT

(puh-TEE vuhr-DOH)

IN THE GLASS

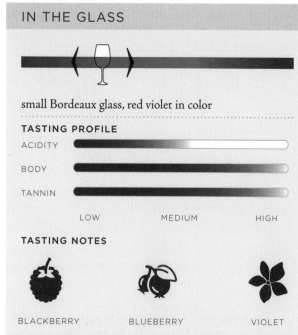

small Bordeaux glass, red violet in color

TASTING PROFILE

	LOW	MEDIUM	HIGH
ACIDITY			
BODY			
TANNIN			

TASTING NOTES

BLACKBERRY   BLUEBERRY   VIOLET

Deep black-fruit notes, such as blackberry and black plum, prevail with lofty aromas of purple flowers. In the mouth, it's full-bodied and opulent with rich ripe fruit flavors and a touch of candied violet flowers in the aftertaste. Expect notes of dried flowers, such as lilac, lavender, and violet, and, when properly oaked, aromas and flavors of toasted hazelnut, cappuccino, and vanilla.

YOU SHOULD KNOW

Petit Verdot ripens very late in the season, and, in Bordeaux blends, it provides great color, additional tannins, and enticing aromas of flowers, olives, or even blueberry when fully ripe.

FOOD PAIRINGS

STEAK   SAUSAGE   CHEESE

Wines made from fully ripened Petit Verdot have a lot of tannins, making them perfect pairings for rich meaty dishes, such as grilled steak, braised lamb, veal roast, pork chops, and spicy sausages. They also pair well with many hard and soft cheeses, such as Manchego, aged Gouda, Grana Padano, and Parmigiano-Reggiano.

RECOMMENDED WINES

BARGAIN

KEVIN Bodegas Luzón Petit Verdot Luzon, Spain
MIKE Chaman, Argentina
Ruca Malen Reserva, Argentina
JEFF Gauchezco Reserva, Argentina

VALUE

KEVIN Clos du Bois Reserve, USA: California
MIKE Opaque, USA: California
Napa Cellars Classic Collection, USA: California
JEFF Michael David Inkblot, USA: California

SPECIAL OCCASION

KEVIN Pahlmeyer Waters Ranch, USA: California
Abadia Retuerta, Spain
MIKE Sannino Spotlight, USA: New York
Trinchero Cloud's Nest Vineyard, USA: California
Marqués de Griñon Single Vineyard Estate Bottled, Spain
Château Malescasse Le Petit Verdot de Malescasse, France
JEFF Lieb Reserve, USA: New York
Grgich Hills Miljenko's Selection, USA: California

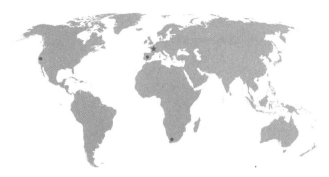

A native of the Gironde in southwestern France, Petit Verdot means "little green one," an amusing name for a red grape. Many Bordelaise chateaux grew and vinified it from the 1700s until the phylloxera plague of the 1800s. Because it requires very specific weather conditions to ripen and ripens so late—hence green—growers here didn't replant it widely. Many winemakers asked, "Why wait for the Petit Verdot when the other grapes are ready to go?" Those who did replant and maintain acreage today largely have ideal growing conditions and ideal levels of patience. Their reward? A grape with a lot of wonderful characteristics.

Some 2,000 acres remain in France, the majority in Bordeaux, chiefly among the noble houses of Château Pichon Lalande in the Médoc, Château Palmer in Margaux, Château Lagrange in St. Julien, and Château Bolaire in the Bordeaux Supérieur region, all of which have impressive plantings.

Outside France, some good producers are making single-varietal wines in regions where Petit Verdot can ripen fully and express its beauty. About 2,500 acres grow in Spain and produce excellent wines. It does extremely well in California, where a number of quality winemakers use it in Meritage blends as well as a single-varietal. In the Golden State, it grows on approximately 2,200 acres, notably in Napa, Santa Barbara, San Luis Obispo, and Sonoma. It also serves as a blending grape in South Africa, but over the last few years producers have begun making quality monovarietal wine as well.

PETITE SIRAH

(puh-TEET see-RAH)

IN THE GLASS

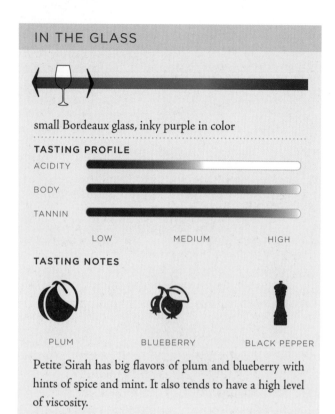

small Bordeaux glass, inky purple in color

TASTING PROFILE

ACIDITY

BODY

TANNIN

LOW   MEDIUM   HIGH

TASTING NOTES

PLUM   BLUEBERRY   BLACK PEPPER

Petite Sirah has big flavors of plum and blueberry with hints of spice and mint. It also tends to have a high level of viscosity.

YOU SHOULD KNOW

Tightly packed clusters of small berries make this variety extremely susceptible to rot in humid or rainy environments. The small berries create a high skin-to-juice ratio, which explains the intense color.

FOOD PAIRINGS

BURGER   CHICKEN   CHEESE

Devour a bacon and blue cheese burger with Petite Sirah. Intense fruit flavors, strong tannins, and delightful acidity all temper the umami and saltiness of the burger. It's also really good with spicy fried chicken and strong cheese.

RECOMMENDED WINES

BARGAIN

KEVIN   Bogle, USA: California
Steele Writer's Block, USA: California

MIKE   Ravenswood Vintners Blend, USA: California
Spellbound, USA: California

VALUE

KEVIN   Trentadue La Storia, USA: California

MIKE   Fiddletown Cellars, USA: California
Recanati Reserve, Israel

JEFF   Concannon, USA: California

SPECIAL OCCASION

KEVIN   Adaptation by Odette, USA: California

MIKE   Montefiore, Israel
Culton Worth Hill Vineyard, USA: California

JEFF   Stags' Leap Ne Cede Malis Estate Grown, USA: California

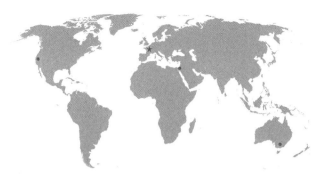

This variety derives from a natural, though somewhat accidental, cross of Peloursin and Syrah that occurred in François Durif's agricultural laboratory in Montpellier, France, in 1880. Durif took credit for the resulting vine that bore dense grape clusters of small berries with highly saturated color, naming the grape after himself. It still goes by the name Durif in Australia and France, though it never caught on in the latter country and barely grows there anymore. (Confusion ensued when Syrah cuttings, sent to California in 1878, earned the nickname "Petite Syrah" because of their low yields.) The most extensive plantings of Petite Sirah grow in America.

Other Notable Countries

AUSTRALIA
Known as Durif (*duh-RIFF*) in Australia, the variety has a similar history here as in its early days in California. It served as a mainstay of the Port-style wines of the world-famous Rutherglen region for almost a century. Winemakers now use it to make deeply colored, powerful dry wines tasting of plum and blueberry with hints of spice and mint. It grows on about 1,000 acres, the majority still in Rutherglen.

ISRAEL
Planted here in the 1970s to add color and backbone to entry-level blends, Petite Sirah recently has been made into single-varietal versions scored highly by international wine critics. Some Israeli winemakers consider it ideally suited to the climate and terroir of Israel, especially the Judean Hills and Galilee. The increase in quality largely has come about from viticulturists dropping grapes to decrease yield, increased attention to the grapes themselves, and improved winemaking techniques. In addition to flavors of blueberry and blackberry, expect notes of thyme, lavender, and anise.

USA: CALIFORNIA
The popularity of Petite Sirah began here when Charles McIver imported it for his Linda Vista Vineyard in Alameda County in 1884. By 1890 the Concannon Family was growing the variety for their own use and also shipped cuttings to wineries in Mexico. In these early days, winemakers vinified it into sweet fortified wines and used it to add color and tannins to entry-level red blends. Today it grows on almost 9,000 acres across California—the largest and most important producer of the variety—representing an increase of more than 30 percent since 2004. You can find large plantings in San Joaquin, San Luis Obispo, Napa, Sonoma, and Lodi Counties, which are producing high quality dry versions in which high tannins contribute to excellent aging potential. Lodi Petite Sirah in particular is becoming a high-profile subcategory (rivaling the region's reputation for Zinfandel), much of it available at desirable price points. The efforts of "PS I Love You," an advocacy group for Petite Sirah growers and producers, no doubt have led to the surge in both acreage and popularity.

· ·

IN HIS OWN WORDS
"There's a brooding, sexy, voluptuous richness in a well-crafted Petite Sirah. Deep blueberry crisp, dark chocolate, plum jam, black pepper all wrapped in teeth-staining color! What's not to like? A well-ripened Petite Sirah aged to give just the right toasted marshmallow and torched crème brûlée tannin-softening layer of character is a stunning wine."

—*Tony Coltrin, winemaker, Spellbound Wines*

· ·

NEXT PAGES Stag's Leap Vineyard in California.

PINOT NOIR

(PEE-no NWAHR)

IN THE GLASS

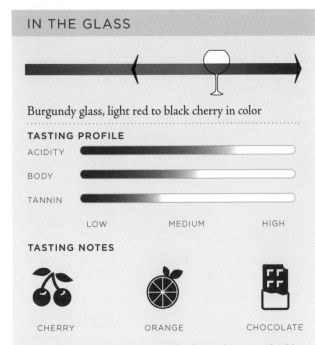

Burgundy glass, light red to black cherry in color

TASTING PROFILE

	LOW	MEDIUM	HIGH
ACIDITY			
BODY			
TANNIN			

TASTING NOTES

CHERRY   ORANGE   CHOCOLATE

Pinot Noir can vary stylistically from elegant to highly extracted. Softer Pinot Noirs from cold-weather regions, such as Burgundy, northern Sonoma, and New Zealand, offer flavors of cherry, chocolate, and orange peel. You'll find intense flavors of blackberry, coffee, and green bell pepper in Pinot Noir from hotter, drier climates, such as California's Central Coast or France's Pays d'Oc.

YOU SHOULD KNOW

Not all French Pinot Noirs are created equal. Some producers who own or source from vineyards in Burgundy also bottle Pinot Noir from Pays d'Oc, a large region spread across southern France. If the price tag seems too good to be true, check the appellation on the label. You can find a decent bottle of Pays d'Oc Pinot Noir, but it will exhibit less complexity than a wine labeled "Bourgogne."

FOOD PAIRINGS

DUCK   TUNA   LOBSTER

Duck and Pinot Noir are one of the world's great pairings. Grab a decent bottle on the way to your favorite Chinese BYOB and enjoy it with Peking or tea-smoked duck. A good Pinot Noir should be light enough to drink with fish, so open a bottle the next time you're eating tuna, grilled salmon, or even lobster with melted butter.

RECOMMENDED WINES

BARGAIN
KEVIN   Josephine Dubois Bourgogne
MIKE   Louis Latour Bourgogne
JEFF   Louis Jadot Bourgogne
    Bouchard Aîné & Fils Bourgogne

VALUE
KEVIN   Côte de Nuits-Villages Drouhin
MIKE   Albert Bichot Mercurey
    Michel Magnien Bourgogne
JEFF   Joseph Drouhin Côte de Beaune-Villages

SPECIAL OCCASION
KEVIN   Domaine Bouchard Père & Fils Chambolle-Musigny
MIKE   Domaine Fernand et Laurent Pillot Chassagne-Montrachet
JEFF   Domaine Bertagna Hautes Côtes de Nuits Les Dames de Huguettes

SPLURGE
KEVIN   Domaine de la Romanée-Conti
MIKE   Domaine Tollot-Beaut Corton-Bressandes
    Domaine Faiveley Nuits-St-Georges Les Damodes Premier Cru
JEFF   Domaine Parent Pommard Premier Cru Les Epenots

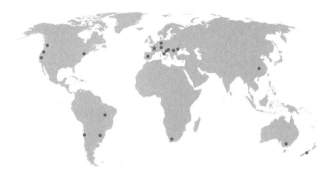

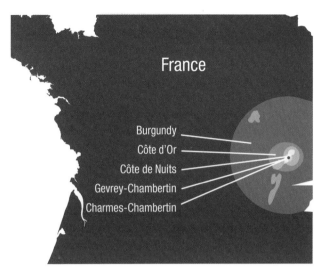

France

- Burgundy
- Côte d'Or
- Côte de Nuits
- Gevrey-Chambertin
- Charmes-Chambertin

t's impossible to know exactly where Pinot Noir originated. French farmers have cultivated it at least since the thirteenth century, though the name—meaning "black pine," after its pinecone-like clusters of grapes—came into fashion only in the nineteenth century. The tight formation in which the dark berries grow makes it susceptible to mold and bacteria, so it requires cool growing areas and diligent farming. Burgundy represents the spiritual (if not native) home of Pinot Noir. For many years in America and Britain, "Burgundy" denoted a generic style of red wine, regardless of grape variety, but a true *vin Bourgogne rouge* contains one grape only: Pinot Noir. Despite worldwide acclaim for French Pinot, it ranks seventh among the nation's red grapes.

Pinot Noir made with grapes sourced from a variety of locations within Burgundy will be labeled Bourgogne AOC, the entry-level category for wine from this region, which has eight major subregions. Four of these have a reputation for exquisite red wines, from north to south: Côte de Nuits, Hautes-Côtes de Nuits, Côte de Beaune, and Côte Chalonnaise.

Kevin likes to describe wine regions in concentric circles: Within France, you have the Burgundy region or Bourgogne AOC. Then you have the Côte d'Or growing region. One of its two designated subregions is the Côte de Nuits. Within that circle, you move to the village level. Some villages, such as Fixin, Gevrey-Chambertin, and Morey-St-Denis, have vineyards classified as Premier Cru, meaning first growth or top level. Gevrey-Chambertin alone has twenty-six Premier Cru appellations, including Clos du Chapître, La Perrière, and La Romanée. It also has nine Grand Cru appellations—the best of the best—that include Chambertin Clos-de-Bèze and Charmes-Chambertin.

This series of circles only scratches the surface of Burgundy wines, but with a little practice and further reading, you can begin to understand wine lists and decode wine labels. For simplicity's sake, we've broken down the major growing regions below, from north to south.

CÔTE DE NUITS The vineyards of the Côte de Nuits extend south of Dijon for more than twelve miles, running through such famed villages as Gevrey-Chambertin, Chambolle-Musigny, Vougeot, Vosne-Romanée, and Nuits-St-Georges. Most red Grand Cru appellations—noted for their rich black cherry flavor with notes of chocolate and herbs that offer luscious tannins and bold acidity—belong to the Côte de Nuits.

HAUTES-CÔTES DE NUITS The lesser-known villages and vineyards of the Hautes-Côtes de Nuits rise on the slopes of the southern part of the Côte de Nuits. Higher altitudes and cooling breezes help grapes retain acidity, giving them a strong, bright backbone. This subregion has no specific village appellations or Premier Cru vineyards; all wines are labeled Bourgogne Hautes-Côtes de Nuits. These fall a step above entry level, but you can find many affordable and highly drinkable bottles.

CÔTE DE BEAUNE Encompassing the next twelve miles south of the Côte de Nuits, the Côte de Beaune centers around the city of Beaune. To the north lie the villages Pernand-Vergelesses and Aloxe-Corton, and to the south of

Beaune you'll find Pommard, Volnay, Meursault, Puligny-Montrachet, and others. This region produces some of the world's finest white wines as well as highly regarded Pinot Noir, offering food-friendly flavors of cherry and vanilla with pleasing aromatics. Vintners make it in a slightly lighter style than wine from the Côte de Nuits to the north.

CÔTE CHALONNAISE South of the Côte de Beaune, the Côte Chalonnaise produces white, red, rosé, and sparkling wines. In the center of the region, the villages of Givry and Mercurey make renowned delicate Pinot Noir wines that offer flavors of raspberry with a touch of smokiness amid soft tannins.

⋮

Some writers have observed that older wine lovers drink regions, such as Burgundy, Bordeaux, and Rioja, while younger folks drink varieties, such as Cabernet Sauvignon, Merlot, and Pinot Noir. This trend has helped spur Pinot Noir's popularity, which in turn has placed much of the really good stuff beyond the financial reach of many people. Its prices now rival those of Cabernet Sauvignon in fine restaurants and at auction, an unimaginable development just twenty years ago. Many excellent bottles cost less than $20, but some Burgundy Grand Crus,

such as Échézeaux, Romanée-Conti, and La Tâche, commonly fetch more than $2,000 *per bottle*. As demand continues rising in China, prices will soar even higher, which will inflate sticker prices on Burgundian Pinot Noir across the board.

Due to its soft tannins and bright acidity, Pinot Noir has the reputation of being a red wine for white-wine drinkers—which makes sense when you consider that Pinot Noir is one of the three grapes allowed in Champagne. In fact, a blanc de noirs Champagne consists entirely of Pinot Noir; minimal skin contact creates a wine with no red color whatsoever, which raises an interesting point: All Pinot varieties—Noir, Gris, Grigio, Blanc—are color-mutations of the same variety. But what a difference those mutations make! Can you think of two more diametrically opposed wines than an elegant, well-made Pinot Noir and a blindingly sweet, citrusy Pinot Grigio?

Pinot Noir may be more difficult to grow than varieties such as Cabernet Sauvignon and Syrah, but that hasn't stopped it from spreading throughout the world and becoming one of the most sought varieties in wine shops and restaurants across the globe. Outside Burgundy, it grows in Champagne, Pays d'Oc, Jura, the Loire Valley, and Alsace. Beyond France, it has grown throughout Europe—particularly in Germany, Austria, Switzerland, and Italy—for centuries. Today growers also cultivate it in Canada, Brazil, Spain, Slovenia, Hungary, Romania, and Moldova.

IN HER OWN WORDS

"Pinot Noir produces elegant, fine, delicate, complex, and sensual wines. This grape variety does not like excess in any form, be it heat, rain, color, tannins, or acidity. Balance is the key word, both in the vineyard and during winemaking. It is certainly the most thrilling and distinguished grape variety but also the most difficult to cultivate and to vinify."

—*Anne Parent, winemaker, Domaine Parent*

Other Notable Countries

ARGENTINA

The new star of the south, Pinot Noir flourished for many years in the Mendoza region, where producers often used it to make white and rosé sparkling wines. More than 4,000 acres of Pinot Noir grow in Argentina—a small fraction of total vineyard land—but old bush-vine Pinot Noir from Neuquén and Río Negro in Patagonia are producing premium reds. Color ranges from medium to deep red, and strong acidity balances the grape's typical flavor profile of cherry and chocolate.

IN HIS OWN WORDS

"Pinot Noir can be considered by some as 'king of all grapes.' Pinot Noir is probably one of the most transparent grapes, as it gives back what it finds in the soils and microclimates of where it is planted. The ones I drink convey incredible elegance, purity, minerality, and balance. It is a very delicate and subtle variety, which provides the most ethereal experience."

—*Piero Incisa della Rocchetta, owner, Bodega Chacra*

RECOMMENDED WINES

BARGAIN
KEVIN Catena Alamos
MIKE Manos Negras
       Alfredo Roca Fincas
JEFF Salentein Reserve

VALUE
KEVIN Luigi Bosca Grand
       Luca
MIKE Ernesto Catena Siesta
       Bodega Chacra Barda

SPECIAL OCCASION
OUR PICKS Pulenta Estate Gran XV
           Salentein PR1MUM

SPLURGE
OUR PICKS Bodega Chacra Treinta y Dos
           Bodega Chacra Cinquenta y Cinco

BELOW Barrel room at Bodega Chacra winery in Argentina.
NEXT PAGES Pinot Noir juice at Bodega Chacra winery in Argentina.

AUSTRALIA

Pinot Noir's best successes in Australia, where it covers more than 12,000 acres, rely on cool climates. The finest examples come from Adelaide Hills, Geelong, Great Southern, Margaret River, Mornington Peninsula, Gippsland, Macedon Ranges, Yarra Valley, and Tasmania. The berries grow very dark on the vine, but the resulting wine usually appears light red to ruby in color. Anticipate tastes of blackberry, cherry, chocolate, coffee, light spice, and orange zest. Age wonderfully benefits Australian Pinot Noirs in a couple of ways: More-mature vines yield wines with increased depth and complexity, and aging in barrel and bottle adds notes of vanilla and Mediterranean herbs.

RECOMMENDED WINES

BARGAIN
KEVIN Jacob's Creek Reserve
Robert Oatley Wild Oats
MIKE Innocent Bystander
JEFF Wakefield Estate
Shoofly

VALUE
KEVIN Shaw & Smith
MIKE Eldridge Estate
Dalrymple Pipers River
JEFF D'Arenberg The Feral Fox

SPECIAL OCCASION
KEVIN Dalrymple Coal River
MIKE De Bortoli Estate Grown
JEFF Giant Steps Applejack Vineyard
Yarra Yering

CHILE

About 6,500 acres of Pinot Noir flourish in the colder climates in the north and south of Chile, such as in Casablanca, San Antonio, and Bío Bío. The severe, sun-filled days of a Chilean summer make for ruby-colored wines. This depth of color often belies the delicate elegance of a well-crafted Pinot Noir, which here has a palate of black cherry and lightly stewed plum balanced by soft chocolate notes and refreshing acidity. Many Chilean winemakers hang their hats on Carménère and Cabernet Sauvignon, but Pinot Noir could turn out to be Chile's little grape that could.

RECOMMENDED WINES

BARGAIN
KEVIN Cono Sur Bicicleta
Montes Limited Selection
MIKE Veramonte
JEFF Santa Rita Secret Reserve
Leyda Pinot Noir Reserva

VALUE
KEVIN Arboleda
MIKE Koyle Costa
JEFF Montes Alpha
Elqui Wines Limited Release

SPECIAL OCCASION
KEVIN Matetic EQ
MIKE William Fevre Quino Noir
JEFF Ventisquero Heru

SPLURGE
OUR PICKS Viña Casablanca Pinot del Cerro
Torres Escaleras de Empedrado

CHINA

As the red wine craze continues in China and vineyard acreage grows, Pinot Noir from the Red Dragon will become an increasingly hot commodity. Pinot Noir grows in small but notable amounts throughout the country, including Shaanxi and Tianjin; the northeast provinces of Beijing, Hebei, and Shandong; and the northwest provinces of Xinjiang, Gansu, and Ningxia.

GERMANY

If you think of Germany exclusively as white wine territory, think again. The grape known here as Spätburgunder (*SHPATE-boor-GOON-dehr*) grows so widely here that Germany ranks as the world's third largest producer of Pinot Noir, behind France and America. Throughout the 1970s, producers sacrificed quality on the altar of quantity, but a handful of winemakers saw Pinot's potential in the late 1980s and reversed that trend. Thanks to them, Pinot Noir acreage doubled here between 1990 and 2010. Most of this wine remains within Germany's borders for domestic consumption, though, making these desirable bottles difficult to find on the international market. The best regions for Spätburgunder are Ahr, Baden, Franken, Pfalz, and Württemberg. German Pinot Noir has a floral aroma and flavors of tart cherry and mocha with earthy and savory notes.

RECOMMENDED WINES

BARGAIN
KEVIN A Diehl Spätburgunder Trocken
MIKE Villa Wolf
Schäfer Estate Bottled
JEFF Thomas Schmitt Private Collection

VALUE
KEVIN Franz Keller
MIKE August Kesseler N
JEFF Markgraf von Baden Gailinger Schloss Rheinburg
Salwey Estate Dry

SPECIAL OCCASION
KEVIN Meyer-Nakel Blauschiefer Trocken
Weingut Rudolf Furst Burgstadter Centgrafenberg
Spätburgunder
MIKE Friedrich Becker B
Huber Alte Reben Trocken Spätburgunder
JEFF Rudolf Fürst Klingenberger Spätburgunder

ITALY

Known as Pinot Nero (*PEE-no NEH-ro*) here, Pinot Noir flourishes in the cooler north of the country, especially Trentino, Alto Adige, Friuli, Lombardy, and the Tyrol. A good portion of it goes into sparkling wines, such as Franciacorta, but you can find a decent amount of good Italian Pinot Noir. The best versions hail from Alto Adige, but a few producers in Friuli and Lombardy do it right as well.

RECOMMENDED WINES

BARGAIN
KEVIN Alta Luna Pinot Noir Dolomiti IGT
Lechthaler Pinot Nero
MIKE Bottega Vinaia
Elena Walch Pinot Nero
JEFF Sartori
St. Michael-Eppan

VALUE
KEVIN Jermann Red Angel on the Moonlight
Franz Haas Pinot Nero
MIKE Castelfeder Burgum Novum Riserva Pinot Nero
Alois Lageder Krafuss
JEFF Tiefenbrunner Linticlarus Pinot Noir Riserva
J. Hofstätter Pinot Nero Meczan Alto Adige

SPECIAL OCCASION
KEVIN Podere Monastero La Pineta Pinot Nero
MIKE Pecchenino Langhe Pinot Nero
JEFF Caldaro Pfarrhof Riserva Pinot Nero

IN HIS OWN WORDS

"Pinot Noir is a very demanding variety and not suitable for weak minds. Pinot Noir spurs the winemaker to peak performances. Pinot Noir is a diva. If you think you know everything about Pinot Noir, you will be astonished by the unexpected."

—*Martin Foradori Hofstätter, owner, Tenuta J. Hofstätter*

NEXT PAGES Chiesa San Michele in the vineyards of the Mazon area in Alto Adige in Italy.

NEW ZEALAND

During the last fifteen years, plantings of Pinot Noir have increased almost nine-fold. More than 12,000 acres of it account for 15 percent of the country's vineyard land, making it New Zealand's most widely planted red grape. About a quarter of it goes into sparkling wine, and the rest into still wine. Central Otago Pinot Noir has everybody talking—and it grows there in nearly equal amounts as in Hawke's Bay—but you can find almost half of the total acreage in Marlborough. Smaller amounts grow in Wairarapa, Gisborne, Nelson, and Waipara.

Dark purple berries produce light red or ruby wines. The maritime climate, dry summers, and cool nights help create flavors of cherry, blackberry, espresso, and orange blossom, though each region has distinct characteristics. Central Otago Pinot Noir exhibits rich herbal notes, bright berry flavors, and a strong tannic structure. Wairarapa showcases the variety's denser, more full-bodied style. Both Marlborough and Nelson produce a version with full fruit and tight tannins. Waipara runs toward pepper and spice.

RECOMMENDED WINES

BARGAIN
KEVIN Brancott Estate
Babich
MIKE The Crossings
Foxes Island Renard
JEFF Peter Yealands
FOX by John Belsham

VALUE
KEVIN Nautilus
MIKE Peter Yealands Single Vineyard
Spy Valley
JEFF Cloudy Bay Marlborough

SPECIAL OCCASION
KEVIN Cloudy Bay Te Wahi
MIKE Seresin Rachel
JEFF Felton Road Bannockburn

SPLURGE
KEVIN Craggy Range Aroha Te Muna
MIKE Dry River
JEFF Mt. Difficulty Bannockburn Long Gully Single Vineyard

SOUTH AFRICA

Producers here commonly use Pinot Noir in sparkling Cap Classique wines, but more vintners are bottling it as a single varietal. It grows in small amounts throughout various areas, the majority in Stellenbosch. Walker Bay Pinot Noir is stirring up interest as well. The berries are dark purple, but the wine often appears ruby or black cherry red. Expect cherry on the nose and palate too, as well as blackberry, chocolate, coffee, and citrus zest.

RECOMMENDED WINES

VALUE
KEVIN Robertson Winery
Paul Cluver
MIKE Reservoir Road
Catherine Marshall Six Barrels Reserve
JEFF B Vintners Black Bream
Meerlust

SPECIAL OCCASION
OUR PICKS Bouchard Finlayson Galpin Peak
Boschendal Appellation Series Elgin
Hamilton Russell Vineyards

SWITZERLAND

Unless you live or lived in Switzerland, you're probably unfamiliar with Swiss wine. Unlike their watches and chocolate, the Swiss wisely keep their wine to themselves. The most widely cultivated red wine grape in the country, Pinot Noir here is called Blauburgunder (*BLAHW-boor-GOON-dehr*). The majority grows in the Valais region, in the far north reaches of the Rhône Valley, but you can find it near Zurich and Graubünden as well. Swiss Pinot Noir has an intense, fruity bouquet with a restrained elegance on the palate.

USA: CALIFORNIA

The Golden State has more than 40,000 acres of Pinot Noir vines—a serious expansion from the 25,000 here in 2004. Sonoma alone features 12,000 acres, and Monterey and Santa Barbara also boast significant plantings. The trend toward lighter, higher-acid, food-friendly wines has helped drive the variety's popularity here .

The best versions come from cool climates. The Sonoma Coast produces a large amount of high-quality, small-batch Pinot Noir that offers flavors of cherry, chocolate, coffee, light spice, and orange zest. Aging in barrel and bottle adds flavors of vanilla and Mediterranean herbs. Once called the coldest region in California, Carneros has been prime Pinot territory for many years. The style here tastes somewhat juicy, with flavors of raspberry and strawberry and touches of vanilla and orange peel. The Russian River Valley—in the far northwest of the Sonoma Coast and farther north in Mendocino County's Anderson Valley—produces the most elegant California Pinot Noir. In addition to cherry and chocolate, flavors include raspberry, violet, and perhaps soft touches of mint. For more intensity, head south to the Santa Lucia Highlands, where the deeply colored Pinot Noir bears flavors of blackberry, anise, and truffle. In Santa Barbara County, Sta. Rita Hills offers Pinot Noir of equal intensity and structure along with flavors of black plum, lingonberry, and mocha. Many California wineries that specialize in Pinot Noir produce multiple bottlings each season using grapes from single AVAs or even single-vineyard sites.

California Pinot Noir also goes into traditional-method sparkling wines.

RECOMMENDED WINES

BARGAIN
KEVIN A by Acacia
MIKE Edna Valley Vineyard Central Coast
Bridlewood Estate Winery Monterey
JEFF DeLoach Vineyards Heritage Reserve

VALUE
KEVIN Talbott Kali Hart
Au Bon Climat
MIKE MacMurray Estate Vineyards Russian River
Smoke Tree Sonoma
Au Contraire Dutton Ranch
JEFF The Calling Russian River Valley ⟶
Frei Brothers Reserve Russian River
Gallo Signature Series Santa
Lucia Highlands

SPECIAL OCCASION
KEVIN Merry Edwards Russian River
MIKE The Calling Patriarch
Maggy Hawk Unforgettable Anderson Valley
Cakebread Cellars Two Creeks Vineyards
JEFF J Vineyards Bow Tie Russian River
Artesa 91D

SPLURGE
KEVIN Williams Selyem Estate Hirsch Vineyard
MIKE J. Rochioli West Block
JEFF Evening Land Occidental Vineyard

IN HIS OWN WORDS

"Pinot Noir is the Mona Lisa. It has an enigmatic smile that one cannot tell if it's amused, laughing, or flirtatious. Each sip is a touch mercurial, showing aspects that no other wine can dare to capture. It has a persistence and pleasure that is unsurpassed by any other wine."

—*Brian Maloney, director of winemaking, Sonoma County, Boisset Collection*

IN HIS OWN WORDS

"The Russian River Valley is a world-class growing region with cool days and cold nights. Cool climates are necessary for Pinot Noir, as the grape is delicate with elegant flavors, and it needs these conditions."

—*Wayne Donaldson, winemaker, The Calling*

NEXT PAGES Vineyard and barn at the Maggy Hawk winery in California.

USA: NEW YORK

Pinot Noir tends to do best in the cooler climates of the Finger Lakes AVA, but it also does well in the altitude of the Hudson Valley and the sea-cooled North Fork of Long Island. Hotter years produce more concentrated fruit flavors, while moderate summers can make for elegant, restrained wines. Expect the typical flavors of freshly picked cherry, black cherry, and a hint of cranberry. Secondary aromas and flavors include coffee, mocha, oolong tea, and a touch of forest floor.

RECOMMENDED WINES

BARGAIN

OUR PICKS Thirsty Owl
Fulkerson
Dr. Konstantin Frank

VALUE

OUR PICKS Shaw Reserve
Inspire Moore Lust
Heron Hill Ingle Vineyard

SPECIAL OCCASION

OUR PICKS Damiani Reserve
Heart and Hands Barrel Reserve
Damiani Reserve Lower Block

IN HIS OWN WORDS

"The joy in making Pinot is in overcoming its challenges and promoting its virtues. Nurture these delicate grapes into a wine that is appreciated by people who understand Pinot Noir, and you have achieved the ultimate success in winemaking. What I really enjoy about making Pinot Noir is when it all comes together to make a wine that Pinot lovers can appreciate."

—*Shawn Kime, winemaker, Thirsty Owl Wine Company*

RIGHT Pinot Noir vines at the Thirsty Owl Vineyard on the shores of Cayuga Lake in New York.

USA: OREGON

Connoisseurs dare compare Oregon Pinot Noirs only with those from Burgundy. Consider the amount of Burgundian investment in Oregon, and you'll understand why. Burgundy's Drouhin family has had a winery here since shortly after the Willamette ("It's *will-AM-it*, damnit!") Valley achieved AVA status in 1983. Burgundy stalwart Maison Louis Jadot released Resonance, its first wine from Oregon, in 2016. The Willamette Valley grows three-quarters of all the grapes in the state, and Pinot Noir shines as its bestseller. Each July, the International Pinot Noir Celebration, a festival extolling the virtues of the grape, takes place in the Willamette Valley. The region is so Pinot Noir–specific that officials have carved it into six sub-AVAs: Chehalem Mountains, Dundee Hills, Eola-Amity Hills, McMinnville, Ribbon Ridge, and Yamhill-Carlton District. Even California wineries are joining the action. Some are trucking grapes from Oregon and making good Pinot Noirs at their own facilities. Expect flavors of black cherry, cranberry, black tea, mocha, and a hint of mushroom or truffle in Oregonian Pinot Noir.

IN HIS OWN WORDS

"The Pinot Noir grape grows well in the Willamette Valley due to the overall cool climate along with the dramatic change of temperature between day and night during growing season. We are enjoying the intensity, volume, and nice precision that we taste within our wines."

—*Thibault Gagey, head of operations,*
Résonance Vineyard and Winery

RECOMMENDED WINES

BARGAIN
KEVIN Erath
MIKE Oregon Territory
JEFF Rainstorm
Eola Hills

VALUE
KEVIN Rex Hill
MIKE Yamhill Valley Estate
Spindrift Cellars
JEFF Gran Moraine Yamhill-Carlton

SPECIAL OCCASION
KEVIN Domaine Drouhin
MIKE Panther Creek Lazy River
Knudsen
JEFF Résonance Résonance Vineyard

SPLURGE
KEVIN Beaux Frères Beaux Frères Vineyard Ribbon Ridge
MIKE Domaine Serene Grace Vineyard
Penner-Ash Pas de Nom
JEFF Zena Crown Vineyard Slope Eola-Amity Hills

RIGHT Barrels at Resonance in Oregon. **OPPOSITE** Zena Crown Vineyard in Willamette Valley in Oregon.

PINOTAGE

(PEE-no-TAHZH)

IN THE GLASS

Burgundy glass, ruby in color

TASTING PROFILE

	LOW	MEDIUM	HIGH
ACIDITY			
BODY			
TANNIN			

TASTING NOTES

BLACKBERRY   BANANA   COFFEE

This wine carries flavors of blackberry and mulberry and can have notes of smoke and leather as well. Flavors include ripe black fruits with secondary notes of tropical fruit and banana as well as smoke, earth, and green bramble. Recent, popular styles have deep coffee and espresso aromas and tastes.

FOOD PAIRINGS

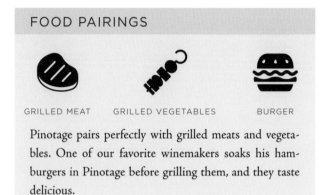

GRILLED MEAT   GRILLED VEGETABLES   BURGER

Pinotage pairs perfectly with grilled meats and vegetables. One of our favorite winemakers soaks his hamburgers in Pinotage before grilling them, and they taste delicious.

RECOMMENDED WINES

BARGAIN

KEVIN Fairview
        Simonsig
MIKE Graham Beck The Game Reserve
        Fleur du Cap Bergkelder Selection
JEFF Barista

VALUE

OUR PICKS Bellingham The Bernard Series Bush Vine
        Beyerskloof Reserve
        Kanonkop

YOU SHOULD KNOW

Early Pinotage smelled like paint or nail polish, and in 1976 a group of British masters of wine described one of the flavor characteristics as "rusty nails." Improved winemaking techniques in recent years have tamed these faults. You can find very bad wines as well as very good ones. It all comes down to the winemaker's skill.

OPPOSITE Kanonkop Estate vineyards in South Africa.

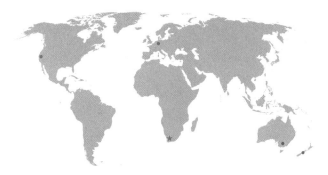

Abraham Perold bred South Africa's signature grape at Stellenbosch University in 1925, crossing Pinot Noir with Cinsaut, known locally as Hermitage—hence the compound name. Perold planted a few vines at his university residence and two years later accepted a job with KWV, the behemoth wine cooperative. His successor, C. J. Theron, tended the vines, but it wasn't until 1941 that Kanonkop Estate—still one of the finest producers of the varietal—planted the first commercial vines. In 1959, a Pinotage won the Cape Wine Show, and two years later the name graced its first wine label. Growers here planted it widely throughout the 1960s, but Pinotage is a hard grape to grow and to vinify. Recent techniques—such as long, cold fermentation and aging in oak barrels—have increased quality immeasurably. The variety grows in all of the country's wine regions most notably in Bot River, Lower Orange, Paarl, Stellenbosch, Swartland, and Walker Bay.

A "Cape Blend" denotes a wine made from Bordeaux varieties blended with Pinotage even if another of the varieties dominates the blend. Pinotage wines range from simple, easy-drinking wines through full, dry reds, to bold wines that taste of coffee and espresso.

IN HIS OWN WORDS

"When Pinotage is young, you will get flavors of plum, black currant, and strawberry. As the wine matures, you will get mushroom, forest floor, and tomato cocktail flavors. I have also tried Pinotage from Australia, New Zealand, Germany, and the United States. Normally the wines are lighter in style, but I think it is the age of the vines."

—*Abrie Beeslaar, winemaker and cellarmaster, Kanonkop Estate*

PLAVAC MALI

(PLAH-vahts MAH-lee)

IN THE GLASS

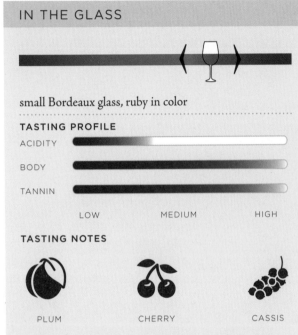

small Bordeaux glass, ruby in color

TASTING PROFILE

ACIDITY

BODY

TANNIN

LOW · MEDIUM · HIGH

TASTING NOTES

PLUM · CHERRY · CASSIS

Aromas include black plum, dried cherry, black raspberry, and cassis. On your palate, expect a big, full-bodied, high-alcohol, viscous wine. Examples from Dingač can have alcohol levels ranging from 13 to 17 percent with a lot of spice up front. Flavors include Damson plum, cassis, blackberry, and black cherry with notes of freshly ground black pepper, licorice, and clove.

FOOD PAIRINGS

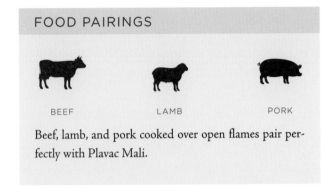

BEEF · LAMB · PORK

Beef, lamb, and pork cooked over open flames pair perfectly with Plavac Mali.

RECOMMENDED WINES

BARGAIN

KEVIN Lirica
MIKE Istravino
JEFF Dingač Winery

VALUE

KEVIN Vuina
       Križ
MIKE Korta Katarina
JEFF Skaramuca Dingač
      Saints Hills Sveti Roko

SPECIAL OCCASION

KEVIN Grgić
MIKE Korta Katarina Reuben's Private Reserve
JEFF Saints Hills Dingač

YOU SHOULD KNOW

If growers harvest the grapes too soon, you can detect a vegetal or farm-stand smell. Alcohol levels legally can reach 17 percent, so these wines may taste too hot for many. Winemakers often let tannins run rampant, but a well-made Plavac Mali has firm or chewy tannins, so age it for a few years before enjoying its complexity fully.

OPPOSITE Saints Hill vineyards in Croatia.

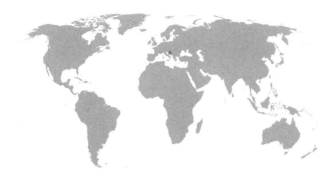

This little-known variety—which means "small blue," accurately describing the berries—grows all over Croatia. The Dingač appellation first registered its use in 1961. During summer months, the sun burns hot, but Adriatic breezes cool the grapes. Evenings and nights run cooler, thus allowing ample time for the grapes to come down in temperature before the next sunrise. Many vineyards here lie on steep slopes that face south and run down to the sea, making it impossible to use mechanized harvest equipment. Most of the viticultural work is done by hand.

This grape has been causing a stir in the wine world for a few decades now. At the urging of Croatian-born California wine luminary Mike Grgich, the University of California at Davis carried out research in the 1980s, hoping to identify Plavac Mali as genetically similar to Zinfandel. Researchers did find similarities between the two varieties, but—unlike Primitivo and Zinfandel—they weren't exactly the same. Plavac Mali, it turns out, is a cross between Tribidrag (ancestral Zinfandel) and Dobričić.

Plavac Mali, which accounts for roughly 10 percent of Croatia's vineyard land, ranks as the most economically important red grape here. It grows throughout the country and goes by different names in different regions: Crljenak, Kaštelanski, Zelenak, among others. Some of the best examples come from the Dalmatian Coast, especially from Dingač and Postup on the Pelješac Peninsula just north of Dubrovnik.

IN HIS OWN WORDS

"Plavac Mali is a very specific grape. It gives the best results in the most beautiful and extreme conditions of the Dalmatian terroir, especially Dingač. Very fruity and complex wines tell the story of sun, stone, and sea, low yields, hard work, and Mediterranean life through every drop. What I love the most is that it cannot be compared to something you know or drank before. It is telling its own story, and it is the story of the Dalmatian way of life through centuries."

—*Ernest Tolj, founder and owner, Saints Hills Winery*

SANGIOVESE

(SAHN-jo-VAY-say)

IN THE GLASS

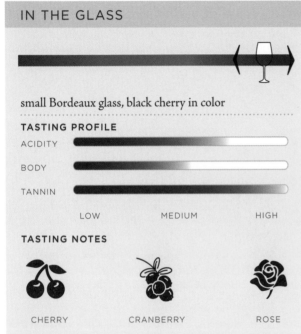

small Bordeaux glass, black cherry in color

TASTING PROFILE

ACIDITY

BODY

TANNIN

LOW   MEDIUM   HIGH

TASTING NOTES

CHERRY   CRANBERRY   ROSE

Primary aromas are cherry, cranberry, oregano, smoke, and rose petal. Young versions, such as Chianti, Morellino di Scansano, and Rosso di Montefalco, have fruit-forward flavors of cherry, strawberry, and rose with touches of dried herbs and tomato. Well-aged Sangiovese exhibits layered flavors of tobacco, smoke, and leather with soft notes of vanilla.

YOU SHOULD KNOW

Sangiovese sometimes hides behind appellation or DOCG names on a wine label, but it's the primary grape in Chianti, Brunello di Montalcino, Vino Nobile di Montepulciano, and Morellino di Scansano.

FOOD PAIRINGS

OLIVES   PASTA   BURGER

The zesty acidity of a young Sangiovese with minimum oak can stand up to capers, olives, and even lemon juice, so try it alongside veal piccata or pasta puttanesca. It marries well with seared beef and gooey cheese, so open a bottle the next time you have a burger. Drink Brunello di Montalcino or Vino Nobile di Montepulciano alongside bistecca Fiorentina or rosemary-studded roast leg of lamb.

RECOMMENDED WINES

BARGAIN

KEVIN   Marchesi Antinori Santa Cristina Chianti Superiore

MIKE   Marchesi de' Frescobaldi Rèmole Toscana
Lunadoro Primosenso Rosso di Montepulciano

JEFF   Podere La Vigna Rosso di Montalcino

VALUE

KEVIN   Col d'Orcia Rosso di Montalcino
Avignonesi Vino Nobile di Montepulciano

MIKE   Tenuta di Arceno Strada al Sasso

JEFF   Castello Banfi Belnero
Tenuta il Poggione Rosso di Montalcino

SPECIAL OCCASION

KEVIN   Castello Banfi Poggio alle Mura

MIKE   Tenute Silvio Nardi Poggio Doria Brunello di
Montalcino Riserva DOCG

JEFF   Poggio di Sotto Rosso di Montalcino

SPLURGE

KEVIN   Marchesi de' Frescobaldi Castelgiocondo Riserva

MIKE   Luce Brunello

JEFF   Biondi Santi Riserva Brunello di Montalcino

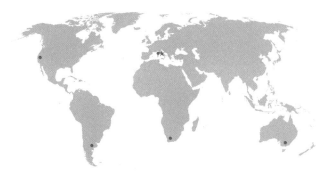

Sangiovese has one of the most exciting origin stories of any grape. Its name derives from the Latin *sanguis Jovis*, or "blood of Jove," referring to the Roman king of the gods, Jupiter, ruler of the heavens. It's also really fun to say if you raise your hands in the air and call out the name like a true Italian.

Although its name and folklore suggest that it has grown here since Roman times, research shows that the grape originated as a spontaneous field crossing between Ciliegiolo, a Tuscan grape, and Calabrese Montenuovo from southern Italy sometime in the sixteenth century. Sangiovese covers about 10 percent of Italy's vineyards, making it the country's number-one grape. It goes by about thirty different synonyms, and clonal differences, terroir, aging requirements, and winemaking style all account for the disparate styles of Sangiovese. In some regions, vintners use it as a blending grape, while in Tuscany in particular it shines as a single varietal. It makes for relatively inexpensive, easy-drinking wines in Chianti and Morellino di Scansano, while Brunello di Montalcino has a reputation as the pinnacle of Italian terroir and winemaking expertise. Our four favorite DOCGs appear below, but you can find good single varietals and Sangiovese-heavy blends in Emilia-Romagna, Umbria, and the Marche.

BRUNELLO DI MONTALCINO is considered the

zenith of Sangiovese. The wine comes from a dark clone of the grape called Sangiovese Grosso, known locally as Brunello (*broo-NEH-lo*). The vineyards lie on hillside slopes and in gently rolling valleys surrounding the beautiful medieval town of Montalcino. Brunello di Montalcino received DOC status in 1968 and, in 1980, Italy's first DOCG classification. It must contain 100 percent Sangiovese, and it must age at least two years in oak and an additional four months in the

bottle. Wines may be sold to consumers no sooner than five years after the harvest. Brunello di Montalcino Riserva wines require at least six months in the bottle and don't release for sale until six years after harvest. These wines exhibit an unmatched intensity and richness of flavor.

CHIANTI, referring to wine made in the Chianti

Mountains between Florence and Siena, dates back to the thirteenth century, although historians don't know for certain which varieties winemakers used then. Baron Bettino Ricasoli receives credit for creating the first modern Chianti using Sangiovese in the 1870s. Since then, the boundaries of the Chianti region have changed several times, and it now includes seven subregions. The largest growing area and style is known simply as Chianti DOCG. Wines produced here must contain a minimum of 75 percent Sangiovese and must age for at least three months in oak. Chianti Classico DOCG represents a

NEXT PAGES Brunello di Montalcino vineyard in Italy.

designated growing area in the heart of the Chianti region, requiring at least 80 percent Sangiovese and at least seven months of oak aging. Chianti Superiore wines come from grapes from the greater Chianti region outside Chianti Classico. These wines require at least nine months of oak aging and geographically equal Chianti DOCG wines with longer aging and therefore increased complexity. The Riserva style, within Chianti Classico, calls for at least two years of aging before sale, a minimum of three months in the bottle.

See the separate chapter on the Chianti style (page 228).

MORELLINO DI SCANSANO

MORELLINO DI SCANSANO received DOCG status in 2007. It lies in the Maremma, the coastal area of Tuscany between Rome and Pisa. The area includes the towns of Scansano, Grosseto, and Magliano, and Morellino is the local name for the Sangiovese grape. Wines must contain a minimum of 85 percent Sangiovese, and Morellino di Scansano DOCG wines may be released for sale as of March 1 in the year after the harvest. These fresh, fruity, easy-drinking wines pair well with seafood dishes. Morellino di Scansano Riserva DOCG wines must age at least two years, with one in wood, which adds a layer of complexity and soft vanilla, toast, and spice flavors.

VINO NOBILE DI MONTEPULCIANO

VINO NOBILE DI MONTEPULCIANO isn't the same as the hilltop Tuscan village of Montepulciano, so don't confuse them! Vino Nobile must consist of at least 70 percent Sangiovese, known locally as Prugnolo Gentile (*proon-YO-lo-JEHN-tee-lay*). Winemakers also may blend Sangiovese with the Canaiolo Nero and Mammolo varieties to make Vino Nobile di Montepulciano DOCG wines. These wines must age for two years, with a minimum of two months in barrel. Riserva wines require three years' aging prior to release. In addition to the traditional Sangiovese flavors of tart cherry and strawberry, Vino Nobile offers notes of hillside herbs, such as thyme and oregano, and a light hint of florality. The region also offers Rosso di Montepulciano, a "little brother" wine, which has less strict production regulations, shorter aging requirements, and a significantly lower price tag.

Beyond Italy, growers cultivate Sangiovese on Corsica (where it also ranks as the most widely planted variety), and it has a presence in Argentina, Australia, and America, thanks to nineteenth-century Italian immigrants who brought their grape cuttings and winemaking skills as they moved across the globe.

IN HIS OWN WORDS

"The author Curzio Malaparte, in his book *Maledetti Toscani* (*Damn Tuscans*), describes perfectly, in a lovingly ironic way, the character of the Tuscans, who manage to bring sarcasm to the most tragic situations they find themselves in and bring discomfort to their greatest moments of joy. Tuscans are cynical, graciously arrogant, sometimes a bit scornful, lovers of liberty, generous, firm and radical in their feelings, magnanimous yet in a highly measured way, and, above all, they are blunt. All that is Sangiovese. Unabashed, noble, and slightly haughty, yet often a bit mischievous; he is a free spirit and knows how to be generous. Sangiovese is simple, spontaneous, and sincere."

—*Rudy Buratti, winemaker, Castello Banfi*

OPPOSITE Detail of Brunello di Montalcino vineyard in Italy. **NEXT PAGES** Plastic baskets in Montalcino in Italy.

BRUNELLO
MONTALCINO
Vend. 1992
n. 70 Bott. Italia

Other Notable Countries

ARGENTINA

Sangiovese grows on more than 5,500 acres of Argentinean vineyards. Wine experts generally consider Sangiovese from here as inferior to the Tuscan variety, but increased quality and a renewed interest in the variety have led to limited quantities of choice Sangiovese coming from Argentina. In them, you'll find primary flavors of cherry, strawberry, and violet. They also can exhibit tomato leaf or mint characteristics usually associated with terroir.

AUSTRALIA

Cultivation of Sangiovese in Australia began in the 1960s and continues today in the King Valley, McLaren Vale, the Adelaide Hills, Canberra, and Mudgee. Sometimes vinified into a refreshing rosé, Sangiovese accounts for only a small percentage of Australia's grape cultivation, scarcely more than 1,500 acres. But winemakers, especially of Italian descent, love it here. Young versions carry flavors of black plum, strawberry, tart cherry, and orange peel. Careful aging can bring on secondary characteristics of earth, tar, and truffle.

FRANCE: CORSICA

No one knows for sure how Sangiovese made it to Corsica. Locals believed for many years that the grape, known here as Nielluccio (*nee-eh-LOO-cho*), was indigenous, although growers probably first planted it when the island formed part of the kingdom of Genoa, sometime prior to the late eighteenth century. Nielluccio grows on about 4,000 acres of Corsican soil, making it the most important grape here. Wines labeled "Vin de Corse AOC" must contain at least 50 percent Nielluccio, and it's the main variety in Patrimonio AOC wines, which must contain at least 95 percent of the grape. Nielluccio wines have strong tannins, high acidity, and flavors of strawberry, black fig, and tomato joined by notes of oregano and a hint of smoke.

USA: CALIFORNIA

Brought over by Italian immigrants, Sangiovese has grown in California since about 1880. It grows in amounts large and small in every region in the state, covering about 1,900 acres, with a fair amount in Sonoma and Napa. You'll often find it as a single varietal, but sometimes winemakers blend it with Cabernet Sauvignon, Merlot, or Cabernet Franc in the Super Tuscan style. Young Californian Sangiovese tastes of tart cherry, black plum, strawberry, and orange peel, while barrel and bottle aging bring out rich notes of forest floor, smoke, or mushrooms.

RECOMMENDED WINES

BARGAIN

KEVIN Frey
Luna

MIKE Terra d'Oro
Barra of Mendocino Estate Grown

JEFF Vino Noceto

VALUE

KEVIN Cent'Anni BuoniAnni

MIKE Palumbo Family Vineyards Bella Vigna Vineyard
Barrel Racer

SPECIAL OCCASION

OUR PICKS Shafer
Staglin Family

OPPOSITE Cellared bottles of Brunello di Montalcino.

SAPERAVI

(SAH-pehr-AH-vee)

IN THE GLASS

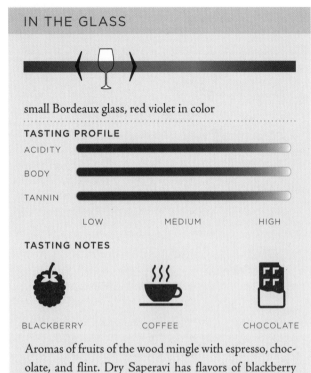

small Bordeaux glass, red violet in color

TASTING PROFILE

	LOW	MEDIUM	HIGH
ACIDITY			
BODY			
TANNIN			

TASTING NOTES

BLACKBERRY   COFFEE   CHOCOLATE

Aromas of fruits of the wood mingle with espresso, chocolate, and flint. Dry Saperavi has flavors of blackberry and plum with notes of cocoa, coffee, and truffle.

YOU SHOULD KNOW

Winemakers vinify this variety into dry, semisweet, and sweet fortified styles. When choosing a bottle, ask the shop's clerk or restaurant's sommelier to make sure you know what you're buying. Saperavi's strong tannins and bright acidity lend themselves to long aging, so don't fear older vintages.

FOOD PAIRINGS

SAUSAGE   STEW   CHILI

This variety goes very well with charcuterie, so pour a glass the next time you have a board of salami, soppresatta, and sausages. As a bold red, it also goes wonderfully with beef stew, but for a more creative pairing try chili instead. Its bold acidity holds up to the brightness of the tomatoes in the dish. Semisweet Saperavi is perfect with blue cheese.

RECOMMENDED WINES

BARGAIN

KEVIN Teliani Valley Kindzmarauli
Pheasant's Tears

MIKE Kindzmarauli Marani →

JEFF Kindzmarauli Marani Kindzmarauli Original

VALUE

KEVIN Standing Stone Vineyards

MIKE Vinoterra
Orgo

JEFF Shalauri Cellars

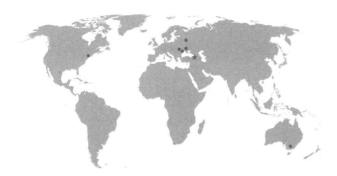

IN HIS OWN WORDS

"Compared with the rare Saperavi from other countries, like Australia and the United States, aromas of Georgian Saperavi are probably a bit less jammy. Due to our climate and terroir, we always get a very good balance between tannins, aromas, and structure. The structure of the wines is softer, the aromas are more elegant and complex, and the finish is longer, especially in wines produced in the Kakheti region."

—*Raphael Genot, winemaker, Marani*

The name of this ancient grape and Georgia's most widely cultivated red variety means "dye" or "paint," thanks to its dark-colored skin and pulp. It comes originally from the southwest of the country, near Turkey, but you'll find most plantings today in the Kakheti region. If you ever have the opportunity to attend a Georgian wine tasting, definitely go, and bring a toothbrush. Most red wine grapes have "black" or red skins and white to green flesh, but Saperavi qualifies as a *teinturier* grape, meaning that both its skin and pulp are red. Winemakers almost exclusively use teinturier grapes in blends to add color to finished wine, but Saperavi stands as the exception.

A bottle labeled just "Saperavi" can come from anywhere in the country and may taste dry or semisweet. It's the main or single variety in wines bearing appellation names such as Akhasheni, Kindzmarauli, Mukuzani, and Napareuli. If the label reads "Akhasheni," the wine also will taste semisweet but hail from the Gurdshaani region. Kindzmarauli wines are late-harvest, semisweet wines from the Kvareli region. The finest dry Saperavi wines come from the Mukuzani and Napareuli regions, which lie on opposite sides of the Alazani River in Kakheti. Aged three years before release, these wines have dark fruit flavors that feature notes of smoke and leather.

Georgian Saperavi had a good reputation throughout the Soviet Union, but tensions arose between Russia and Georgia in 2006, and exports of Georgian wine to Russia halted. Since then, the Georgian wine industry has been pushing to sell more wine into America, Britain, Canada, and other large wine markets. You'll have an easier time finding Mukuzani wines, which have a better presence on the international market than Napareuli.

In addition to Georgia, Saperavi grows throughout the former USSR in Bulgaria, Moldova, Russia, and Ukraine. You can find small plantings in New York's Finger Lakes region and in McLaren Vale and the Barossa Valley in South Australia.

ABOVE Grape bud on the vine at Marani vineyard in Georgia.
NEXT PAGES Stainless steel fermentation tanks at Marani winery in Georgia.

SYRAH

(suhr-AH)

IN THE GLASS

large Bordeaux glass, black cherry color

TASTING PROFILE

	LOW	MEDIUM	HIGH
ACIDITY			
BODY			
TANNIN			

TASTING NOTES

CHERRY   BLUEBERRY   CASSIS

Intoxicating aromas fill the nose with black cherry, blueberry, vanilla, and savory notes of olive leaf and thyme. Dark fruit flavors abound, including blackberry, plum, and cassis that some interpret as sweetness, though serious Syrah is always dry. A well-made Syrah will wash across the palate with rich berry flavors and strong notes of spice, dried herbs, smoke, and black pepper.

YOU SHOULD KNOW

Old World Syrah, especially from France, exhibits elegance and restraint. New World versions, particularly from Australia, South Africa, and California's Central Coast, may taste jammy.

FOOD PAIRINGS

CHINESE FOOD   CHICKEN   KEBABS

New World Syrah's abundant fruit flavors, spice notes, and bold acidity make it a good match for foods with touches of sweetness and spice. Try it with Chinese take-out—in particular spareribs, pepper steak, and spicy sesame noodles. French Syrah pairs naturally with roasted chicken with herbes de Provence or Moroccan-spiced lamb kebabs.

RECOMMENDED WINES

BARGAIN

KEVIN   Domaine Alain Voge Les Peyrouses Côtes du Rhône
MIKE   La Forge Estate
JEFF   Michel Gassier Les Piliers Costières de Nîmes
     Château des Crès Ricards Stécia

VALUE

KEVIN   Paul Jaboulet Aîné Crozes Hermitage Les Jalets
MIKE   Château Paul Mas Clos des Mûres
JEFF   Vidal-Fleury Saint-Joseph Red
     Château des Crès Ricards Oenothera

SPECIAL OCCASION

KEVIN   Domaine Jean-Louis Chave Saint-Joseph
MIKE   Jean-Luc Colombo Les Ruchets Cornas
     Les Vins de Vienne L'Arzelle Saint-Joseph
JEFF   Jean-Michel Gerin Côte Rotie La Viallière

SPLURGE

KEVIN   E. Guigal Château d'Ampuis Côte Rôtie
MIKE   M. Chapoutier Les Greffieux Ermitage Hermitage
JEFF   E. Guigal La Turque Côte Rôtie
     Paul Jaboulet Aîné Domaine de Roure Crozes
     Hermitage

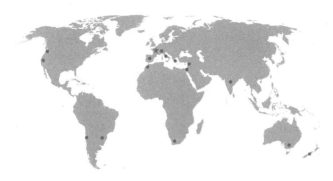

The origin of the grape's name remains shrouded in mystery. Some researchers theorize that it descended from an ancient Syrian grape or from a grape originating in the city of Shiraz in the Persian Empire. Others believe that its name comes from the Sicilian city of Syracuse or the Greek island Syros (sometimes called Syra). As with humans, grapes can far surpass their parents in success and popularity. Syrah, for example, hails from two little-known, practically extinct varieties: Dureza and Mondeuse Blanche. It's this parentage that points definitively to French origins.

This dark-skinned variety falls among the ten most widely planted grapes worldwide, which you wouldn't know by looking only at wine lists or store shelves. Most restaurants and wine shops overflow with Cabernet Sauvignon, Pinot Noir, Merlot, and proprietary red blends. The retail market vastly underrepresents this variety, which is good news for wine lovers in the know. With the exception of a handful of French AOCs, Syrah often presents great value in restaurants and wine shops alike.

When it comes to real estate, Syrah has excellent, expensive taste. "Syrah likes a view," winemakers often say because this variety prefers hilltop vineyards with plenty of light and proximity to the sea. Syrah lives for the sun and hot climates. The altitudes at which it thrives offer breezes and nighttime coolness that prevent sugar levels from going too high and also help retain acidity for fresh and invigorating flavors.

It's the main grape in the wines of Hermitage, Côte-Rôtie, Cornas, and St. Joseph in the northern Rhône, and it also goes into the Grenache-dominant blends of Gigondas, Châteauneuf-du-Pape, and the Côtes du Rhône. France has the largest amount of Syrah vines of any country, and they grow widely throughout both the northern and southern Rhône and Languedoc-Roussillon. Syrah somewhat fell from favor in the 1960s but rebounded later in the twentieth century thanks to

ABOVE Syrah juice during the crush in Woodinville in Washington.

high scores and accolades bestowed by wine critics as well as the popularity of Australian Shiraz on the global market. French Syrah, especially at the high end, elegantly features flavors of blackberry, cassis, black olive, anise, and smoked meat. Here are our favorite Syrah locations:

HERMITAGE, the pinnacle of Syrah, consists of 345 acres near the village of Tain-l'Hermitage. The majority of the vineyards here—which include L'Hermite, La Chapelle, Le Méal, Les Greffieux, Murets, and Les Bessards—face south, where all-day sun transmits power and flavor to the finished wines. Winemakers here may add up to 15 percent of two white grapes, Marsanne and Roussanne, to their Syrah. In addition to an intense earthiness, Hermitage wines have an acute minerality and a floral lift. Deep-seated tannins and vibrant acidity allow for long aging, making these some of the priciest Syrahs on the market.

CORNAS, from a Celtic word for "burned earth," has red-tinged soils featuring rock and sand that provide a near-perfect environment for growing Syrah. The winemaking prestige of Cornas stretches back to the tenth century. This is among the smallest appellations in the Rhône Valley, and vineyards on the right bank of the Rhône grow Syrah vines almost exclusively. Wines from here are noted for their long age-ability, though some producers now create a more fruit-forward style meant to be drunk on or shortly after release. Any wine labeled "Cornas" must contain 100 percent Syrah. Expect strong tannins and fruit-of-the-wood flavors on the palate joined by black olive and mocha.

CÔTE-RÔTIE, the northernmost appellation in the Rhône Valley, runs through three communes, or counties, on the right bank of the Rhône: St-Cyr-sur-le-Rhône, Ampuis, and Tupin-et-Semons. Narrow terraces carve up steep riverside vineyards that range in altitude from about 600 feet to more than 1,000. The wines of Côte-Rôtie must contain at least 80 percent Syrah and can include up to 20 percent Viognier, a white grape that softens Syrah's tannins and adds floral notes. Deep ruby in color, these wines offer flavors of blackberry, raspberry, violet, and clove with a hint of leather.

ST. JOSEPH, once known as Vin de Mauves, extends for thirty miles along the right bank of the Rhône River and also carries a historic reputation. Charlemagne prized Mauves among his favorite wines, and Victor Hugo mentioned it in *Les Misérables*. The name St. Joseph comes from an area vineyard owned by Jesuits in the seventeenth century, although officials didn't formalize the appellation until 1956. Syrah from here may contain up to 10 percent Marsanne and Roussanne. Many of the region's almost 3,000 acres bear old-vine Syrah up to one hundred years in age. Even with their storied past and great age, you'll find red wines from St. Joseph

among the most approachable and affordable in the northern Rhône. Their fruit-forward style centers on easy-drinking flavors of black plum and black cherry with smooth tannins and notes of black pepper and vanilla.

Syrah has a dual identity: Australia and South Africa call it Shiraz (*sheer-AZZ*). The name on a label can offer insight into the style of the wine inside. "Syrah" often connotes an Old World winemaking technique, while "Shiraz" indicates more of a New World approach and flavor profile. To add yet more confusion, the grape sometimes is called Hermitage in France, Australia, and South Africa, although only Hermitage (*erm-mee-TAHZH*) AOC wines may use that designation on the label.

In addition to France and the countries detailed below, Syrah grows in Morocco, Switzerland, Greece, and Lebanon.

Other Notable Countries

ARGENTINA

This spicy red variety grows on about 32,000 acres, or roughly 6 percent of Argentina's vineyard land. It's most abundant in the Mendoza, San Juan, Catamarca, and La Rioja regions, and vintners often blend it with Malbec to add freshness of fruit and richness of mouthfeel. As a single varietal, it can become a powerful fruit bomb or a wine of delicate complexity. Regardless of style, a glass of Argentinean Syrah will have flavors of plum, black cherry, anise, pepper, and some touches of smoke or earth.

RECOMMENDED WINES

BARGAIN
OUR PICKS Pascual Toso Maipú
Luigi Bosca Reserva
Trapiche Oak Cask

VALUE
OUR PICKS Luca Laborde Double Select
Viña Alicia San Alberto
Trivento Golden Reserve
O. Fournier

AUSTRALIA

James Busby, the father of Australian viticulture, brought cuttings of what became known here as Shiraz in 1832. Today you can't miss it: A whopping 28 percent of Australian vineyards—more than 100,000 acres!—grow Shiraz vines, and wines from the Barossa Valley, Eden Valley, Heathcote, Beechworth, Canberra, Great Western, McLaren Vale, Margaret River, and the Hunter Valley regions earn high points with critics and consumers alike. Whether bottled on its own or in a Rhône-style GSM blend, Shiraz is far and away Australia's most widely planted and wildly popular variety. It often packs a powerhouse punch from the first scent of blackberry, blueberry, violet, spice, and black pepper, through tastes of black cherry, cassis, jalapeño, chocolate, and espresso, to a long, chewy finish. Aged Syrah takes on flavors of earth, tobacco, and truffle as well, making this a wine that begs to share the table with grilled red meat. Winemakers sometimes add small amounts of Viognier—a white grape and one of Syrah's grandparents—to add more florality to the nose and palate. If you come across an Australian bottle labeled "Syrah," expect a more elegant, French-style wine.

- -

IN HIS OWN WORDS

"Some of Australia's oldest Shiraz vines can be found in the Barossa. The magical combination of climate (low rainfall) and ancient soils results in vines that deliver beautifully balanced fruit with excellent color and varietal definition. The result is rich and full-bodied wines that are true expressions of the region."

—*Ian Hongell, winemaker, Peter Lehmann*

- -

RECOMMENDED WINES

BARGAIN

KEVIN Jacob's Creek Reserve Shiraz

MIKE Hope Estate Basalt Block Shiraz
 Redbank The Long Paddock Shiraz

JEFF Peter Lehmann Portrait Shiraz

VALUE

KEVIN Penfolds Bin 28 Kalimna Shiraz

MIKE St. Hallett Blackwell Shiraz
 Kilikanoon Testament Shiraz

JEFF Yangarra Estate Vineyard Shiraz

SPECIAL OCCASION

KEVIN D'Arenberg The Dead Arm Shiraz

MIKE Standish Andelmonde Barossa Valley Shiraz
 D'Arenberg The Swinging Malaysian Single
  Vineyard Shiraz

JEFF Hickinbotham Clarendon Vineyard Brooks Road
  Shiraz
 Thorn-Clarke Ron Thorn Single Vineyard Barossa
  Shiraz

SPLURGE

KEVIN Henschke Mount Edelstone

MIKE Penfolds Grange
 Torbreck RunRig Shiraz Viognier

JEFF Casella 1919 Shiraz
 Henschke Hill of Grace

NEXT PAGES Barrels at Yangarra Estate Vineyard in Australia.

CHILE

Nonexistent in Chile until the mid-1990s, Syrah now grows on more than 13,000 acres, quickly gaining cult status as a must-have wine. Whether planted at high altitudes in the Elqui Valley, the seaside foothills of Colchagua, or the cherished soils of Apalta, Chilean Syrah offers intense flavors of blackberry, spice, and black pepper that wine connoisseurs appreciate widely. Cooler-climate versions from San Antonio and Elqui develop a fiery complexity with notes of smoked meat and herbs that make it an accompaniment for grilled or roasted foods.

RECOMMENDED WINES

BARGAIN
KEVIN Santa Rita Reserva
Arboleda
MIKE Echeverria Reserva
JEFF Emiliana Natura
Koyle Reserva

VALUE
KEVIN Matetic EQ
MIKE Lagar de Bezana Edicion Limitada
JEFF MontGras Antu
Lapostolle Collection El Rosario

SPECIAL OCCASION
KEVIN Viña Casablanca Nebulus
MIKE Ventisquero Pangea Apalta Vineyard
JEFF Matetic San Antonio

SPLURGE
KEVIN Montes Folly
MIKE Concha y Toro Gravas del Maipo
JEFF Errazuriz La Cumbre

INDIA

Syrah is becoming India's signature red grape. Grown primarily in Nashik, India's premier winegrowing region, the variety thrives in the hot climate here. Having garnered the highest points and accolades from several international wine magazines and competitions, the Dindori subregion is earning recognition for producing premium-quality wine. Depending on the winery, the grape goes by Syrah or Shiraz, which often indicates the winemaking style. Expect a red-violet wine with bright cherry and blueberry flavors, smooth tannins, and touches of spice and black pepper.

ABOVE Harvesting grapes at Sula Vineyards in India.
OPPOSITE Handpicking during the harvest at Sula Vineyards in India.

ISRAEL

Widely planted throughout Galilee and the Judean Hills, Syrah has made itself at home in Israel's hot, sunny, Mediterranean climate. As Israeli vintners continue forging a national identity in the wine world, they are doing some of their finest work with grape varieties native to the Rhône Valley, especially Syrah. Israeli Syrah features a harmonious interplay of tannins and acidity with flavors of black cherry, blueberry, coffee, and mountainside herbs.

RECOMMENDED WINES

BARGAIN
KEVIN Mt. Tabor
MIKE Jerusalem Wineries 3400 Premium Shiraz
JEFF Recanati Shiraz
Golan Heights Winery Gilgal

VALUE
KEVIN Dalton Reserve Shiraz
MIKE Recanati Reserve
JEFF Pelter Matar Stratus Shiraz

SPECIAL OCCASION
KEVIN Tulip Winery Reserve
MIKE Binyamina The Chosen Ruby
JEFF Flam Reserve

ITALY

Almost every Italian wine region grew at least some Syrah from the late nineteenth century through the mid-twentieth century, often for adding color to native varieties. In the 1950s and 1960s, however, it almost disappeared as growers replanted vineyards with more commercially desirable grapes. It's on the upswing again, though, especially in Tuscany, Lazio, and Sicily. You can find Sicilia IGT Syrah relatively easily, especially from the communes of Menfi, Erice, and Monreale. Valle d'Aosta in the northern Alps and Cortona in Tuscany also produce it, as do Abruzzo, Apulia, Sardinia, and the Marche. Italian Syrah has intense dark berry flavors with notes of clove and anise.

RECOMMENDED WINES

BARGAIN
OUR PICK Cusumano

VALUE
KEVIN Tenuta Rapitala Nadir
Fantodi Case Via
MIKE Rinieri Regina di Rinieri
Planeta
JEFF La Braccesca Bramasole

SPECIAL OCCASION
KEVIN Marchesi Antinori La Braccesca
MIKE Monteverro Tinata
JEFF Marchesi de'Frescobaldi Ammiraglia
Michele Satta Toscana

SPLURGE
KEVIN Duemani Suisassi
MIKE Tua Rita Toscana
JEFF Le Macchiole Scrio

. . . .

IN HIS OWN WORDS

"I believe that the soils and the weather of the south Maremma are best suited for the production of amazing Syrah. The region has a dry, hot climate, which is tempered by significant diurnal temperature shifts and drip irrigation. These are the reasons that Syrah has had such great success in the Maremma."

—*Lamberto Frescobaldi, president, Frescobaldi Toscana*

. . . .

NEW ZEALAND

Very little Syrah grows in New Zealand—just 1 percent of cultivated vineyards here—but that small amount wows across the board. Hawke's Bay has 78 percent of New Zealand's Syrah vines, producing wines that exhibit intense plum and cassis flavors backed by strong tones of black pepper and anise. A modest amount of Syrah grows in the Auckland region, particularly on Waiheke Island. Northland, Gisborne, Wairarapa, Marlborough, and Waipara have smaller but still noteworthy amounts. Unlike neighboring Australia, New Zealand tends toward the name Syrah and a more elegant French style.

IN HIS OWN WORDS

"Syrah can be very expressive, and the emergence of many styles of New Zealand Syrah is exciting. We are proud of the Syrah grown within the Gimblett Gravels for its vivid blue-purple floral and fruit profile as well as unique tannin feel. This is a completely different expression from the wines made from vineyards on surrounding soils."

—*Matt Stafford, chief winemaker, Craggy Range*

RECOMMENDED WINES

BARGAIN

KEVIN Okahu Estate Shipwreck Bay
MIKE Mission Estate
JEFF Pask Hawke's Bay

VALUE

OUR PICKS Man O' War Dreadnought
Maimai Hawke's Bay
Trinity Hill
Te Mata Bullnose

SPECIAL OCCASION

KEVIN Villa Maria Reserve Gimblett Gravels
MIKE Sacred Hill Deerstalkers Reserve
JEFF Esk Valley Winemakers Reserve Gimblett Gravels
Reserve

SPLURGE

OUR PICKS Craggy Range Le Sol Gimblett Gravels
Trinity Hill Homage

BELOW Craggy Range vineyard in New Zealand.
NEXT PAGES Gimblett Gravels vineyards in New Zealand.

SOUTH AFRICA

Like the Aussies, South Africans call it Shiraz, though some winemakers use the French name. The grape covers about 10 percent of South Africa's vineyards, especially in Stellenbosch, Franschhoek, and Paarl, and it stands as another wonderful example of a French variety thriving in the ancient soils of the Southern Hemisphere. A big, round, jammy wine here, it has flavors of black cherry, plum, cassis, licorice, black pepper, smoke, and leather. It's a powerful wine perfect with a braai covered with red meat. Some versions start with the delicate fruit and floral notes of a Rhône-style version, then open up to juicy berry flavors and touches of freshly ground black pepper and gingerbread spice. The more restrained South African style features flavors of black plum and blackberry backed by notes of truffle and smoked meat.

IN HIS OWN WORDS

"Syrah ticks all the boxes. It is rich, textured, medium- to full-bodied, and concentrated. It produces deeply colored wines with great structure. The tannins are full and round without being aggressive. The wine can be enjoyed in its youth without the need to cellar for extensive time."

—*Carl van der Merwe, winemaker, DeMorgenzon*

RECOMMENDED WINES

BARGAIN
KEVIN Nederburg the Winemaster's Reserve Shiraz
Groot Constantia Shiraz
MIKE Jam Jar Sweet Shiraz
Porcupine Ridge
JEFF DeMorgenzon DMZ

VALUE
KEVIN Fairview The Beacon Shiraz
MIKE Topiary Shiraz
Mullineux
JEFF Rudi Schultz

SPECIAL OCCASION
KEVIN Boekenhoutskloof
MIKE Stark-Condé Three Pines
Simonsig Merindol
JEFF Fable Mountain Tulbagh

SPLURGE
OUR PICKS Hartenberg The Stork Shiraz
Mullineux Granite

ABOVE A tank of Shiraz 2016 at the Delaire Graff Estate in Stellenbosch in South Africa. **OPPOSITE** Speaker playing music in the vineyards at DeMorgenzon in South Africa.

SPAIN

Given its hot, Mediterranean climate, Spain should be growing acre upon acre of Syrah, but Syrah's blending partner Garnacha has a far bigger presence here. That said, you can find significant plantings of Syrah in Castilla–La Mancha, Catalonia, Aragon, Extremadura, and Murcia. It has a small presence in the Sierras de Málaga as well. Some of the best single-varietal versions come from the Priorat DOQ in Catalonia. Spanish Syrah offers sweetness on the palate with spicy overtones and bracing acidity.

RECOMMENDED WINES

BARGAIN
KEVIN Alceño 50 Baricas
Bodegas Borsao Zarihs
Marqués de Griñon
MIKE Marqués de la Concordia Hacienda Zorita Natural Reserve
JEFF Pagos del Moncayo

VALUE
KEVIN Abadia Retuerta Pago La Garduña
MIKE Marques de Griñon Single Vineyard Estate Bottled
JEFF Alta Alella Privat Orbus
Clos Berenguer del Molar Selecció

USA: CALIFORNIA

Syrah covers more than 19,000 acres of California hillsides and valleys for now, its numbers as strong here as its rich, fruity flavor, although plantings may decline as winemakers replant more commercially viable varieties. San Luis Obispo has the most extensive plantings, but San Joaquin, Sonoma, Madera, Monterey, and Santa Barbara feature considerable acreage. You'll find it in GSM and other red blends as well as on its own as a big, powerful wine with flavors of plum, black cherry, cassis, anise, black pepper, and leather. A more elegant style puts emphasis on the savory notes of Mediterranean herbs and earth. California Syrah also makes for a luscious rosé with the refreshing qualities of white wine and the rich mouthfeel of a red.

RECOMMENDED WINES

BARGAIN
KEVIN Clos du Bois Shiraz
MIKE Terre Rouge Les Côtes de l'Ouest
JEFF Graziano
Kendall-Jackson Vintner's Reserve

VALUE
KEVIN Bonny Doon Le Pousseur
MIKE Finestra Estate
San Simeon
JEFF Presqu'ile Presqu'ile Vineyards

SPECIAL OCCASION
KEVIN Alban Vineyards
MIKE Calcareous Devil's Canyon
Ojai Bien Nacido Vineyard
JEFF Storm Slide Hill Vineyard

SPLURGE
KEVIN Shafer Relentless
Galatea Effect Genception of Giants
JEFF Justin Focus
Sanguis 1/1

USA: WASHINGTON STATE

Production of Syrah here has nearly doubled since 2010. The state's best comes from the steep, rocky soils of Walla Walla, which bring out the grape's dense berry flavors and floral tones dusted with savory notes of smoke, black olive, and roasted meats. Ample amounts of Syrah grow in Yakima Valley as well. Unlike Syrah from other countries and regions, Syrah from Washington can command a higher price than more typically expensive varieties, including Cabernet Sauvignon.

RECOMMENDED WINES

BARGAIN

KEVIN Columbia Crest Grand Estates

MIKE Snoqualmie
Castle Rock

JEFF Purple Star

VALUE

KEVIN Chateau Ste. Michelle Ethos
Charles Smith K Vintners Clifton Hill

MIKE Woodinville Wine Cellars
Stevens Black Tongue

JEFF W. T. Vintners Gorgeous Destiny Ridge Vineyard

SPECIAL OCCASION

KEVIN Gramercy Cellars John Lewis Reserve

MIKE Sequel Columbia Valley
Stolen Horse

JEFF Ardor Red Heaven Vineyard

SPLURGE

KEVIN Silverback Reserve

MIKE Charles Smith Royal City

JEFF Reynvaan Family Vineyards Stonessence
In The Rocks Vineyard

RIGHT Red Willow Vineyard Chapel in Yakima Valley in Washington.

TANNAT

(tah-NAH, tah-NAHT)

IN THE GLASS

small Bordeaux glass, red violet in color

TASTING PROFILE

	LOW	MEDIUM	HIGH
ACIDITY			
BODY			
TANNIN			

TASTING NOTES

PLUM   RASPBERRY   CHERRY

Expect aromas of black plums, raspberry jam, and a touch of wet river rocks. It has full, voluptuous body with dark fruit flavors, grippy tannins, and a persistent finish.

YOU SHOULD KNOW

Uruguayan Tannat can have less tannin than French versions. Besides climatic differences, the major reason for this difference is that the New World vines descend directly from pre-phylloxera vines brought from France in the nineteenth century.

FOOD PAIRINGS

SAUSAGE   KEBABS   CHEESE

Spicy chorizo and lamb skewers on the grill. The smoky notes in Tannat also make it a great match for oven-roasted meats and game, such as venison loin and wild boar. It pairs well with grilled venison or venison sausage, too. The strong tannic structure also holds up to the strongest of cheeses—English Stilton, aged cheddars, and Goudas.

RECOMMENDED WINES

BARGAIN

KEVIN Château Peyros
Domaine Berthoumeiu Cuvée Charles de Batz
MIKE Château Peyros Tannat-Cabernet Franc
Château Viella Tradition Red
JEFF Château d'Aydie Laplace

VALUE

KEVIN Domaine Labranche-Laffont Vieilles Vignes
MIKE Château de Gayon Dou Hauret Red
JEFF Producteurs Plaimont Plénitude

SPECIAL OCCASION

OUR PICK Brumont Château Montus

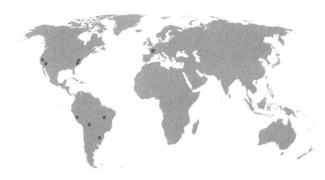

Other Notable Countries

URUGUAY

The end of the nineteenth century brought a wave of immigrants here from Italy and especially the Basque region of northern Spain. They brought rootstock and vines with them—Cabernet Sauvignon, Merlot, Cabernet Franc—to make wine in the New World.

They originally called the Tannat transplants "Harriague" in honor of the French Basque settler who introduced the varietal to the region.

With an average annual rainfall of 63 inches, Uruguayan winemakers need a sturdy thick-skinned grape. Tannat ranks as the most widely planted grape in the country (about 4,500 acres). Many winemakers in the Canelones, Colonia, Maldonado, and Montevideo departments are making very good Tannat either as a single varietal or in interesting blends. Here it has a dark red, bluish, almost black color, often with violet reflections, and aromas of mature, ripe dark fruits, tobacco, and saddle leather. In the best varietal examples, the tannins are strong but supple.

Many wines from Uruguay—including Tannat, Tannat blends, and other international varietals—have won medals at prestigious international wine competitions, including Bacchus, Challenge du Vin, Chardonnay du Monde, Ljubljana, Mondial de Bruxelles, and Vinitaly. Many of these award-winning wines are made only for domestic consumption or export to other South American countries, though, and never make it to the American or British wine markets.

Tannat has two homes, one in the Old World and another in the New. It originated in southwestern France, in the foothills of the Pyrenees, in the Madiran region, where it still grows widely. In addition to single-varietal versions, the French use Tannat to make full-bodied rosés as well as Armagnac. In 2009, scientists in London revealed the antioxidant benefits of Tannat grown in Madiran. They found it has high levels of compounds that help prevent cancer and heart disease. Madiran has twice the national average of men over age ninety—conclusive or coincidental? Either way, it might be worth adding a glass of Tannat to your daily health regimen.

About 7,000 acres of Tannat grow in France, especially in areas surrounding Madiran. It also grows in Irouleguy, Tursan, and Bearn. Wines produced in Madiran contain 40 to 80 percent Tannat, while wines made in the village of St. Mont must have at least 60 percent Tannat. Blending partners include Cabernet Sauvignon and Cabernet Franc, both of which make for rounder, more approachable wines. But winemakers use other techniques to soften Tannat's strong tannins. One of the most popular, micro-oxygenation introduces a slow stream of oxygen into the barrel or tank, while others use two- or three-year-old oak barrels for aging, which impart less tannin to the wine.

Tannat's spiritual home lies in France, but it also grows extensively in Uruguay, its second home, where the grape has sparked national pride. It grows to a lesser extent in other South American countries, including Argentina, Brazil, Peru, and Bolivia, as well as in America in Maryland, Virginia, Arizona, and California.

IN HIS OWN WORDS

"Tannat has a long history, originating in France, but it is now the undisputed grape varietal of Uruguay. Tannin management is critical in calling the perfect pick. For a winemaker, walking the vineyards daily to check everything is invigorating. I love the hands-on approach that this varietal requires of us."

—*Germán Bruzzone, winemaker, Bodega Garzón*

RECOMMENDED WINES

BARGAIN

KEVIN Pueblo del Sol

MIKE Bodega Garzón
Viñedo de los Vientos

JEFF Antiqua Bodega Stagnari Prima Donna

VALUE

KEVIN Bodega Bouza B2 Parcela Única
Viñedo de los Vientos Alcyone

MIKE Familia Deicas
Bodega Bouza A8

JEFF Ariano Hermanos Don Nelson

SPECIAL OCCASION

OUR PICK César Pisano E Hijos Don César Gran Reserva

ABOVE Concrete fermentation pods at Bodega Garzón in Uruguay. **RIGHT** Alejandro Bulgheroni and his son Alejandro Bulgheroni Jr. in Tannat vineyards at Bodega Garzón in Uruguay.

TEMPRANILLO

(TEHM-prah-NEE-yo)

IN THE GLASS

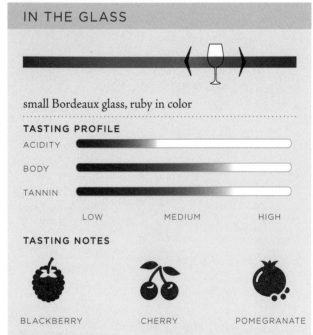

small Bordeaux glass, ruby in color

TASTING PROFILE

ACIDITY
BODY
TANNIN

LOW   MEDIUM   HIGH

TASTING NOTES

BLACKBERRY   CHERRY   POMEGRANATE

This wine has aromas of cassis, black plum, caramel, and mocha. Expect flavors of blackberry and black cherry marked by fresher notes of strawberry and pomegranate combined with touches of baking spice, saddle leather, and tobacco.

YOU SHOULD KNOW

The Spanish aging system offers a reliable indicator of time spent in barrel and bottle prior to release, and many of the spice, vanilla, and coffee elements of Tempranillo derive from time spent in oak barrels. Fresh and fruity Tempranillos are well worth seeking as well. Discovered in the late 1980s, Tempranillo Blanco, a white mutation, also exists.

FOOD PAIRINGS

STEAK   PASTA   PORK

Tempranillo is a meat lover's dream. Serve Reserva or Gran Reserva wines with well-marbled cuts of steak, such as porterhouse and rib eye. Tempranillo with a few months to one year of oak aging will work well with pasta Bolognese or slightly sweet grilled pork ribs.

RECOMMENDED WINES

BARGAIN
KEVIN   Castillo de Monjardin Clasico
Val de los Frailes Cigales
MIKE   Matsu El Recio Tinta de Toro
Bodegas Ochoa Tempranillo Crianza
JEFF   Bodegas Maximo Edicion Limitada
Poema Red Wine

VALUE
KEVIN   Bodegas Ontañon Reserva
MIKE   El Coto del Rioja Coto Real Reserva Rioja
Alma de Vino Old Vine
JEFF   Campo Viejo Rioja Gran Reserva

SPECIAL OCCASION
KEVIN   Triennia by Bodegas Portia
MIKE   Bodegas Cepa 21 Malabrigo
JEFF   Marqués de Riscal Baron de Chirel Rioja Reserva

SPLURGE
KEVIN   Dominio de Pingus
MIKE   Bodegas Muga Aro
JEFF   Remírez de Ganuza Gran Reserva
Bodega Contador La Cueva del Contador

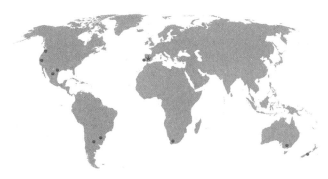

Cultivation of this thick-skinned black grape on the Iberian Peninsula dates back to the Phoenician Empire, more than 2,500 years ago. In the days of the Roman Empire, merchants sold wine most likely made from Tempranillo all over Europe and the Mediterranean. Taking its name from *temprano*, the Spanish word for "early," Tempranillo grapes ripen early in the season, often weeks ahead of other varieties. They grow in almost every wine region here—except Galicia in the northwest and Andalucia in the south—and cover more than 500,000 acres. Spaniards consider their number-one grape variety a national treasure, and arguments among friends about which region makes the best wine can last long into the night, as they open bottle after bottle and pour glass after glass for comparison.

The grape's name varies from region to region. Common synonyms within Spain include Tinta del Pais, Tinta de Toro, Aragonez, Tinto Fino, Cencibel, and Ull de Llebre. You'll come across about twenty more nationwide and a dozen others internationally. Only Spain has a strict set of aging requirements for Tempranillo-based wines. The terms Joven, Crianza, Reserva, and Gran Reserva offer a guarantee of the length of time that a wine aged prior to release, with minimum barrel time followed by bottle aging. Post-barrel bottle aging softens the tannins from the barrel, rendering the wine ready to drink on purchase.

This aging system allows you to determine the style you prefer and choose it consistently. Some wine drinkers enjoy a heavy oak profile, while others prefer wines aged only a short time. The latter of these are called Joven, or young, reds. They may age no more than one year in oak, but many release within several months of the harvest, having spent little or no time in wood. These wines have aggressive acidity and full-on blackberry and cassis flavors. Any well-made, well-stored Tempranillo will have vibrant acidity despite lengthy aging.

Crianza wines from Rioja, Ribera del Duero, and Navarre age for two years, with at least one in barrel, while other regions stipulate two years of aging, with a minimum of six months in oak. A Crianza usually offers dark berry flavors joined by notes of vanilla, clove, and anise. Reserva wines age for three years, at least one in barrel. In addition to dark fruit favors, a Reserva features stronger spice and vanilla notes along with leather and tobacco flavors. Gran Reserva wines age for five years prior to sale, with a minimum of two years in barrel, but many producers extend barrel aging beyond that. Gran Reservas offer the most complex flavor profile: stewed fruit flavors layered with notes of clove, baking spice, butterscotch, and truffle.

Ribera del Duero, Rioja, and Toro are making the best Tempranillos. The variety also grows in just about every New World country or emerging wine region, including America, Argentina, Australia, New Zealand, Portugal, Mexico, South Africa, and Uruguay. Base flavors remain somewhat similar from region to region, but differing soils, clonal selections, climates, and winemaking techniques have a profound effect on the final wine's taste profile.

ABOVE Tempranillo vines at Viñas del Cénit in Zamora in Spain.

Ribera del Duero

Winemaking here dates back more than 2,000 years, yet Ribera del Duero didn't receive DO status until July 1982. The growing region follows the Douro River, east to west, for about seventy miles. Most vineyards lie in the province of Burgos, and many sit at elevations of between 2,500 and 3,000 feet above sea level. Such great heights, combined with limestone soil, create a complexity of flavor in the grape. Some of the most sought wines in the country hail from Ribera del Duero, especially Reservas and Gran Reservas from vineyards close to the town of Peñafiel, in an area known as the Golden Mile.

Locals more commonly call Tempranillo either Tinta del Pais or Tinto Fino. Wines either consist solely of Tempranillo or feature small blending amounts of Cabernet Sauvignon, Merlot, Malbec, Garnacha Tinta, or Albillo, the last a local white grape. Some producers use American oak barrels, which impart stronger flavors and a creamier texture than those from France.

Rioja

King Peter I of Navarre and Aragon recognized wine from Rioja in 1102, and by the late thirteenth century merchants were selling wine from this region throughout Europe. Today medieval villages surrounded by ancient stone walls give way to space-age wineries, hotels, and tasting rooms designed by a veritable who's who of internationally renowned architects. The Rioja designation encompasses vineyards in the Autonomous Community of La Rioja, the Basque province of Álava, and parts of Navarre. It has three subregions: Rioja Alta, Rioja Baja, and Rioja Alavesa. Bordered to the north by the Cantabrian Mountains and nourished by the Ebro River and its many tributaries, Rioja provides a special climate for growing red grapes, especially Tempranillo. Spaniards here refer to Tempranillo as Tinto Fino. Garnacha, Cariñena, and Graciano also grow well here and often go into blends with Tempranillo. What other regions would label as Joven, here is simply "Rioja."

See the separate chapter on the Rioja style (page 244).

RECOMMENDED WINES

BARGAIN
KEVIN O. Fournier Urban Ribera Tinta del Pais
MIKE Portia Ebeia
JEFF Cruz de Alba Crianza
Arrocal Seis Meses en Barrica

VALUE
KEVIN Dominio de Pingus
Viña Mayor Secreto Roble
MIKE Montebaco Alma de Vino
Legaris Reserva
JEFF Portia Crianza

SPECIAL OCCASION
KEVIN Alion Ribera del Duero
MIKE O. Fournier Alfa Spiga
JEFF Pago de los Capellanes Parcela El Nogal

SPLURGE
KEVIN Viña Sastre Pesus
MIKE Vega Sicilia Unico
JEFF Legaris Calmo
Emilio Moro Malleolus de Valderramiro

RECOMMENDED WINES

BARGAIN
KEVIN El Coto Crianza
MIKE Ramón Bilbao Crianza
JEFF Bodegas Bilbainas Viña Zaco Tempranillo
Bodega Classica El Pacto Crianza

VALUE
KEVIN Marqués de Cáceres Reserva
MIKE Sierra Cantabria Reserva
JEFF Faustino I Gran Reserva
Pagos del Rey Arnegui Reserva

SPECIAL OCCASION
KEVIN Marqués de Murrieta Dalmau Reserva
MIKE Bodegas Bilbainas Viña Pomal Alto de la Caseta
JEFF Mirto Rioja
El Coto Coto de Imaz Gran Reserva

SPLURGE
KEVIN La Rioja Alta Gran Reserva Selección Especial
MIKE Bodegas Roda Cirsion
JEFF Artadi Viña El Pison
Marqués de Murrieta Castillo Ygay Gran Reserva

OPPOSITE Harvesting Tempranillo in Lanciego in Spain.

Toro

Vintners have been making wine here since the first century BC, but Toro didn't receive DO recognition until 1987. Its sandy soils protect vines from phylloxera, so plants that predate the European epidemic of the late nineteenth century make a great deal of old-vine Tempranillo here. Toro has a hotter climate than Rioja or Ribera del Duero, and Tinta del Toro (*TEEN-tah dehl TOH-ro*), the Tempranillo synonym here, offers opulent flavors in an almost New World style that can have a lot of fruit and occasionally little complexity, especially at entry-level prices. More expensive, longer-aged bottles from Toro offer similar quality as from Spain's other major players. In addition to Crianza, Reserva, and Gran Reserva designations, Toro wineries produce Joven wines—which may have no oak aging and should be consumed within one year of release— and Roble wines, which have aged for between three and six months.

RECOMMENDED WINES

BARGAIN

KEVIN François Lurton Hermanos
Bodegas Farina Dama de Toro
MIKE Telmo Rodriguez Dehesa Gago
JEFF Pagos del Rey Bajos Crianza
Viña Mayor Vendimia Seleccionada

VALUE

KEVIN Bodega Carmen Rodriguez Carodorum Crianza
MIKE Numanthia Termes
JEFF Pipeta Toro

SPECIAL OCCASION

KEVIN Bodegas del Palacio de los Frontaura Aponte Reserva
MIKE Maurodos San Román
JEFF Vatan Toro
Liberalia Cinco

SPLURGE

KEVIN Elias Mora Reserva
MIKE Teso La Monja Alabaster
JEFF Numanthia Termanthia

Other Notable Countries

ARGENTINA

Grown mainly in Mendoza, Tempranillo is the fifth most widely planted grape in the nation. Bottled on its own, it often has young, vibrant fruit flavors with a touch of spice. It also frequently goes into blends with Cabernet Sauvignon and other Bordeaux varieties in high-end icon wines.

RECOMMENDED WINES

BARGAIN

KEVIN Luigi Bosca Finca La Linda
MIKE O. Fournier Urban Uco
JEFF Santa Julia Made with Organic Grapes

VALUE

KEVIN Altocedro Año Cero
MIKE Finca El Retiro Reserva Especial
JEFF Zuccardi Q
Bodega Calle El Olvidado Reserva

PORTUGAL

The Portuguese refer to Tempranillo as Tinto Roriz (*TEEN-toh ROH-ress*) in the Douro and Dão regions and as Aragonez (*a-rah-GO-nehs*) in the Alentejo. In Douro, much of it goes into making Port, but more and more winemakers are vinifying it as a high-quality single-varietal table wine. Producers in Dão have been bottling Tempranillo on its own for a longer time, and many experts compare these wines to those from Ribera del Duero in Spain. It's one of the most important grapes in the Alentejo, but the hot climate tends to produce an overripe style.

RECOMMENDED WINES

BARGAIN
KEVIN Herdade de São Miguel Ciconia
MIKE J. Portugal Ramos Vila Santa Aragonez
JEFF Terras de Alter Terra d'Alter

VALUE
KEVIN Quinta do Monte d'Oiro Têmpera
MIKE Cortes de Cima Aragonez
JEFF Quinta de Lemos Tinto Roriz

SPECIAL OCCASION
KEVIN Quinta do Pôpa Pôpa Tinto Roriz
MIKE Quinta do Portal Douro
JEFF Quinta do Crasto Douro

USA: CALIFORNIA

Around 1,000 acres of Tempranillo grow throughout the Golden State. For many years, it bore the name Valdepeñas (*vahl-deh-PAYN-yas*) and went into inexpensive table wine blends. Today winemakers are producing a single-varietal wine in both fresh and more heavily oaked styles. It grows throughout the Central Valley, in San Luis Obispo County, and to smaller degrees in other wine regions.

RECOMMENDED WINES

VALUE
OUR PICKS Twisted Oak
Bodegas Paso Robles Viva Tu!
Curran Santa Ynez
Tejada Reserve
Matchbook
Rob Murray Vineyards Force of Nature
Truchard Vineyards

SPECIAL OCCASION
OUR PICKS Jarvis Estate Grown Cave Fermented
Epoch Estate

BELOW The harvest at Bodegas Casa Primicia in Rioja Alavesa in Álava in Spain.

USA: TEXAS

Some wine critics have hailed Tempranillo as the Lone Star State's signature red grape, but Texas is far too large and geographically diverse for one grape to thrive statewide. Tempranillo from the High Plains AVA has shown the most promise, having garnered awards in major wine competitions across the country. Vineyard elevations of between 3,000 and 4,000 feet provide the nighttime cooling effect necessary for the preservation of acidity in grapes. High Plains has only a handful of wineries at this time, but other Lone Star wineries source Tempranillo from vineyards here. Expect flavors of cassis and blackberry with notes of spice and tobacco.

RECOMMENDED WINES

BARGAIN

OUR PICKS Alamosa Wine Cellars El Guapo
Pedernales Cellars Texas
Llano Estacado Newsome Vineyard

SPECIAL OCCASION

OUR PICKS Spicewood Vineyards Estate
Brushy Creek
Inwood Estates Vineyards "Cornelious"
Ground Up
Fall Creek Salt Lick Vineyard

BELOW Storm over Gramercy Cellars vineyards in Washington.

USA: WASHINGTON STATE

Plantings of Tempranillo are relatively small here, but it remains a winemaker favorite, with limited-edition bottlings in tasting rooms in Woodinville and the Columbia Valley. The finished wine usually has fresher fruit flavors and brighter acidity than its Spanish counterparts.

. . . .

IN HIS OWN WORDS

"Walla Walla has a very suitable climate for Tempranillo, which loves the high desert. As in Rioja, we have a very fine, sandy-type soil that drains freely. But most important, the temperature difference between the day and night allows perfect ripening for the grape. One of the primary benefits of this climate in Walla Walla is that Tempranillo can achieve full ripeness before sugars become excessive."

—*Greg Harrington, winemaker, Gramercy Cellars*

. . . .

RECOMMENDED WINES

VALUE

OUR PICKS Upland Estates Snipes Mountain
College Cellars Anderson Vineyard
Indian Creek Winery Snake River Valley
David Hill Vineyards & Winery Rogue Valley
Plaisance Ranch Papa Joe's Private Stash
Idilico

SPECIAL OCCASION

OUR PICKS Gramercy Cellars Inigo Montoya Columbia Valley
Palencia Wine Co. El Viñador
Valley View Winery Pioneer Reserve
Zerba Cellars

SPLURGE

OUR PICK Cayuse Vineyards

TERAN

(tehr-AHN)

IN THE GLASS

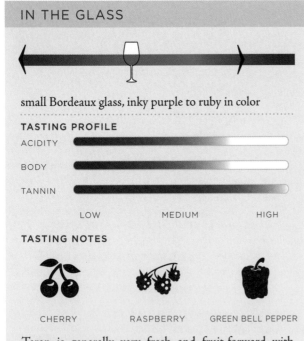

small Bordeaux glass, inky purple to ruby in color

TASTING PROFILE

	LOW	MEDIUM	HIGH
ACIDITY			
BODY			
TANNIN			

TASTING NOTES

CHERRY   RASPBERRY   GREEN BELL PEPPER

Teran is generally very fresh and fruit-forward with pleasant tannins and fresh acidity in the finish. Aromas include freshly picked red cherries, red raspberry, blackberry, and sometimes a touch of green bell pepper, farm stand, or wet hay. Flavors include a combination of red and black fruits with a pleasant mouthfeel.

FOOD PAIRINGS

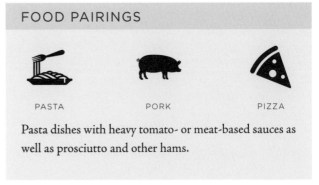

PASTA   PORK   PIZZA

Pasta dishes with heavy tomato- or meat-based sauces as well as prosciutto and other hams.

RECOMMENDED WINES

BARGAIN
OUR PICKS Castelvecchio Terrano IGT Venezia Giulia, Italy
Vina Stoka Izbrani, Slovenia

VALUE
OUR PICKS Trapan Terra Mare, Croatia
Kozlović, Croatia
Zidarich Teran Terrano Carso, Italy

SPECIAL OCCASION
OUR PICK Coronica Gran Teran, Croatia

YOU SHOULD KNOW

Many winemakers in Croatia grow Teran in iron-rich soils, which adds farm-stand aromas and flavors and imparts a slightly metallic taste to the wines. Single-varietal Teran doesn't age particularly well. Drink it within a few years of production.

OPPOSITE Teran grapes at Trapan Wine Station in Croatia.
NEXT PAGES Barrels at Trapan Wine Station in Croatia.

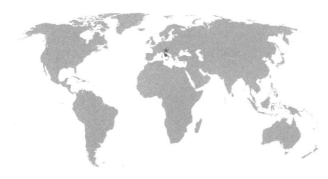

Teran originated on the plateau of Istria, which includes southwestern Slovenia, a smidge of northeastern Italy, and western Croatia. The variety grows in the Friuli-Venezia-Giulia region of Italy, the Kras and Slovenska Istra regions of Slovenia, and the Istrian region of Croatia. The dark, thick-skinned grape grows in large clusters of densely packed berries and ripens late in the growing season, producing wines with character, potency, and strength. Younger wines tend to have slightly higher acidity and more aggressive tannins, while barrel-aged versions have more rounded acidity and a more pleasant tannic structure. Vintners often blend Teran with varieties that can round out the flavor profile and increase age-ability, such as Merlot and Cabernet Sauvignon.

"In order to make good wine from Teran," an older winemaker here once told us, "you must first tame it, like you would tame a wild horse." Another winemaker, whose family has been growing Teran on the same land for generations, said that his great-grandfather lived in Austro-Hungary, his grandfather lived in Italy, his father lived in Yugoslavia, and he lives in Croatia—but no one has ever moved from the family house. Given this international turnover, it's no surprise that Teran goes by a number of names. Italians call it Terrano (*teh-RAH-no*), and it's also known as Refosco d'Istria (*reh-FOHS-ko DISS-tree-ah*) or Refosco Terrano (*reh-FOHS-ko teh-RAH-no*), but don't confuse it with other well-known Refoscos on the market.

IN HIS OWN WORDS

"Teran is special to me because it is a very wild grape, a very wild wine, but, if you learn how to control it, it gives big but smooth and elegant wines. It's a smooth criminal! I also have tasted Terans from Italy and Slovenia, and the biggest difference is in the soil, the terroir. Istrian versions are generally more full bodied because they come from red soil, which is rich in minerals."

—*Bruno Trapan, owner and winemaker, Trapan Winery*

TOURIGA NACIONAL

(too-REE-gah NAHS-yoh-NAHL)

IN THE GLASS

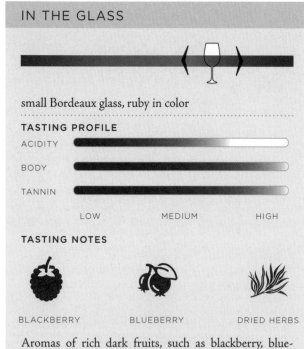

small Bordeaux glass, ruby in color

TASTING PROFILE

	LOW	MEDIUM	HIGH
ACIDITY			
BODY			
TANNIN			

TASTING NOTES

BLACKBERRY   BLUEBERRY   DRIED HERBS

Aromas of rich dark fruits, such as blackberry, blueberry, and currant, prevail as well as notes of Earl Grey tea, dried Mediterranean herbs, and candied violets. It's full-bodied with good acidity in the mouth, a bold but pleasant tannic structure, and great persistence in the finish.

YOU SHOULD KNOW

Touriga Nacionals produced in Portugal's Algarve region tend to have lower acidity levels and more jammy and cooked fruit characteristics because of the hot climate.

FOOD PAIRINGS

LAMB   STEW   SAUSAGE

Dry red wines made from Touriga Nacional pair perfectly with grilled and roasted lamb as well as meaty soups and stews. Try it with oven-roasted Italian sausage or chorizo on the grill. It also goes great with vegetarian bean dishes and tomato-based casseroles.

RECOMMENDED WINES

BARGAIN

KEVIN Aveleda Follies
Delaforce

MIKE DFJ Vinhos Scancio Reserva Touriga Nacional–Syrah Red
Fiuza Touriga Nacional–Alicante Bouschet Red

JEFF José Maria da Fonseca Domini Douro

VALUE

KEVIN Quinta do Passadouro

MIKE Quinta da Pacheca

JEFF Prats & Symington Post Scriptum de Chryseia Douro
Quinta do Noval Cedro do Noval

SPECIAL OCCASION

OUR PICK Quinta do Crasto

OPPOSITE Fonseca vineyards in Portugal. **NEXT PAGES** Harvest at Fonseca vineyards in Portugal.

use it for both sweet fortified wines and dry reds. Wines made from Touriga Nacional have strong acid and tannin levels, which makes them great for aging and a great choice for people who like well-priced, full-bodied reds from warmer climates.

Ostensibly Touriga Nacional was the only red grape cultivated in Dão region, where it likely originated, until the twentieth century. The name comes from the town of Tourigo. Traditionally it has played a major role in the production of Port wine, but younger winemakers have been experimenting with dryer, less alcoholic single varietals and blended dry red wines in the last few years. About 18,000 acres grow across Portugal with approximately 3,500 of those in the Douro. Globally, the grape grows in California, Virginia, Argentina, Australia, and New Zealand, where winemakers

XINOMAVRO

(KSEE-no-MAHV-ro)

IN THE GLASS

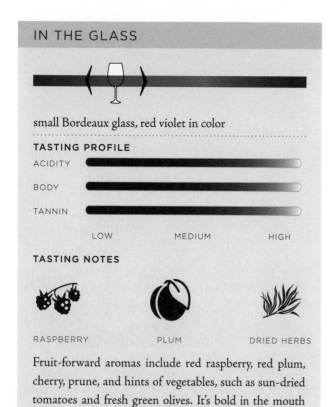

small Bordeaux glass, red violet in color

TASTING PROFILE

	LOW	MEDIUM	HIGH
ACIDITY			
BODY			
TANNIN			

TASTING NOTES

RASPBERRY   PLUM   DRIED HERBS

Fruit-forward aromas include red raspberry, red plum, cherry, prune, and hints of vegetables, such as sun-dried tomatoes and fresh green olives. It's bold in the mouth with flavors of red fruits, summer vegetables, and a touch of dried Mediterranean herbs in the finish.

FOOD PAIRINGS

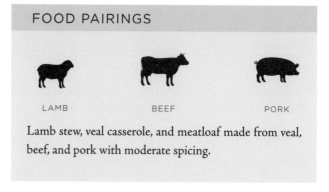

LAMB   BEEF   PORK

Lamb stew, veal casserole, and meatloaf made from veal, beef, and pork with moderate spicing.

RECOMMENDED WINES

BARGAIN

KEVIN   Thymiopoulos Young Vines
MIKE   Alpha Estate Axia Red Blend
JEFF   Tsantali

VALUE

KEVIN   Dalamara Paliokalias
        Alpha Estate Old Vine Reserve
MIKE   Chatzivariti Staphylus Red Blend
        Boutari Naoussa
        Kir-Yianni Ramnista

YOU SHOULD KNOW

Styles vary widely depending on terroir, growing conditions, and winemaker's hand. Some are elegantly fruit-forward, while others can prove overpowering.

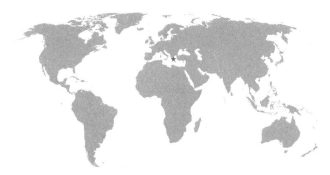

This second most planted red grape in Greece ranks as number one in the country's northern Macedonia region. The variety grows near Mount Olympus in the south and Goumenissa in the east. The blue-black grapes grow in tight clusters—berry size depending on the clonal variety—but generally they ripen later in the growing season. Some experts have compared Xinomavro to Pinot Noir and Nebbiolo, but DNA testing doesn't support a genetic relation to either of those varieties. The name means "acid-black" or "sour-black" in Greek, but don't let the name fool you: It makes for many excellent wines.

Many vintners are making a young, fresh style of Xinomavro, and many also age it carefully in oak barrels or continue the tradition of aging it in locally sourced walnut barrels that don't overwhelm the flavors of the wine. Xinomavro has characteristically high acidity and tannins, which gives it excellent potential for aging. In the right hands, it can have great elegance and finesse.

Wines bearing the Naoussa and Amyntaio appellations must contain 100 percent Xinomavro. Other areas may allow other varieties in the bottle, and many winemakers are experimenting with the addition of Syrah and Merlot as well as other indigenous Greek varieties.

ZINFANDEL

(ZINN-fahn-dehl)

IN THE GLASS

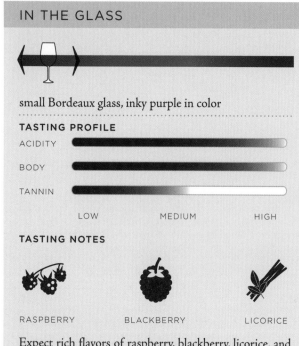

small Bordeaux glass, inky purple in color

TASTING PROFILE

ACIDITY		
BODY		
TANNIN		
LOW	MEDIUM	HIGH

TASTING NOTES

RASPBERRY   BLACKBERRY   LICORICE

Expect rich flavors of raspberry, blackberry, licorice, and black pepper. Depending on how long it has been barrel-aged, you'll taste vanilla, chocolate, or soft leather flavors as well. Cooler-climate versions exhibit a bit more restraint, with hints of herbal notes or green bell pepper.

YOU SHOULD KNOW

Some winemakers produce Zinfandel with levels of alcohol of up to 17 percent. At more than about 14.5 percent, the wine can taste too "hot," and it becomes difficult to pair with food. If growers harvest the grapes before they reach full ripeness, the resulting wine can have notes of green bell pepper or summer farm stand.

FOOD PAIRINGS

BURGER   PIZZA   PORK

This cookout wine goes great with burgers and steaks. High acidity makes it a good match for pizza or pasta with red sauce, while strong fruit sweetness gives it the power to pair with slightly sweet foods, such as pork teriyaki and Peking duck.

RECOMMENDED WINES

BARGAIN

KEVIN Cantele Primitivo Salento
MIKE Cantine Due Palme San Gaetano
JEFF Cantine Paolo Leo Primitivo di Manduria
Torrevento Ghenos

VALUE

OUT PICKS Zlatan Crljenak
Radunić Crljenak Kaštelanski
Sladić Tribidrag
Krolo Crljenak
Putalj Crljenak Kaštelanski

SPECIAL OCCASION

OUR PICK Gianfranco Fino Es Primitivo di Manduria

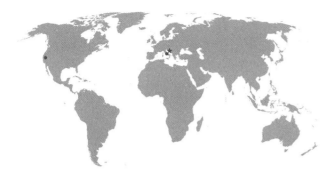

As far back as the fourteenth century, this was one of the most important varieties around the Adriatic Sea. Zinfandel nearly went extinct in Croatia, but it's experiencing a resurgence in its home country—known here as Crljenak Kaštelanski (*TSUHRL-yen-ahk KASH-tel-AHN-skee*) and Tribidrag (*TREE-be-drahg*)—thanks to the research linking it to the popular versions that grow in California and Italy. It grows mainly on the Dalmatian Coast between Split and Dubrovnik. Some of the best-known producers in Croatia, such as Zlatan Plenković, Nicola Bura, and Mare Mrgudić, are growing and vinifying it under the name Tribidrag, but very few of these bottles make their way to the international market.

Two of the wine world's great mysteries are how Zinfandel reached California and how it got its name. According to genetic studies at the University of California at Davis, Zinfandel is the same grape as Croatian Tribidrag and Italian Primitivo. (Carole Meredith, the Davis ampelographer who confirmed its genetic identity, refers to the variety as ZPTC.) In the 1820s it was growing in two nurseries on Long Island, New York, but evidence supports the claim that it made its way to California via the Austrian Imperial Vine Collection in or around the 1830s. In this scenario, the name appears to be Austrian in origin, though the grape likely originated in Croatia, then a part of the Austrian Empire. Whatever the case, Zinfandel has reached superstar status in California, thanks in part to Zinfandel Advocates and Producers (ZAP), a group dedicated to the study and celebration of this flavorful grape.

Other Notable Countries

ITALY

A little more than a quarter of the world's Zinfandel vines grow here—mainly in Puglia, the heel of Italy's boot—where the variety is called Primitivo (*pree-mee-TEE-vo*). Italian winemakers vinify it in a more Old World style than their Californian counterparts. Primitivo appears red violet in color, tastes less jammy, and has stronger notes of mountainside herbs in addition to rich berry flavors. The most complex wines come from the Primitivo di Manduria subregion. Less well-known than the red wines from farther north in Italy, Primitivo wines often represent a good value; you'll be hard-pressed to find a bottle at the splurge level.

RECOMMENDED WINES

BARGAIN
KEVIN Cantele Primitivo Salento
MIKE Cantine Due Palme San Gaetano
JEFF Cantine Paolo Leo Primitivo di Manduria
Torrevento Ghenos

VALUE
KEVIN Tormaresca Torcicoda
Vigneti del Salento Vigne Vecchie Gold Series
MIKE Masseria AlteMura AlteMura
Ognissole Essentia Loci Primitivo di Manduria
JEFF Feudi di San Gregorio Primitivo di Manduria

SPECIAL OCCASION
OUR PICK Gianfranco Fino Es Primitivo di Manduria

NEXT PAGES Zinfandel vine and grapes at Kunde Winery in California.

USA: CALIFORNIA

Some 50,000 acres of the world's 71,000 Zinfandel vines grow in California. Much debate surrounds how Zinfandel came here and acquired its name, but its success is solid fact. The Golden State's third most prolific grape, Zinfandel grows throughout the state. with some of the best examples coming from Napa, Sonoma, Lodi, and the Sierra Foothills. Many old-vine Zinfandel vineyards include plantings of other varieties—such as Cariñena, Petite Sirah, and Alicante Bouschet—sometimes called "mixed blacks." Producers accidentally included them in field blends in the past, but now they intentionally blend them together. Because of its high sugar content, Zinfandel easily makes high-alcohol wine, but a more elegant, lower-alcohol style is trending. Most bottles fall into the bargain and value categories, but look for an increasing number of high-end bottles coming onto the market.

RECOMMENDED WINES

BARGAIN

KEVIN Ravenswood Vintners Blend Old Vine
Rosenblum Cellars Contra Costa County

MIKE LangeTwins
Ghost Pines
Klinker Brick Old Vines

JEFF Frei Brothers Reserve Dry Creek
Angry Bunch Lodi

VALUE

KEVIN Ridge Vineyards Lytton Springs

MIKE Bedrock Old Vines
Tres Sabores Rutherford Napa Valley

JEFF Robert Biale Vineyards Founding Farmers
Napa Valley
Girard Old Vine

SPECIAL OCCASION

KEVIN Martinelli Jackass Vineyard

MIKE Gallo Signature Series
Renwood Grand Wren
Epoch Estate Paderewski Vineyard

JEFF Kunde Reserve Century Vines
Louis M. Martini Gnarly Vine Monte Rosso

IN HER OWN WORDS

"I love the history of Zinfandel in the Dry Creek Valley. We had some amazing Italian settlers come here and begin planting Zinfandel in the late 1800s. You could really call them visionaries because many of those same spots are still planted to Zinfandel today. I believe these immigrants were planting Zinfandel because they were so familiar with it from their Italian homeland. They were interesting in that they managed the land for its best use, from the tops of the hills down to the valley floor. They planted the valley floor with produce, prunes, and other fruit trees, using the ideal loamy, well-draining benchland hillside soils for Zinfandel. It is remarkable how successful they were in their vision because vineyards are still flourishing in these spots today."

—*Gina Gallo, winemaker, Gallo Signature Series*

IN HIS OWN WORDS

"Zinfandel is incredibly adaptable to different foods because of its natural acidity, fine-grained tannins, and forward fruit, and many chefs have paired it amazingly well with duck and pork dishes—meats that love fruit. Asian flavors can be a delicious adventure; try glazing grilled chicken with hoisin, garlic, and rice wine vinegar."

—*Dave Pramuk, cofounder, Robert Biale Vineyards*

ABOVE Kunde Winery vineyards in California.

IN HIS OWN WORDS

"I respect a vine that tends to be unruly as a rule! A viticulturist spends a lifetime trying to achieve vine balance, a philosophy often debated and rarely agreed upon. A perfect Cabernet vineyard is often viewed as one of uniformity. Zinfandel is chaos! The more uniformly you attempt to grow this cultivar, the less interest and depth you tend to find in the finished wine. Head-trained, sprawling, old Zinfandel vines offer the idea of a timeless tradition that seems to steer clear of the prim and proper Bordeaux selections and give this variety its own hipster attitude."

—*Zach Long, winemaker, Kunde Family Winery*

ZWEIGELT

(TSVY-guhlt)

IN THE GLASS

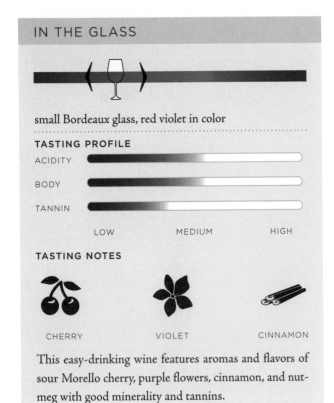

small Bordeaux glass, red violet in color

TASTING PROFILE

ACIDITY

BODY

TANNIN

LOW   MEDIUM   HIGH

TASTING NOTES

CHERRY   VIOLET   CINNAMON

This easy-drinking wine features aromas and flavors of sour Morello cherry, purple flowers, cinnamon, and nutmeg with good minerality and tannins.

YOU SHOULD KNOW

Some producers make a lightly oaked or no-oak version that appears more red violet and has softer tannins. Zweigelt responds well to small amounts of old oak. Too much or new oak can overpower some of the grape's more subtle aromas and flavors.

FOOD PAIRINGS

PORK   SAUSAGE   BURGER

Open a bottle with your next plate of Wiener schnitzel and Kartoffelsalat. Its body, flavors, and tannic structure stand up to deep-fried pork and mayonnaise-laden potato salad. It's also great for a picnic or a grill out with pork ribs, sausage, and burgers.

RECOMMENDED WINES

BARGAIN

KEVIN Weingut Willi Brundlmayer
Umathum

MIKE Markus Altenburger

JEFF Scheiblhofer Andau
Esterházy Classic

VALUE

KEVIN Leo Hillinger

MIKE R&A Pfaffl Zweigelt Burggarten Reserve
Gernot and Heike Heinrich

JEFF Netzl Rubin

SPECIAL OCCASION

KEVIN Weinlaubenhof Alois Kracher Zweigelt
Beerenauslese

MIKE Arndorfer Die Leidenschaft

JEFF Leth Gigama Grande Reserve
Artner Steinacker

OPPOSITE Adelheid Pfaffl at harvest at Weingut R&A Pfaffl in Austria. **NEXT PAGES** Vineyard near Pinnacles National Park in Central California.

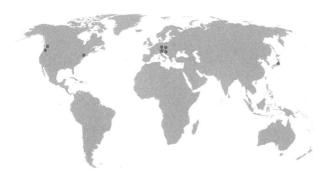

This wine has a tough name. It's not sexy or even romantic, and many critics crinkle their noses when pronouncing it in a *Hogan's Heroes* German accent. But let's be honest, it's better than the variety's original moniker: Rotburger. Nevertheless, it has become Austria's most consumed wine. In 1922, viticulturist Fritz Zweigelt created it in Klosterneuburg by crossing Blaufränkisch and St. Laurent, two *Vitis vinifera* varieties. Since then, Zweigelt (the grape) has made great strides. The most widely planted red variety in Austria, it grows well in Austria's climate and in just about every wine region in the country, to the tune of almost 17,000 acres, mostly north of Vienna in Niederosterreich. It can grow well in a variety of soil types, and Austrian winemakers take great care in leaf canopy management and yield regulation to produce good wines, which have varying levels of body and intensity depending on where the grapes grew. The bigger, bolder wines generally come from Carnuntum and Neusiedlersee in Burgenland. Considerable amounts grow in Germany as well as Canada's Niagara Peninsula and British Columbia wine regions. You'll find smaller plantings in Czechia, Slovakia, Hungary, Washington State, and, interestingly, about 500 acres in Japan.

IN HIS OWN WORDS

"Zweigelt is such a great grape variety when it comes to fruit. You can hardly find these distinctive cherry notes in any other variety. Combined with the smooth, soft tannins, you can make very charming wines with Zweigelt."

—*Roman Josef Pfaffl, winemaker, Weingut R&A Pfaffl*

STYLES &
BLENDS

AMARONE

(ah-mah-RO-nay)

IN THE GLASS

large Bordeaux glass, red violet in color

TASTING PROFILE

ACIDITY		
BODY		
TANNIN		
LOW	MEDIUM	HIGH

TASTING NOTES

PLUM   CASSIS   LICORICE

This concentrated, high-alcohol wine offers intense aromatics at first whiff. It features notes of dried dark fruit and cherry cola. Its balance exhibits great strength and power, with fruit flavors of prune, dark plum, black raspberry, cassis, and dried black cherry and secondary flavors of anise, licorice, espresso, and dark chocolate. Oak aging imparts a softer vanilla essence and toast notes. Don't let the potentially sweet descriptors above fool you, though. The name of this wine literally means "bitter one."

YOU SHOULD KNOW

The grapes undergo a three- to four-month drying process that concentrates the flavors, but this traditional process also can allow bacteria to grow on the grapes, resulting in volatile acidity in the finished wine. Newer, scientifically controlled methods decrease the odds of the wine going sour.

FOOD PAIRINGS

TRUFFLES   GRILLED MEATS   CHEESE

Anything rich, flavorful, and opulent. Risotto made with red wine and topped with shaved truffles. Braised wild boar with roasted root vegetables. Oven-roasted loin of venison served with a puree of butternut and acorn squash. Powerful stinky semi-hard and hard cheeses, such as Stilton, Époisses, Gorgonzola, aged Gouda, and four-year-old Vermont Cheddar.

RECOMMENDED WINES

VALUE

KEVIN   Antiche Terre Venete Valpolicella
MIKE   Cantine di Ora Amarone della Valpolicella
JEFF   Corte Giona Amarone della Valpolicella
     Villa Annaberta Amarone della Valpolicella

SPECIAL OCCASION

KEVIN   Santi Valpolicella
     Allegrini Amarone della Valpolicella Classico
MIKE   Masi Agricola Costasera Amarone della
     Valpolicella Classico
JEFF   Sartori Corte Bra

SPLURGE

KEVIN   Bertani Amarone della Valpolicella Classico
MIKE   Le Salette Pergole Vece Amarone della
     Valpolicella Classico
JEFF   Tommasi Ca' Florian Riserva Amarone della
     Valpolicella Classico

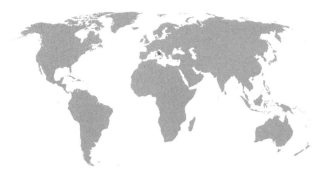

M ost wine historians agree that newly bottled wine underwent an accidental second fermentation in the bottle, causing unplanned carbonation and creating what we now call Champagne. The second-greatest wine mistake happened in Valpolicella, Italy, when winemakers were trying to make sweet wine from dried grapes and ended up with Amarone instead. It also seems they left the wine to ferment too long, and the yeast consumed *all* of the sugars, resulting in a dry red wine with an unusually high alcohol content.

Amarone della Valpolicella—the style's full name—must come from Valpolicella, north of Verona. This hilly area runs about twenty miles wide at the foot of the Dolomite Mountains. The Valpolicella Classico zone lies northwest of Verona, and Valpolicella Est to the northeast. The areas have similar rolling hillsides and climates, but winemaking techniques have differed among them for centuries. All feature the same harvesting practice, however. The grapes for an Amarone blend must be harvested separately due to different ripening times for different styles. Growers harvest by hand, so they make multiple passes through the vines over the course of a few weeks. The main grape is Corvina, which must comprise between 45 and 95 percent of the final blend. Rondinella may account for between 5 and 30 percent. No more than 25 percent may come from other red grapes. The Amarone process uses about 22 pounds of grapes to make one bottle of wine, while standard winemaking techniques require only 2.2 pounds per bottle. Now you know why Amarone costs so much; it's expensive but worth it!

The winemaking process for Amarone resembles that of sweet wines such as Passito. Rather than going straight to the crushers and de-stemmers, workers lay the grapes out in bunches, stems and all, on straw mats or in shallow wooden crates in airy barn lofts, where they dry for three to four months.

This process is called *appassimento* and generally takes place in the traditional barn setting, although some winemakers are using modern, controlled environments and machine-generated warm air to prevent the damaging effects of rain and high humidity that can ruin the grapes—which allows them to relax for the four-month drying period rather than worrying.

The Amarone della Valpolicella DOC sets the duration of the drying process and stipulates that dried clusters not be de-stemmed and crushed before the end of the January following harvest. In extremely hot years, the DOC has made exceptions and permitted producers to crush on December 15 to preserve the fresh fruit characteristics of the finished wine. Recently winemakers have succeeded in moving the crush date to December 1 in response to changing climate conditions.

What this means for you is that producers using more scientific techniques and earlier crush dates will produce more modern-style wines with brighter, fresher, fruit characteristics. Vintners maintaining the traditional techniques will produce traditional-style wines with velvety flavors of dried fruit. Try each style to see which you prefer. Also note that most Amarones have alcohol levels between 15 and 16.5 percent, and many exceed 17 percent!

BELOW Amarone cellars at Bertani winery in Italy. **OPPOSITE** Allegrini Villa della Torre in Italy. **NEXT PAGES** Valpantena vineyards at Bertani winery in Italy.

IN HER OWN WORDS

"The history of producing wines with the use of dried grapes, such as those used to make Amarone, goes back millennia in my region. Two thousand years ago, Roman emperors would enjoy these wines at court. Roman generals were also known to fortify themselves with the rich and powerful wines from the Valpolicella before making the trek over the Alps on their endeavors of conquest. Naturally, using the appassimento technique would yield grapes particularly well suited for travel-worthy and age-worthy wines."

—*Marilisa Allegrini, CEO, Allegrini Estates*

BIKAVÉR

(bee-kah-VEER)

IN THE GLASS

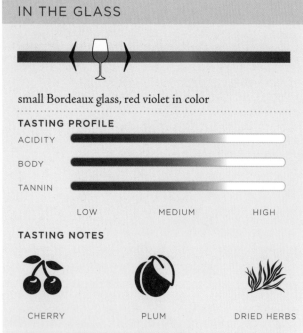

small Bordeaux glass, red violet in color

TASTING PROFILE

ACIDITY

BODY

TANNIN

LOW   MEDIUM   HIGH

TASTING NOTES

CHERRY   PLUM   DRIED HERBS

Aromas include black cherry, plum, and dried herbs. Expect flavors of dried cherry, cranberry, pomegranate, and a touch of savory Mediterranean herbs. Smooth tannins support the finish of modern, well-made Bikavérs, and sometimes you'll find a burst of fresh fruit at the very end.

FOOD PAIRINGS

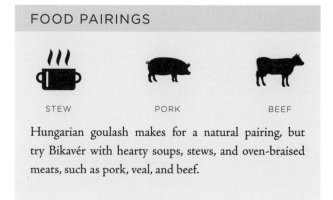

STEW   PORK   BEEF

Hungarian goulash makes for a natural pairing, but try Bikavér with hearty soups, stews, and oven-braised meats, such as pork, veal, and beef.

RECOMMENDED WINES

BARGAIN

OUR PICKS Takler Szekszárdi Bikavér Reserve
Demeter Egri Bikavér Reserve
Besenyei Egri
Gál Lajos Pajados Egri
Kovács Nimród
Bodri Szekszárdi Bikavér Faluhely

VALUE

OUR PICKS Csaba Sebestyen Iván-Völgyi
St. Andrea Merengo Egri Bikavér Superior
Grof Buttler Nagy Eged Egri
Heimann

YOU SHOULD KNOW

In cooler years, Bikavérs appear less purple and more red, have less tannin, and can taste very harsh.

OPPOSITE Szekszárd vineyards in Hungary.

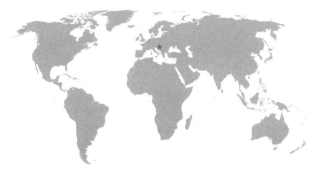

Winemaking in Hungary dates to before AD 1000, but area winemaking gained notoriety in 1010. That year, King Stephen founded the Eger Bishopric and established the region's tithes stipulating that winemakers had to give the church 10 percent of their finished wine each year. The first wine cellars built here belonged to the Church. The rest of the eleventh century brought Walloon settlers with their French traditions and winemaking techniques. The region soon embraced the use of wood barrels, rather than animal skins, for aging their wines. As quality improved, profits from sales significantly contributed to the area's defense against Ottoman invaders, resulting in the digging of tunnels for both protection and wine storage. The Ottomans eventually prevailed, however, and took control of Eger in 1596. Islam forbids the consumption of alcohol, but the Ottomans continued collecting wine and taxes from winegrowers to finance their reign. After the Ottoman occupation ended in 1718, Eger sold its wines to Austria, Poland, and Russia until phylloxera hit in the late nineteenth century.

Prior to phylloxera, Hungarian winemakers in Eger and Szekszárd made field blends heavy on the Kadarka grape variety. After phylloxera, vineyard owners replanted grape varieties separately, harvested and fermented them separately, and then blended the finished wines to make Bikavér. Replanting included the traditional Kadarka as well as Kékfrankos (the local name for Blaufränkisch), Médoc Noir (Hungarian Merlot also known as Menoir), Kékoportó (called Blauer Portugieser elsewhere), and Cabernet Sauvignon. These blends worked well until the Communist Party disqualified Kadarka and Médoc Noir because of their low yields and required the planting of Zweigelt, Kékfrankos, and Cabernet Sauvignon.

If, during the Cold War, you drank a wine called Bull's Blood, that was a Bikavér. It wasn't great, but it was cheap. It was also very strong with an extremely high alcohol content and harsh tannins. The problem wasn't the underlying style but rather that the Soviets emphasized quantity over quality. The fall of Communism in 1989 gave rise to a new sense of national pride, and quality soon became winemakers' goal as they reclaimed their great-grandparents' principles. Legislation in the 1997 Wine Code added new villages to the Eger and Szekszárd appellations and allowed the planting of new varieties, including Cabernet Franc and Merlot. It also stipulated that Bikavér must contain a blend of at least three permitted grape varieties, the most popular being Kékfrankos, Zweigelt, Cabernet Sauvignon, Merlot, and Kékoportó. A little more than 10,000 acres of these varieties grow in the two designated regions, and today's vintners are making excellent wines from them.

BORDEAUX

(bor-DOH)

IN THE GLASS

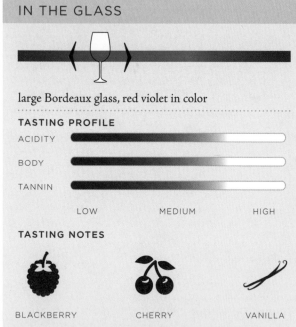

large Bordeaux glass, red violet in color

TASTING PROFILE

ACIDITY

BODY

TANNIN

LOW · MEDIUM · HIGH

TASTING NOTES

BLACKBERRY · CHERRY · VANILLA

The finest Bordeaux wines are made to age for years, which softens the tannins. A good vintage aged for twenty-plus years will feature dark fruit, such as blackberry, black cherry, and cassis, on the nose and palate. Cooked fruit flavors such as stewed plums or cherry jam may persist as well. Secondary tastes include vanilla, spice, and leather. Fine tannins will coat your mouth, and a refreshing note of orange zest or cranberry will punctuate a smooth, lingering finish.

YOU SHOULD KNOW

If a chateau appears on the label, it must exist and belong to the winemaker or winery owner and be attached to a vineyard with a specific number of acres and winemaking and storage facilities on site. You may also see the word *domaine*, meaning "estate."

FOOD PAIRINGS

CHICKEN · BURGER · PASTA

Any uncomplicated, unfussy food, such as fried chicken, burgers, or spaghetti Bolognese. For a First Growth Bordeaux, go big with a truffle-studded breast of veal in a red wine and cream sauce, or try roast leg of lamb with shallots and morels. For a Pomerol, have pork medallions in mustard sauce or roast cod with a red bell pepper reduction.

RECOMMENDED WINES

BARGAIN

KEVIN Château Belgrave
MIKE Château Bellevue Bordeaux Supérieur
Château Franc Cardinal Francs Côtes de Bordeaux
JEFF Château Lafite Monteil Bordeaux Supérieur →

VALUE

KEVIN Château Greysac Médoc Cru Bourgeois
MIKE Château Rollan de By Médoc Cru Bourgeois
JEFF André Lurton Château de Rochemorin

SPECIAL OCCASION

KEVIN Château Cantemerle
MIKE Domaine de l'A Castillon Côtes de Bordeaux
Château Smith Haut Lafitte
JEFF Château Haut Condissas Médoc

SPLURGE

KEVIN Château Latour Pauillac
MIKE Château Cheval Blanc Saint-Émilion
JEFF Château Haut-Brion Pessac-Léognan

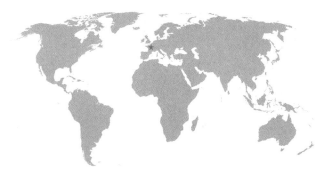

First let's dispel one of the biggest wine myths: Not all Bordeaux wine costs a lot of money. Yes, some of the world's priciest bottles come from this esteemed region in southwestern France, but Bordeaux has some 7,000 chateaux that make wine at a variety of quality levels and prices, so there's something here for everyone.

Bordeaux abuts the Atlantic Ocean and forms a major part of the traditional region of Aquitaine. In 1152, Eleanor, Duchess of Aquitaine, married the future king Henry II of England, and control of the region passed to the English crown for three centuries. Why does this matter? During those 300 years, the wine merchants of Bordeaux shipped their wares tax-free to England, where both royalty and nobility enjoyed them. Bordeaux wine has ruled the export market for nearly 900 years, so it's no wonder that the region has such an outsized reputation.

Bordeaux has fifty-seven subregions that produce high-quality wine and that may use an AOC designation on their label. The five most important are:

THE MÉDOC This large area lies between the left bank of the Gironde Estuary and the Atlantic Ocean, just north of the city of Bordeaux. Its 40,000 acres produce only red wines, and the seven most important appellations within it are Haut-Médoc, St. Estèphe, Pauillac, St. Julien, Margaux, Moulis, and Listrac.

GRAVES AND PESSAC-LÉOGNAN These two contiguous regions lie just south of the Médoc, on the left bank of the Garonne River. They contain almost 13,000 acres of grapevines and produce both red and dry white wine. (The Sauternes region, noted for its ambrosial sweet white wine, sits wholly within Graves.)

POMEROL This small commune on the right bank of the Dordogne River produces only red wines, predominantly Merlot. Pomerol has no officially classified chateaux.

ST. ÉMILION This commune also falls on the right bank of the Dordogne, just south of Pomerol, and the more than 23,000 acres of vines consist primarily of Merlot.

Cabernet Sauvignon dominates the left bank of the Garonne—the Médoc, Graves, and Pessac-Léognan—while wines from the right bank of the Dordogne, including Pomerol and St. Émilion, contain mostly Merlot.

Quality Levels

In addition to knowing the major regions, it's important to understand the three different quality levels of Bordeaux wine:

BORDEAUX Wines labeled "Appellation Bordeaux Controlée," the lowest level, cost the least. Many of these agreeable, consistent wines go by a brand name, such as Mouton-Cadet, rather than by an individual subregion or vineyard.

REGION Only grapes and wines produced in one of the fifty-seven AOC subregions can go by a regional name, such as St. Émilion or Pauillac. These wines cost a little bit more than entry-level Bordeaux.

REGION + CHATEAU Chateau wines come from individual estates and vineyards. In 1855, Bordeaux officially classified the quality level of some chateaux. Since then hundreds have been recognized for their quality. For example, in the Médoc, the 61 highest-level chateaux are known as Grand Cru Classé, while 246 chateaux there are called Cru Bourgeois, which is a step below Grand Cru Classé. Other areas, including St. Émilion and Graves, have their own classification systems.

Classifications

Various subregions within Bordeaux—though not all of them—have classified their wines over the years. Here are the five most important:

MÉDOC GRAND CRU CLASSÉ features sixty-one chateaux as listed in the 1855 Bordeaux Classification, further broken down into tiers or growth levels. For the full listing, see the table on page 224

MÉDOC CRU BOURGEOIS has 246 chateaux originally classified in 1920. Revisions followed in 1932, 1978, and 2010. It includes Château Chasse-Spleen, Château Monbrison, and Château Greysac.

GRAVES GRAND CRU CLASSÉ features twelve chateaux classified in 1959. This list includes Château Smith-Haut-Lafitte, Château La Mission–Haut Brion, and Château Haut-Bailly.

ST. ÉMILION PREMIER GRAND CRU CLASSÉ has eighteen chateaux originally designated in 1955. Revisions followed in 1996 and 2006. Noteworthy chateaux include Angelus, Ausone, and La Mondotte.

ST. ÉMILION GRAND CRU CLASSÉ features eighty-five chateaux, also designated in 1955. This list includes Château Monbousquet, Château La Tour-Figeac, and Château Faugères. Pomerol—which contains Château Petrus, Château Le Pin, and Château Bourgneuf—doesn't have any official classifications despite its prestige as a regional appellation.

OPPOSITE Bottling at Château Fontcaille Bellevue in Bordeaux.

THE OFFICIAL CLASSIFICATION OF
THE GREAT RED WINES OF BORDEAUX (1855)
THE MÉDOC

FIRST GROWTHS/PREMIERS CRUS

VINEYARD	AOC
Château Lafite-Rothschild	Pauillac
Château Latour	Pauillac
Château Margaux	Margaux
Château Haut-Brion	Pessac-Léognan (Graves)
Château Mouton-Rothschild	Pauillac

SECOND GROWTHS/DEUXIÈMES CRUS

VINEYARD	AOC
Château Rausan-Ségla	Margaux
Château Rausan Gassies	Margaux
Château Léoville-Las-Cases	St. Julien
Château Léoville-Poyferré	St. Julien
Château Léoville-Barton	St. Julien
Château Durfort-Vivens	Margaux
Château Lascombes	Margaux
Château Gruaud-Larose	St. Julien
Château Brane-Cantenac	Margaux
Château Pichon-Longueville-Baron	Pauillac
Château Pichon-Longueville-Lalande	Pauillac
Château Ducru-Beaucaillou	St. Julien
Château Cos d'Estournel	St. Estèphe
Château Montrose	St. Estèphe

THIRD GROWTHS/TROISIÈMES CRUS

VINEYARD	AOC
Château Giscours	Margaux
Château Kirwan	Margaux
Château d'Issan	Margaux
Château Lagrange	St. Julien
Château Langoa-Barton	St. Julien
Château Malescot-St-Exupéry	Margaux
Château Cantenac-Brown	Margaux
Château Palmer	Margaux
Château La Lagune	Haut-Médoc
Château Desmirail	Margaux
Château Calon-Ségur	St. Estèphe

VINEYARD	AOC
Château Ferrière	Margaux
Château d'Alesme (formerly Marquis d'Alesme)	Margaux
Château Boyd-Cantenac	Margaux

FOURTH GROWTHS/QUATRIÈMES CRUS

VINEYARD	AOC
Château St. Pierre	St. Julien
Château Branaire-Ducru	St. Julien
Château Talbot	St. Julien
Château Duhart-Milon-Rothschild	Pauillac
Château Pouget	Margaux
Château La Tour-Carnet	Haut-Médoc
Château Lafon-Rochet	St. Estèphe
Château Beychevelle	St. Julien
Château Prieuré-Lichine	Margaux
Château Marquis de Terme	Margaux

FIFTH GROWTHS/CINQUIÈMES CRUS

VINEYARD	AOC
Château Pontet-Canet	Pauillac
Château Batailley	Pauillac
Château Grand-Puy-Lacoste	Pauillac
Château Grand-Puy-Ducasse	Pauillac
Château Haut-Batailley	Pauillac
Château Lynch-Bages	Pauillac
Château Lynch-Moussas	Pauillac
Château Dauzac	Haut-Médoc
Château d'Armailhac (Château Mouton-Baron-Philippe 1956–1988)	Pauillac
Château du Tertre	Margaux
Château Haut-Bages-Libéral	Pauillac
Château Pédesclaux	Pauillac
Château Belgrave	Haut-Médoc
Château Camensac	Haut-Médoc
Château Cos Labory	St. Estèphe
Château Clerc-Milon-Rothschild	Pauillac
Château Croizet Bages	Pauillac
Château Cantemerle	Haut-Médoc

BOX SCORE OF THE 1855 CLASSIFICATION

COMMUNE	1ST	2ND	3RD	4TH	5TH	TOTAL
Margaux	1	5	10	3	2	**21**
Pauillac	3	2	0	1	12	**18**
St. Julien	0	5	2	4	0	**11**
St. Estèphe	0	2	1	1	1	**5**
Haut-Médoc	0	0	1	1	3	**5**
Graves	1	0	0	0	0	**1**
CHÂTEAUX	**5**	**14**	**14**	**10**	**18**	**61**

The Bordeaux Classification of 1855 grew from a request from Emperor Napoléon III to brokers from the wine industry to select the best wines to represent France at the International Exposition of 1855. The brokers ranked the top wines from the Médoc according to price, which at that time directly correlated to quality. The only amendment ever made to the 1855 system took place in 1973, when Château Mouton-Rothschild rose from Second Growth to First.

Bordeaux wines are almost always blends of Merlot, Cabernet Sauvignon, and Cabernet Franc. Merlot accounts for about 60 percent of the red grapes cultivated here. Cabernet Sauvignon covers roughly a quarter of the vineyard area, and Cabernet Franc 12 percent. The last 3 percent consists of Petit Verdot, Carménère, and Malbec, also used for blending.

Single-varietal wines dominate the international market, but red blends are growing in popularity again. A true Bordeaux wine can come from Bordeaux only, but in America and other countries the Meritage style (page 232) also uses only these grapes.

Even with this knowledge of regions, quality levels, and classifications, you might still wonder what really separates a $30 Bordeaux from one that costs $300. Primary considerations include where the grapes grew, the age of the vines, the yield of the vines, winemaking technique, and the vintage. Older vines usually produce better wine, and fewer grapes on the vines generally translate to higher-quality wine.

You'll need ten years minimum to age a great vintage of a great chateau wine. Down a step, you'll need at least five years to age a Cru Bourgeois from the Médoc or a second label wine from a great chateau. Store a regional wine for no more than two or three years, and drink an Appellation Bordeaux Contrôlée wine as soon as you buy it.

Look for a great vintage if you want a wine to put away for a long time. If you want a great wine to drink now, look for a lesser vintage. (For a comprehensive list of vintages, see Kevin's *Complete Wine Course*.) If you want a great wine from a great vintage, go to the lesser known chateaux, and always remember that Bordeaux wines are blends. If you prefer the Merlot style from St. Émilion or Pomerol, you can drink these sooner because Merlot has softer tannins. If you favor the Cabernet Sauvignon style from the Médoc or Graves, look for an older wine.

IN HIS OWN WORDS

"Wine is the symbiosis between man and his land. It is not made to be looked at through plexiglass; it is meant to be drunk and enjoyed. Much of Bordeaux has lost touch with that. We haven't."

—*Matthieu Guyon, proprietor, Domaines Rollan de By*

NEXT PAGES Vineyards at Lafite Monteil.

CHIANTI

(kee-AHN-tee)

IN THE GLASS

small Bordeaux glass, black cherry in color

TASTING PROFILE

ACIDITY

BODY

TANNIN

LOW   MEDIUM   HIGH

TASTING NOTES

CHERRY   PLUM   DRIED HERBS

Aromas include cherry, strawberry, fig, violet, leather, and Mediterranean herbs. Expect flavors of slightly tart cherry, strawberry, black plum, lavender, thyme, smoke, and leather. Chianti that spends significant time in oak barrels, especially Chianti Superiore and Chianti Classico Riserva, will exhibit additional flavors of vanilla and baking spices.

YOU SHOULD KNOW

The *Gallo Nero*, or "Black Rooster," is the symbol of Chianti Classico and always appears on bottles of Chianti Classico and Chianti Classico Riserva.

FOOD PAIRINGS

PIZZA   PASTA   CHEESE

Chianti and pizza are a great combination. The rich berry flavors and strong acidity pair wonderfully with cheese, so open a bottle with fondue or a grilled cheese sandwich. Chianti also holds a place of honor alongside traditional Italian-American dishes with red sauce, such as spaghetti and meatballs, lasagna, and eggplant Parmesan.

RECOMMENDED WINES

BARGAIN

KEVIN   Castello di Gabbiano Chianti Classico
Castello Banfi Chianti Classico

MIKE   Marchesi de'Frescobaldi Castiglioni

JEFF   Rocca delle Macie Chianti Classico Famiglia Zingarelli

VALUE

KEVIN   Rocca delle Macie Chianti Classico Riserva

MIKE   DaVinci Chianti Riserva
Tenuta di Arceno Chianti Classico Riserva

JEFF   Fonte Alla Selva Chianti Classico

SPECIAL OCCASION

KEVIN   Marchesi Antinori Badia a Passignano Chianti Classico Gran Selezione
Fontodi Vigna del Sorbo Chianti Classico Gran Selezione

MIKE   Castello di Verrazzano Sassello Chianti Classico Gran Selezione

JEFF   Brancaia Chianti Classico Riserva

SPLURGE

OUR PICKS   Isole e Olena Gran Selezione Chianti Classico
Volpaia Il Puro Gran Selezione Chianti Classico

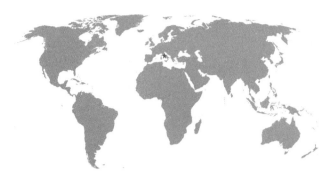

First things first: Chianti isn't a grape; it's a place—a beautiful place that lies in the heart of Tuscany. It contains mainly the Sangiovese grape, and a wine labeled Chianti must have at least 75 percent of this grape in the blend. The name Chianti dates back to the thirteenth century, when it referred to wine made from grapes grown in the Chianti Mountains between Florence and Siena, although researchers don't know which varieties winemakers used at the time. Baron Bettino Ricasoli receives credit for creating the first modern Chianti using Sangiovese in the 1870s. Since then, the boundaries of the Chianti zone have changed several times, and today the Chianti region includes seven subregions. The most important points to remember are that Chianti wine consists primarily of Sangiovese and comes from central Tuscany. With that as your starting point, you can explore the different styles and find the one you like the best.

Chianti can come only from the Chianti DOCG region, which has seven districts within it:

1. Rufina (east of Florence)
2. Montalbano (west of Florence)
3. Montespertoli (southwest of Florence)
4. Colli Pisane (west of Montespertoli)
5. Colli Fiorentini (south of Florence)
6. Colli Senesi (around Siena)
7. Colli Aretini (around Arezzo)

The Italian grapes Canaiolo Nero and Colorino traditionally go into a Chianti blend, but winemakers also can use Cabernet Sauvignon, Merlot, and Syrah.

Chianti has four quality levels, which differ based on growing areas, production and yield requirements, alcohol levels, and aging requirements. In increasing levels of quality, these are Chianti, Chianti Superiore, Chianti Classico, and Chianti Classico Riserva. Wine drinkers of a certain age may recall drinking Chianti poured from a straw-wrapped bottle while eating pizza, then placing a candle in the empty bottle's mouth and allowing the wax to drip down the sides. Most of us have come a long way since then, and so has Chianti.

Quality Levels

Here's how the different quality levels of the Chianti style vary:

CHIANTI

These wines offer the best value within the Chianti family.

* Grapes may come from anywhere within the Chianti region.
* Bottle must contain at least 70 percent Sangiovese.
* Other allowable grapes include Canaiolo Nero, Cabernet Sauvignon, Colorino, Merlot, and Syrah.
* Wines must age for at least three months.
* Minimum alcohol level is 11.5 percent.

CHIANTI SUPERIORE

This quality level distinguishes wines produced within the Chianti region that fall outside the historic growing area.

* Grapes may come from anywhere in the region except the Chianti Classico subregion.
* Wines must age for at least nine months. This additional oak influence imparts greater complexity.
* Minimum alcohol level is 12 percent.

CHIANTI CLASSICO

This region represents the historic heart of the growing area.

* All grapes must come from the Chianti Classico subregion.
* Wines must contain at least 80 percent Sangiovese but may contain 100 percent.
* The wine must age for seven months in oak barrels.
* Minimum alcohol level is 12 percent.
* The label will feature the Black Rooster.

CHIANTI CLASSICO RISERVA

These are the most complex wines in the family and can age the longest.

* Grapes may come only from the Chianti Classico subregion.
* Bottles must contain a minimum of 80 percent Sangiovese.
* Wines must age at least two years before release, including three months in the bottle.
* Minimum alcohol level is 12.5 percent.
* The label will feature the Black Rooster.

IN HER OWN WORDS

"The wines of Chianti for me are an icon of Tuscany and of Italy as well. This wine is a part of our beautiful country dating back to 300 years ago when Grand Duke Cosimo III de' Medici identified the four most highly prized territories of Tuscany for the production of wines."

—*Eleonora Marconi, winemaker, Castello di Nipozzano, Frescobaldi*

ABOVE The Chianti black rooster. **RIGHT** Vineyard in Chianti in Italy.

MERITAGE

(MEHR-it-ij)

IN THE GLASS

large Bordeaux glass, red violet to black cherry in color

TASTING PROFILE

	LOW	MEDIUM	HIGH
ACIDITY			
BODY			
TANNIN			

TASTING NOTES

BLACKBERRY   PLUM   CHOCOLATE

Aromas of raspberry, blueberry, and black cherry with notes of violet and flint will prepare your palate for flavors of blackberry, black plum, chocolate, and anise. Supple tannins and a lengthy, expressive finish hallmark a well-made Meritage wine.

YOU SHOULD KNOW

Meritage rhymes with heritage, and many American wineries reserve the designation for their finest wines, so some can cost quite a lot. That said, many fine Meritage wines won't break the bank, especially those from beyond Napa County.

FOOD PAIRINGS

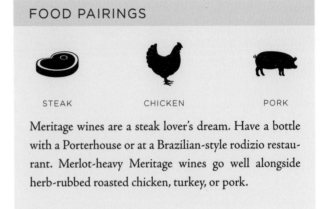

STEAK   CHICKEN   PORK

Meritage wines are a steak lover's dream. Have a bottle with a Porterhouse or at a Brazilian-style rodizio restaurant. Merlot-heavy Meritage wines go well alongside herb-rubbed roasted chicken, turkey, or pork.

RECOMMENDED WINES

BARGAIN

KEVIN Sterling Vintner's Collection, USA: California
MIKE Lock & Key, USA: California
JEFF Lyeth Red, USA: California

VALUE

KEVIN Estancia Estate Red Meritage Reserve, USA: California
MIKE Kunde Meritage 202, USA: California
JEFF Girard Artistry, USA: California
Lieb Meritage Red, USA: New York

SPECIAL OCCASION

KEVIN Napanook by Dominus, USA: California
MIKE St. Supery Elu Red, USA: California
Cosentino The Poet Red, USA: California
JEFF The Calling Our Tribute, USA: California

SPLURGE

KEVIN Joseph Phelps Insignia, USA: California
Opus One, USA: California
MIKE Bryant Family Vineyards Bettina, USA: California
JEFF Stonestreet Legacy Meritage Red, USA: California

OPPOSITE Sunset in Sonoma, California.

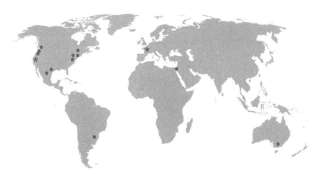

n 1988, a group of American winemakers led by Agustin Huneeus Sr., Mitch Cosentino, Julie Garvey, and David Stare created a new category of blended wines, choosing the name Meritage (merit + heritage) from a contest that fielded more than 6,000 entries. The term designates red or white wines made in America and several other countries using a blend of the classic Bordeaux grape varieties.

The primary varieties for red blends include Cabernet Sauvignon, Merlot, Cabernet Franc, Petit Verdot, and Malbec. Winemakers also may use Carménère, Gros Verdot, and St. Macaire. In blended wines, each variety brings something beautifully different to the final product. Merlot's soft tannins loosen the grip of Cabernet Sauvignon, making it more drinkable at an earlier age. Petit Verdot adds color, tannins, and florality. Malbec brings color and smoothness, while Cabernet Franc offers spice, black pepper, and a touch of earthiness.

Meritage wines must use at least two Bordeaux grapes but cannot contain more than 90 percent of any single variety. As in Bordeaux, Cabernet Sauvignon remains the dominant grape, but vintners are making quite a few Merlot-heavy blends. In America, any Meritage wine with more than 75 percent of a given variety can include that varietal name on the label. A wine with less than that amount of a single variety qualifies only as table wine, which doesn't do justice to the many fine wines that use more balanced amounts of multiple varieties. To feature the name "Meritage" on a label, a winery must belong to and pay a licensing fee to the Meritage Alliance, which has trademarked the word.

Despite the lingering misconception, not just California or America produces Meritage wines. New York, Oregon, Washington State, Virginia, Texas, and Pennsylvania also have a healthy group of Meritage producers, and the alliance includes more than 320 member wineries in 26 states and 6 other countries: Argentina, Australia, Canada, France, Israel, and Mexico.

Thanks to the growing popularity of premium red blends, particularly in America and China, demand for Meritage wines is increasing, which is great news for both producers and drinkers. You can drink these wines on release or age them for many years. They offer a complexity difficult to attain in single-varietal wines, especially in years in which a particular grape struggles to ripen fully. The blending process also allows the character of each variety to shine, offering the best possible expression of the vineyards and the art of winemaking.

PORT

(POHRT)

IN THE GLASS

Port glass, ruby to black cherry in color

TASTING PROFILE

ACIDITY			
BODY			
TANNIN			
	LOW	MEDIUM	HIGH

TASTING NOTES

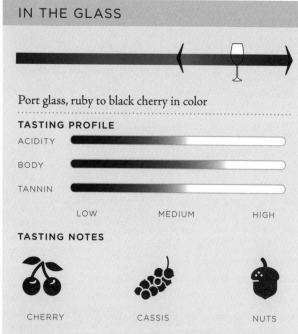

CHERRY	CASSIS	NUTS

RUBY: Aromas include blueberry, cherry, and cassis, and these Ports have great weight on the palate. They taste sweet with delicious notes of ripe red and black fruit.

TAWNY: These wines have nutty, oxidized aromas, especially toasted almond and hazelnut, as well as caramel, leather, and butterscotch. They taste sweet and have flavors of dried fruit, nuts, and caramel.

YOU SHOULD KNOW

Many winemakers around the world produce wine labeled "Port," but EU laws stipulate Portugal as the designated origin for Port and Porto wines. Portuguese vintners also make white and rosé Ports, many of which never leave the country, so try them if you visit.

FOOD PAIRINGS

CHEESE	NUTS	ICE CREAM

Classic pairings with Ruby Port include blue cheese, Époisses, and Stilton—the stinkier the better. Tawny Port wines pair perfectly with creamy desserts, such as cheesecake, crème brûlée, and flan.

RECOMMENDED WINES

BARGAIN
KEVIN Churchill's Finest Reserve
MIKE Niepoort Ruby
JEFF Fonseca NV Bin 27 Porto
      Croft NV Fine Ruby

VALUE
KEVIN Fonseca 10 Year Old Tawny
      Taylor Fladgate Late Bottled Vintage
MIKE W. & J. Graham's Late Bottled Vintage
JEFF Quinta do Passadouro Ruby Port Reserva

SPECIAL OCCASION
KEVIN Taylor Fladgate Porto Vintage Quinta de Vargellas
MIKE Quinta do Vesuvio Vintage
JEFF Quinta do Vale Meao Vintage

SPLURGE
KEVIN Quinta do Noval Vintage
MIKE Taylor Fladgate Scion 1855 Vintage Tawny
JEFF W. & J. Graham's NV 90 Year Old Tawny

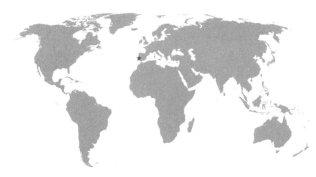

Port wine originated in Portugal, and the grapes used in the blending process grow in the Demarcated Region of the Douro in the Douro River Valley, one of the world's most beautiful wine regions. (UNESCO has named the terraced vineyards here a World Heritage Site.) The Port houses lining both sides of the Douro bear the names of British gentry: Taylor Fladgate, Symington, Churchill. These names denote the strong ties between Portugal and England, which have influenced the making of this fortified wine also known as Porto or vinho do Porto.

In 1662, King Charles II of England married Catherine of Braganza, the Portuguese infanta and sister of King Peter II of Portugal. She strongly supported the Treaty of Methuen, also called the Port Wine Treaty, which solidified military and trade alliances between the two countries. Several years prior, Charles had prohibited the importation of all French goods, including wine, into England, allowing Portugal to fill the void. The Treaty of Methuen abolished import taxes on English wool sold to Portugal, and it lowered taxes on Portuguese wines brought into England.

Because of the steep incline of the river valley, growers initially planted vineyards on narrow terraces. This terracing, combined with the Douro's many hairpin turns, adds to the region's unique beauty. After phylloxera decimated the area in the 1870s, broader, angled terraces became the norm. In the 1960s, bull-dozers carved wider and steeper terraces, or *patamares*, into the valley walls. Quinta do Bom Retiro receives credit for first using these *patamares*. Planting techniques improved again in the late 1970s when growers widely adopted the *vinha ao alto* system, which uses a perpendicular planting orientation.

Located just inland from the Atlantic Ocean in northern Portugal, the Douro River Valley consists of three separate areas: Baixo Corgo (Lower Corgo), in which about 15,000 farmers manage roughly 35,000 acres of vines; Cima Corgo (Upper Corgo), with around 16,000 farmers tending 50,000 vine acres; and Douro Superior (Upper Douro), where roughly 7,300 growers look after 25,000 acres of vines.

Of the more than 100,000 acres of vines, Portuguese law has authorized only 65,000 for the production of Port. Those vines must be at least five years old and must follow strict criteria, including geographic location, altitude, slope angle, exposure to sun, soil type, amount of stones, grape variety, vine density, vine age, vine training, and productivity. Growers train the vines close to the ground here and may not use trellises, which are popular in many other winegrowing regions.

The Montemuro and Marão mountains protect the Douro from Atlantic winds, leading to hot, dry summers and freezing cold winters. Rainfall is heaviest in December and January, and the vines in this region can extend their roots downward more than 25 feet in search of water.

Port wine consists primarily of five grape varieties:

TINTA CÃO, which means "red dog," adds bite. It has notable acidity, and strong tannins allow for decades of aging. This very low-yielding grape almost went extinct until experiments at the University of California at Davis and changes in vine training techniques saved it. Tinta Cão favors cooler areas of the Douro Valley and accounts for just 1 percent of the vineyards (about 1,000 acres). Aromas include wildflowers and red fruits. It tastes powerful, well rounded, and slightly acidic on the mid-palate and has a great deal of persistency in the back of the throat.

TINTA RORIZ, often called Aragones in southern Portugal, is genetically identical to Tempranillo grown in Spain. About 42,000 acres grow in the country, and it ranks as the second most planted variety in the Douro Valley. Aromas include dark fruits and freshly ground black pepper. Big, bold, and generous in the mouth, it has luscious fruit and spice flavors.

TOURIGA FRANCESA, also known as Touriga Franca, grows widely in the Douro as well, with 22,000 acres under vine. Aromas include red fruits, such as raspberry and strawberry, purple flowers, and Mediterranean herbs. It tastes juicy with firm but fine tannins.

TOURIGA NACIONAL grows on about 18,000 acres in Portugal. Aromas include rich dark fruits, such as blackberry and currant, as well as Earl Grey tea and candied violet. It is full-bodied and has good acidity. Its high tannins also add good aging potential to blends.

See the separate chapter on Touriga Nacional (page 196).

TINTA BARROCA covers roughly 11,000 acres in Portugal. Aromas include red and black fruits. Expect flavors of red cherry and blackberry.

Winemakers may use other red grape varieties: Bastardo, Cornifesto, Donzelinho, Malvasia, Mourisco Tinto, Periquita, Rufete, Tinta Amarela, Tinta da Barca, and Tinta Francisca—but in extremely small amounts. Portuguese law limits the yield per 2.5 acres to 16,500 pounds of grapes. Most producers striving for quality limit their yields even further, though, typically to just 9,000 pounds per 2.5 acres.

In winter months, workers prune vines by hand to coax the correct number of grape bunches to grow the following summer. Farmers who don't use herbicides weed at this time also. In February come fertilizer and replanting. In March, workers lay out the training wires and posts as well as graft new vines onto rootstock. April brings growth for both the vines and the surrounding grass, which prevents erosion but also must not compete with the vines. Flowering begins in May, followed by continuously hand-tying new growth to the wires. By June, clusters of hard, green berries are hiding under the thick, lush leaves. Workers cull the excess grapes—now the size of black-eyed peas—in July. Their color changes in a process known as *veraison*, which marks the beginning of ripening. Come August, the grapes have stopped growing, but they continue to ripen, increasing their sugars, tannins, acids, and pigments, all vital components for the final wine.

Mid to late September brings the harvest. Workers pick the grapes and place them in flat, shallow containers so as not to crush the skins prematurely. A gentle crush takes place in the winery before the grapes go into shallow granite tanks, or *lagares*. Villagers, migrant workers, winemakers, wine writers, college students, and field hands alike roll up their pants, wash their feet, and jump into the tanks to crush grapes to the sounds of accordions and drums. The smell of yeast and sweet grapes fills the air as the crushed grapes warm underfoot, marking the start of the fermentation process. That process can last as little as forty-eight hours, as opposed to the week or ten days it lasts for dry wines, but a high level of maceration during that short time must extract a great deal of flavor, color, and tannin from the grape skins. That's why wineries have used foot crushing for centuries; only recently has mechanization taken over to simulate this effect.

At the precise moment when the yeasts have converted half of the grapes' sugars into alcohol, the winemaker adds neutral brandy, or *aguardente*, to halt fermentation, giving Port its characteristic voluptuous sweetness.

Different varieties of grapes either coferment or become finished wines blended together to make the different styles of Port:

RUBY-STYLE PORTS include Ruby, Reserve, Late Bottled Vintage, and Vintage versions. Ruby—the youngest and most fruit-forward of the family—usually consists of blends of a few different vintages and age two or three years before bottling. Reserve Rubies come from premium grapes and generally age for three to five years. Late Bottled Vintage (LBV) Ports come from a single harvest year and age for four to six years before bottling. Vintners make Vintage Ports from the best wines from a single, exceptional harvest. They age in wood for approximately two years prior to bottling and will continue aging in the bottle for many more years. Vintage Ports come only from "declared" years. (Each producer declares a vintage year.) Enjoy Ruby and Reserve Ports while you wait for your LBV and Vintage Ports to age. All of them make excellent dessert wines and can accompany a variety of cuisines.

TAWNY PORTS have aged in either vats or barrels. They pick up their tawny color (yellowish brown) and oxidative character from time and wood. The four types of Tawny Port are Tawny, Tawny Reserve, Tawny with an age indication (10, 20, 30, 40 years old), and Colheita. Only Colheita must come from a single vintage, and it also must age in wood for at least seven years. The other three types may contain a blend of different vintages. Long barrel aging gives aged Tawnies remarkable complexity.

"Port is the ideal wine to accompany humorous conversations. There's nothing like sharing a bottle with friends around the table when you're finished with the business of eating. It's extraordinary how quickly the Port disappears when the jokes and witty banter get going!"

—*Rupert Symington, joint managing director, Symington Family Estates*

ABOVE Mechanical crusher at W. & J. Graham's winery in Portugal. **RIGHT** Barrels of W. & J. Graham's Six Grapes in Portugal. **NEXT PAGES** Vesuvio vineyards in Portugal.

RHÔNE VALLEY

(ROHN VAL-ee)

IN THE GLASS

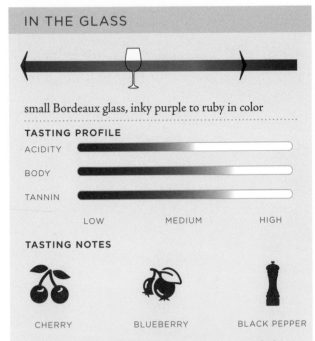

small Bordeaux glass, inky purple to ruby in color

TASTING PROFILE

ACIDITY

BODY

TANNIN

LOW · · · · · · MEDIUM · · · · · · HIGH

TASTING NOTES

CHERRY · · · · · BLUEBERRY · · · · · BLACK PEPPER

Aromas include blackberry and blueberry with hints of violet, black pepper, and spice. Flavors include black cherry, cassis, blueberry, vanilla, lavender, thyme, and black pepper. A lingering fruit sweetness in the finish counters the intense tannins and zesty acidity.

YOU SHOULD KNOW

Winemakers are using the traditional Rhône varietals to make delicious GSM (Grenache, Syrah, Mourvèdre) blends worldwide. Hotbeds for this style include California, especially Paso Robles, and Australia, particularly Barossa Valley, Clare Valley, and McLaren Vale. Excellent examples also come from Spain's Priorat region—home of Garnacha and Monastrell—and Washington State's Columbia Valley. These wines may appear on lists under the headings GSM or Rhône-Style Blends.

FOOD PAIRINGS

STEAK · · · · · · PORK · · · · · · CHEESE

Pair an easy-drinking Côtes du Rhône with dry-rubbed and grilled spareribs. Consider a Cornas or Côte-Rôtie with a porterhouse steak, topped with a little blue cheese. Enjoy the first glass of an Hermitage on its own and slowly, then pair it with a pot of French onion soup.

RECOMMENDED WINES

BARGAIN

KEVIN Domaine Saint-Nabor Côtes du Rhône Villages

MIKE Domaine des Pasquiers Côtes du Rhône

JEFF Jean-Luc Colombo Les Abeilles Côtes du Rhône

VALUE

KEVIN Domaine Roger Perrin Les Galet Château Cabrières

MIKE Lavau Châteauneuf-du-Pape
Tardieu-Laurent Guy Louis Côtes du Rhône

JEFF Château Pégau Cuvée Setier Côtes du Rhône Villages

SPECIAL OCCASION

KEVIN Domaine Bosquet des Papes

MIKE J. Vidal-Fleury Châteauneuf-du-Pape

JEFF Louis Bernard Châteauneuf-du-Pape
Domaine du Colombier Cuvée Gaby Crozes-Hermitage

SPLURGE

KEVIN Famille Perrin Château de Beaucastel Châteauneuf-du-Pape

MIKE Château La Nerthe Cuvée Cadettes Châteauneuf-du-Pape

JEFF Domaine Santa Duc Habemus Papam Châteauneuf-du-Pape

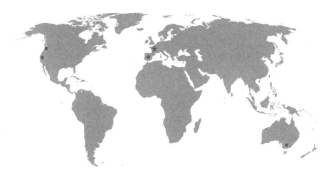

Grapes have grown on the steep slopes of the Rhône River since Greek and Roman times, but the region's modern winemaking history dates to the mid-seventeenth century. In 1737, wine barrels from this region bore the initials "CDR," indicating Côte du Rhône, specifically the right bank of the river. Some of the first rules of what has become the French AOC system began here. More than a century later, wines from the left bank received protected status under the same initials, which now abbreviate the plural Côtes du Rhône. The overall appellation received AOC status in 1937. Revisions followed in 1996 and 2001.

The Rhône Valley region consists of two major areas, the northern Rhône and the southern Rhône. Each has its own rules for production, but both have a hot climate featuring long hours of sunshine, which helps grapes develop more sugar, which in turn boosts alcohol levels. The rocky soil here retains the intense summer heat through the day and into the night. Vintners make rosé and white wines here, but 91 percent of Rhône Valley wine is red. The main red grapes of the region are Grenache and Syrah. Other grapes—used primarily for blending, although some producers make single-varietal versions—include Mourvèdre and Cinsaut.

The basic quality level is simply called Côtes du Rhône, and it accounts for 58 percent of the wine that comes from the region. The next levels up are Côtes du Rhône Village and Côtes du Rhône Crus. The most famous red wines from the northern region, all Syrah-based, include Hermitage, Crozes-Hermitage, Cornas, Côte-Rôtie, and St. Joseph. The most famous red wines from the southern region, both Grenache-based, are Châteauneuf-du-Pape and Gigondas.

Northern Rhône

These are the main red Crus:

HERMITAGE

Many wine critics consider these 345 acres near the village of Tain-l'Hermitage the pinnacle of Syrah. Vineyards here include L'Hermite, La Chapelle, Le Méal, Les Greffieux, Murets, and Les Bessards, and the majority face south. All-day sun transmits incredible power and flavor to the finished wines. Up to 15 percent of Marsanne and Roussanne, two white grapes, may go into a Syrah blend here. In addition to intense earthiness, Hermitage wines have acute minerality and a floral lift. Deep-seated tannins and vibrant acidity allow for long aging. These Syrahs are among the most expensive in the world.

CORNAS

This is one of the smallest appellations in the Rhône Valley, but its reputation stretches back to the tenth century. Celtic for "burned earth," Cornas has red-tinged rock and sandy soils that provide a nearly perfect environment for cultivating Syrah. These vineyards on the right bank of the Rhône almost exclusively grow Syrah vines, and any wine labeled "Cornas" must contain 100 percent of the variety. Strong tannins and fruit-of-the-wood flavors mingle on the palate with black olive and mocha. Traditionally these wines have long age-ability, but some producers are making a more fruit-forward style meant to be drunk on or shortly after release.

CÔTE-RÔTIE

The northernmost appellation in the Rhône Valley, Côte-Rôtie stretches through three counties on the right side of the Rhône: St. Syr sur Rhône, Ampuis, and Tupin-et-Semons. Riverside vineyards lie on steep, narrow terraces that range in altitude from about 600 feet to more than 1,000. Côte-Rôtie wines must contain at least 80 percent Syrah and may include up to 20 percent Viognier, a white grape, which softens Syrah's tannins and adds floral notes to the finished wine. Deep ruby in color, Côte-Rôtie wines proffer flavors of blackberry, raspberry, violet, and clove with a hint of leather.

ST. JOSEPH

Once known as Vin de Mauves, St. Joseph extends for thirty miles along the right bank of the Rhône. It reportedly ranked among Emperor Charlemagne's favorite wines, and Victor Hugo mentioned it in *Les Misérables*. The appellation name comes from an area vineyard owned by the Jesuit order in the seventeenth century, although formal AOC recognition didn't come until 1956. Many of the region's almost 3,000 acres bear old-vine Syrah plants up to a century old, and winemakers may blend Syrah with up to 10 percent Marsanne and Roussanne. These wines are among the most approachable and affordable in the northern Rhône. Their fruit-forward style centers on easy-drinking flavors of black plum and black cherry with smooth tannins and notes of black pepper and vanilla.

Southern Rhône

These are the main red Crus:

GIGONDAS

The name of this appellation has two possible origins: *gignit undas*, meaning "it springs from the waves," or the joyful name of St. Jucunda. A blend here may use up to 80 percent Grenache, and the balance must contain at least 15 percent Syrah and/or Mourvèdre and 10 percent maximum of the other Rhône varietals, excluding Carignan. Allowed varieties include Cinsaut, Clairette, Counoise, Picardan, and Terret Noir.

CHÂTEAUNEUF-DU-PAPE

This fanciful-sounding appellation takes its name from the palace where the Avignon popes resided during the fourteenth century. Baron Le Roy, owner of Château Fortia, created the concept of French AOC regulations here in 1923. Grenache accounts for about 75 percent of the vines that grow here, but winemakers may use twelve other varieties: Bourboulenc, Cinsaut, Clairette, Counoise, Mourvèdre, Muscardin, Picardan, Piquepoul, Roussanne, Syrah, Terret, and Vaccarèse.

For the last forty years, the red wines of Burgundy and Bordeaux have overshadowed those from the Rhône Valley. Today wines from all three regions stand on equal footing in terms of quality, but the best value proposition comes from the Rhône Valley. The region has had great weather for the last decade, which helped create terrific wines at a reasonable cost. Every thirteen seconds, someone in the world opens a bottle of Rhône Valley wine, and the top export market is America. Are you doing your part?

When choosing a Rhône Valley wine, determine whether you want a lighter style Côtes du Rhône or a bolder, more flavorful Hermitage or Châteauneuf-du-Pape. If you want to buy wine to cellar, know that Côtes du Rhône wines should age for no more than three years, Crozes-Hermitage and lower-priced Châteauneuf-du-Pape wines within five, and higher-priced Châteauneuf-du-Pape or those from excellent vintages for ten years or more. Hermitage wines age to perfection within eight years, but if they come from a great vintage you can cellar them for fifteen years or more. Many Hermitage wines still drink well even after fifty years!

OPPOSITE Vineyard in Pilat village in the northern Rhône Valley.

RIOJA

(ree-OH-hah)

IN THE GLASS

small Bordeaux glass, ruby in color

TASTING PROFILE

	LOW	MEDIUM	HIGH
ACIDITY			
BODY			
TANNIN			

TASTING NOTES

CHERRY

STRAWBERRY

POMEGRANATE

Typical aromas include black currant, dark plum, caramel, and chocolate-covered espresso bean. Expect flavors of black cherry and fruits of the wood along with juicier notes of strawberry and pomegranate and hints of cinnamon, star anise, aged leather, and pipe tobacco.

YOU SHOULD KNOW

Many of the coffee, spice, and vanilla elements of Rioja wine derive from oak aging. The Rioja regulation committee rules for labeling reliably indicate time in barrel and bottle prior to release. Worthy fresh and fruity versions of Tempranillo exist, but complexity and price increase with aging.

FOOD PAIRINGS

STEAK

PORK

PASTA

Drink Reserva or Gran Reserva with well-marbled cuts of steak, such as New York strip or Argentine-style ojo de bife. Rioja Crianza is terrific with a plate of jamón Serrano, salchichón, and Manchego. Riojas with less than a year of aging work well with roasted chicken or pork tenderloin.

RECOMMENDED WINES

BARGAIN
KEVIN Bodegas Campo Viejo Reserva
MIKE Bodegas Ontañón Crianza
Valserrano Crianza
JEFF Ramón Bilbao Reserva ➞

VALUE
KEVIN Ramelluri Granja Nuestra Señora
MIKE CVNE Viña Real Reserva
Bodegas Campo Viejo Gran Reserva
JEFF Faustino I Gran Reserva

SPECIAL OCCASION
KEVIN Bodegas Fernando Remirez de Ganuza
Reserva
MIKE Bodegas de Los Herederos Marqués
de Riscal Gran Reserva
JEFF Bodegas Lan Rioja Edición Limitada

SPLURGE
KEVIN CVNE Imperial Real de Asúa Reserva
MIKE Bodegas Roda Cirsion
JEFF Bodegas Muga Aro
Bodegas y Viñedos Artadi La Poza de Ballesteros

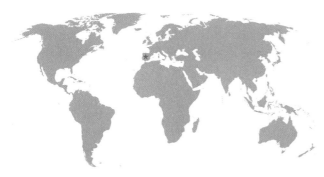

King Peter I of Navarre and Aragon gave the first formal acknowledgment of Rioja wine in 1102, and wine merchants were selling it across Europe by the thirteenth century. The region gained further renown in the late nineteenth century as phylloxera ravaged the vineyards of France. Rioja received DO status in 1926.

That's right: Rioja is a place, not a grape! The name has grown so tied to the style of wine made here that otherwise knowledgable wine drinkers sometimes confuse the region for its primary variety, Tempranillo (page 184), which Spaniards call Tinto Fino. The region has more than 63,000 acres of vineyards growing in three provinces: the majority in Rioja Province and the balance in the Basque provinces of Álava and Navarre. The region has three subregions: Rioja Alavesa and Rioja Alta, which enjoy a continental climate influenced by the Atlantic, and Rioja Baja, which has a warmer, drier Mediterranean climate.

DOCa rules also allow the making of Rioja wines from the Cariñena (Mazuelo), Maturana Tinta, Graciano, and Garnacha varieties, but wines here consist predominantly—typically at least 60 percent—of Tempranillo. A common blend looks like this: 85 percent Tempranillo, 10 percent Graciano, 5 percent Mazuelo. (A handful of producers releases single-varietal bottlings of Garnacha, Graciano, Mazuelo, and Tempranillo, but these are hard-to-find cult wines.)

Why all the fuss over blending? Think about chili: Different ingredients serve different functions. Tempranillo, the main ingredient, brings essential flavors, in this case black plum and cassis, along with age-ability. A moderate amount of Garnacha imparts color, alcohol, and backbone. Add a little Mazuelo for juicy fruit flavors and spice as well as a touch of Graciano for aroma and structure. Now the blend appeals irresistibly to both nose and palate.

The aging system—Crianza, Reserva, Gran Reserva—guarantees the time that a wine aged prior to release. Use these terms to determine the style you prefer, and stick with it. All wines from DOCa Rioja will have a "Rioja Trustseal" below the back label, authenticating the origin, vintage, aging, and quality category. Let's look at what each of these categories means.

RIOJA

Wine labeled "Joven" (meaning "young") in other regions here is simply Rioja. The front label will feature the word *cosecha*, meaning "harvest" or "vintage," followed by the year, without further designation. These wines have aged either completely in stainless steel or for a few months in oak. They generally release within a few months to one year after harvest. Expect bright acidity and full-on blackberry and cassis as well as other fresh fruit flavors.

CRIANZA

These wines age for two years, with at least one in barrel. If you like some oak in your wine but not a lot, this style hits that sweet spot. Soft notes of vanilla and toast join flavors of fruit and spice. Crianza wines offer great value.

RESERVA

Wines labeled Reserva age for three years, with at least one year in barrel and the remainder in the bottle. Those regulations represent minimum requirements, and many winemakers add barrel-aging time. Reserva wines usually come from grapes carefully selected from among the best plots, and some producers make them only in exceptional years. If you like oak, but not *too* much, try this style. This wine offers fruit flavors that retain all the brightness of youth along with caramel, spice, and coffee bean notes.

GRAN RESERVA

This style represents the pinnacle of winemaking in Rioja. These wines age for five years prior to sale, with a minimum of two years in barrel. Many producers extend that period beyond the minimum. Gran Reservas offer the most complex flavor profile of all Rioja wines: Stewed fruit flavors layer among notes of clove, baking spice, butterscotch, and truffle. Any well-made, well-stored Rioja will have vibrant acidity despite the lengthy aging process.

IN HIS OWN WORDS

"A Rioja wine can be enjoyed with many different meals, but I like it with paella. Some seafood, such as shrimp or mullet, is also very good with it. But a glass of old, mature Rioja after dinner, continuing the conversation on the sofa talking about life, travel with friends, is my favorite pairing."

—*Rodolfo Bastida, winemaker, Ramón Bilbao*

BELOW Faustino winery in Spain. **OPPOSITE** Vineyards at Faustino winery in Spain.

SUPER TUSCAN

(SOO-purr TUHS-kuhn)

IN THE GLASS

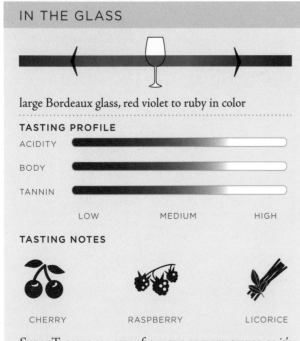

large Bordeaux glass, red violet to ruby in color

TASTING PROFILE

ACIDITY

BODY

TANNIN

LOW   MEDIUM   HIGH

TASTING NOTES

CHERRY   RASPBERRY   LICORICE

Super Tuscans can come from one or many grapes, so it's hard to give them a specific tasting profile. They all have a complex tannic structure to allow for lengthy aging, though, which makes them all quite powerful.

YOU SHOULD KNOW

When the Super Tuscan style first hit the market, many of the wines retailed for more than $100 per bottle. Many of the better-known wineries retained these prices, but you can find quite a few good bottles for less than $50. If you can wait, age them for a few years. If you can't wait and don't dislike the fruit-bomb style, decant the wine for a few hours before drinking.

FOOD PAIRINGS

STEAK   PASTA   CHEESE

Because these wines have high tannins and intense power, choose bold foods that will complement their robustness. Thick steaks on the grill always work, as do spicy tomato-sauced pastas and strong cheese.

RECOMMENDED WINES

BARGAIN

KEVIN   Santa Martina Toscana Rosso

MIKE   Ceralti Scire Bolgheri

JEFF   Tenuta Argentiera Poggio ai Ginepri

VALUE

KEVIN   Tenuta Sette Ponti Crognolo

MIKE   Brancaia Tre
Guado al Tasso Il Bruciato Bolgheri Superiore

JEFF   Arcanum Il Fauno di Arcanum
Le Macchiole Bolgheri

SPECIAL OCCASION

KEVIN   Castello Banfi Summus
Cabreo Il Borgo

MIKE   Castello Banfi Excelsus
Poggio al Tesoro Dedicato a Walter

JEFF   Brancaia Ilatraia
Rocca delle Macie Roccato Toscana IGT

SPLURGE

KEVIN   Luce della Vite Luce Toscana
Tenuta dell'Ornellaia Ornellaia

MIKE   Arcanum
Tenuta dell'Ornellaia Masseto

JEFF   Mazzei Siepi Toscana IGT
Tenuta San Guido Sassicaia Bolgheri Sassicaia

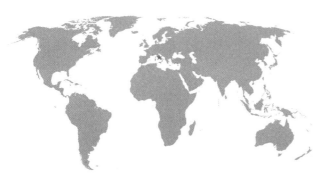

You can't tell an Italian what to do—but that's exactly what prompted a group of rogue Tuscan winemakers to take matters into their own hands. The "Super Tuscan" phenomenon started quite innocently, gaining momentum only gradually, taking several decades to achieve recognition and then notoriety.

In the mid 1940s, Marchese Mario Incisa della Rocchetta and his wife moved to a horse ranch in the town of Bolgheri on the Tuscan coast. He imported Cabernet Sauvignon vines from Bordeaux and planted his beloved Tenuta San Guido estate to make wine only for personal consumption. He aged his wine in small French oak barrels rather than the large wooden casks used in the rest of Tuscany. A few years later, a relative, Piero Antinori of the Chianti winemaking dynasty, persuaded the marchese to sell 250 cases of his wine commercially. Its individuality and quality made it an international hit. Around the same time, the Antinori family also decided to buck convention and eliminate the required white grapes from their Chianti blend. (Chianti laws allowed winemakers to use up to 30 percent Malvasia, a white grape, to soften the Sangiovese.) The Antinoris added 10 percent Cabernet Sauvignon and 5 percent Cabernet Franc to 85 percent Sangiovese, more or less establishing the now-classic Tignanello blend. But tempers flared.

Because of supply and demand, winemakers conforming to Chianti DOC regulations had to sell their wines for very low prices (some less than $10 per bottle) while unregulated but highly sought wines cost more than $100 per bottle on the open market. The conformists found this irritating—to put it *mildly*—so the Chianti DOC punished the rule-breakers, forcing their wines to bear the shameful name of *vino da tavola*, or table wine. This move made the nonconformists, dissatisfied with prevailing regulations, hot under the collar, so they marshaled their ingenuity and created the *indicazione*

geografica tipica (IGT) designation. This step helped set these new Chianti-style wines apart, but the key marketing development and the magic stroke of luck came with the all-important nickname, "Super Tuscan." The catch-all term can apply to a wine produced with aging in mind but made from either a single varietal or a blend.

A Super Tuscan doesn't have to be a blend, but most are, which is why it falls here in the Styles & Blends part of the book. Winemakers began using international varieties, eventually dropping the white grapes. Some even dropped Sangiovese from the blend. That's right, a Super Tuscan doesn't have to contain any Sangiovese! Some amazing Super Tuscans consist solely of Merlot—Tenuta dell'Ornellaia Toscana Masseto, for example. Some examples contain a blend of Cabernet Sauvignon, Merlot, and Syrah, while others consist of different percentages of completely different varieties.

Since the turbulent late 1960s and 1970s, Bolgheri, where all the agitation began, has restructured its percentages and aging requirements. A DOC Bolgheri wine can contain from no to all Cabernet Sauvignon, from no to all Merlot, from no to all Cabernet Franc, from no to half Syrah, from no to half Sangiovese, and less than 30 percent of "complementary" grapes defined by DOC Bolgheri's official website as "Petit Verdot, etc." To ensure quality, grape yield must fall below 9 tons per 2.5 acres, and the wine can't release until September 1 of the year following harvest. A DOC Bolgheri Superiore wine must meet all the same percentage requirements, but the maximum yield is more stringent (8 tons per 2.5 acres) and the wine must age at least two years, calculated from January 1 of the year following harvest, with at least one year in oak barrels.

IN HIS OWN WORDS

"It is interesting to discover wines that challenge the rules of their regions and create something new. The choice by wine producers to focus on something so innovative shows a lot of courage. It is equally interesting to see how the choice of different grapes in the blend is dictated by their potential to perform in the terroir."

—*Nicolò Incisa della Rocchetta, owner,*
Tenuta San Guido / Sassicaia

BELOW House at Tenuta San Guido in Italy.   **OPPOSITE** Wine cellar at Montalcino in Tuscany.   **NEXT PAGES** Vineyard at Arcanum estate in Tuscany in Italy.

ACKNOWLEDGMENTS

A book of this magnitude takes a village, a town, or even a small city to create. It's impossible to thank everyone who helped us on this journey, but we'll try.

First, we thank the president of Sterling Publishing, Theresa Thompson, for the opportunity to write this book and for her steady hand on the rudder in the turbulent sea of book publishing. We thank Marilyn Kretzer for her undying advocacy in bringing this book to the table and James Jayo for his excellent editorial skills and keeping the three of us in line and on time. We thank Igor Satanovsky for the beautiful cover design, Christine Heun for her deft skills in designing and laying out the book, Linda Liang for coordinating all of the artwork, and Katherine Furman and Margaret Moore for their eagle eyes in the copyediting process.

We can't thank Peter Miller, Jeff and Mike's literary manager, enough for his friendship and unwavering advocacy of author's rights. We also thank our three assistants, Michelle Woodruff, Judy Cohen, and Christina An.

Space constraints don't allow us to thank all of the people from each appellation, consejo, consorzio, grower's alliance, or importer who assisted us in our quest for information. Please know that we appreciate all of your help as we say danke, gracias, grazie, merci, and thank you.

Lastly but certainly not least, we thank our families and wine friends—you know who you are—for putting up with us as we wrote this book.

Now let's have a glass of wine!

—Kevin, Mike & Jeff

FURTHER READING

American Vintage by Paul Lukacs

American Wine by Jancis Robinson and Linda Murphy

The Art and Science of Wine by James Halliday and Hugh Johnson

Australian Wine Companion by James Halliday

Bordeaux by Oz Clarke

Bordeaux by Robert M. Parker Jr.

The Bordeaux Atlas and Encyclopedia of Chateaux by Hubrecht Duijker and Michael Broadbent

Bordeaux Legends by Jane Anson

Burgundy by Anthony Hanson

Burgundy by Robert M. Parker Jr.

Buyer's Guide to New Zealand Wines by Michael Cooper

The Complete Bordeaux by Stephen Brook

The Essential Wine Book by Oz Clarke

Exploring Wine by Steven Kolpan, Brian H. Smith, and Michael A. Weiss

The Far Side of Eden by James Conaway

The Finest Wines of Bordeaux by James Lawther

The Finest Wines of Rioja and Northwest Spain by Jesus Barquin, Luis Gutierrez, and Victor de la Serna

Food & Wine Pocket Guide

From Vines to Wine by Jeff Cox

The Gault Millau Guide to German Wines by Armin Diel and Joel Payne

Grands Vins by Clive Coates

Grapes & Wines by Oz Clarke

The Great Domaines of Burgundy by Remington Norman and Charles Taylor

Great Tastes Made Simple by Andrea Immer

Great Wine Made Simple by Andrea Immer Robinson

Hugh Johnson's Modern Encyclopedia of Wine

Hugh Johnson's Pocket Encyclopedia of Wine

The Illustrated Greek Wine Book by Nico Manessis

Italian Wine by Victor Hazan

Italian Wines for Dummies by Mary Ewing-Mulligan and Ed McCarthy

Making Sense of Burgundy by Matt Kramer

Making Sense of California Wine by Matt Kramer

Making Sense of Wine by Alan Young

The New and Classical Wines of Spain by Jeremy Watson

The New California Wine by Jon Bonné

The New Spain by John Radford

The Northwest Wine Guide by Andy Perdue

The Original Grand Crus of Burgundy by Charles Curtis

The Oxford Companion to the Wines of North America by Bruce Cass and Jancis Robinson

The Oxford Companion to Wines edited by Bruce Cass and Jancis Robinson

Oz Clarke's Pocket Wine Guide

Peñín Guide to Spanish Wine edited by José Peñín

Perfect Pairings and Daring Pairings by Evan Goldstein

Platter's South African Wine Guide

Pocket Guide to Wine Tasting by Michael Broadbent

The Port Companion by Godfrey Spence

The Simon & Schuster Pocket Guide to Italian Wines by Burton Anderson

The Ultimate Austrian Wine Guide by Peter Moser

Vino Italiano by Joseph Bastianich and David Lynch

Vintage Canada by Tony Aspler

Vintage Port by James Suckling

Vintage Timecharts by Jancis Robinson

The Vintner's Apprentice by Eric Miller

Washington Wines & Wineries by Paul Gregutt

The Wine Atlas of California and the Pacific Northwest by Bob Thompson

The Wine Atlas of Canada by Tony Aspler

Wine Atlas of Italy by Burton Anderson

The Wine Bible by Karen MacNeil

Wine for Dummies by Ed McCarthy and Mary Ewing-Mulligan

Wine Grapes by Jancis Robinson, Julia Harding, and José Vouillamoz

Wine Guide Hungary by Gabriella Rohaly and Gabor Meszaros

The Wine Lover's Guide to the Wine Country by Lori Lyn Narlock and Nancy Garfinkel

The Wine Project by Ron Irvine and Walter J. Clore

The Wines of Austria by Philipp Blom

The Wines of Burgundy and Côte d'Or by Clive Coates

The Wines of Chile by Peter Richards

The Wines of Greece by Konstantinos Lazarakis

Wines of the New South Africa by Tim James

Wines of the Pacific Northwest by Lisa Shara Hall

The Wines of the Rhône Valley by Robert M. Parker Jr.

The World Atlas of Wine by Hugh Johnson and Jancis Robinson

IMAGE CREDITS

WINE CHECKLIST

- ☐ Agiorgitiko
- ☐ Aglianico
- ☐ Alicante Bouschet
- ☐ Amarone
- ☐ Baco Noir
- ☐ Barbera
- ☐ Bikavér
- ☐ Blaufränkisch
- ☐ Boğazkere
- ☐ Bordeaux
- ☐ Cabernet Franc
- ☐ Cabernet Sauvignon
- ☐ Cariñena
- ☐ Carménère
- ☐ Chianti
- ☐ Cinsaut
- ☐ Dolcetto
- ☐ Fetească Neagră
- ☐ Gamay
- ☐ Garnacha
- ☐ Malbec
- ☐ Marselan
- ☐ Mavrud
- ☐ Meritage
- ☐ Merlot

- ☐ Mission
- ☐ Monastrell
- ☐ Montepulciano
- ☐ Nebbiolo
- ☐ Nero d'Avola
- ☐ Öküzgözü
- ☐ Petit Verdot
- ☐ Petite Sirah
- ☐ Pinot Noir
- ☐ Pinotage
- ☐ Plavac Mali
- ☐ Port
- ☐ Rhône Valley
- ☐ Rioja
- ☐ Sangiovese
- ☐ Saperavi
- ☐ Super Tuscan
- ☐ Syrah
- ☐ Tannat
- ☐ Tempranillo
- ☐ Teran
- ☐ Touriga Nacional
- ☐ Xinomavro
- ☐ Zinfandel
- ☐ Zweigelt

FOOD PAIRING INDEX

Olives
aging: caponata, 116
Mission, 102
Nero d'Avola, 116
Sangiovese, 150

Paella, Monastrell with, 104
Pasta
about: macaroni and cheese, 108; pasta puttanesca, 150; with red sauce, 202, 228; spaghetti Bolognese, 76, 220; Thai noodle dishes, 56; tortellini with ragu, 76
Aglianico, 6
Barbera, 14
Bordeaux, 220
Chianti, 228
Cinsault, 56
Dolcetto, 58
Malbec, 76
Marselan, 84
Montepulciano, 108
Nebbiolo, 110
Öküzgözü, 120
Rioja, 244
Sangiovese, 150
Super Tuscan, 248
Tempranillo, 184
Teran, 192
Zinfandel, 202
Pizza
Aglianico, 6
Barbera, 14
Chianti, 228
Dolcetto, 58
Malbec, 76
Marselan, 84
Montepulciano, 108
Teran, 192
Zinfandel, 202

Pork. *See also* Hams and prosciutto; Sausage
about: barbecue, 24; braised, 48, 218; chops, 122; deep-fried, 208; grilled, 86, 208; pulled sandwiches, 24; ribs. *See* Pork, ribs; roast, 10, 48, 232; tacos, 108; tenderloin, 244; teriyaki, 202
Alicante Bouschet, 10
Bikavér, 218
Cabernet Franc, 24
Cariñena, 48
Mavrud, 86
Meritage, 232
Mission, 102
Monastrell, 104
Montepulciano, 108
Petit Verdot, 122
Plavac Mali, 148
Rhône Valley, 240
Rioja, 244
Teran, 192
Xinomavro, 200
Zinfandel, 202
Zweigelt, 208
Pork, ribs
about: grilled, 184, 208
Cabernet Franc, 24
Monastrell, 104
Rhône Valley, 240
Tempranillo, 184
Zweigelt, 208
Poultry. *See* Chicken; Duck; Turkey

Ribs. *See* Pork, ribs
Risottos
Amarone, 212
Barbera, 14
Cabernet Sauvignon, 30
Nebbiolo, 110

Salads, Gamay with, 66
Salami. *See* Sausage
Salmon
about: grilled, 128
Nero d'Avola, 116
Pinot Noir, 128
Sandwiches, pork, Cabernet Franc with, 24. *See also* Gyros
Sausage
about: chorizo, 180, 196; spicy, 122, 180
Baco Noir, 12
Petit Verdot, 122
Saperavi, 160
Tannat, 180
Zweigelt, 208
Seafood. *See specific seafood*
Smoked foods
Cariñena, 48
Nebbiolo, 110
Öküzgözü, 120
Soups and stews
about: Hungarian goulash, 86, 218
Baco Noir, 12
Bikavér, 218
Blaufränkisch, 20
Boğazkere, 22
Cabernet Franc, 24
Fetească Neagră, 64
Garnacha, 70
Mavrud, 86
Saperavi, 160
Spaghetti. *See* Pasta
Steak. *See* Beef, steak
Stews. *See* Soups and stews

Tacos
Merlot, 88
Montepulciano, 108
Tapas, Mission with, 102
Tex-Mex chili. *See* Chili
Thai curries, Garnacha with, 70

Thai noodle dishes, Cinsault with, 56
Tomatoes (sauces and tomato-based dishes)
about: bruschetta, 116
Nero d'Avola, 116
Öküzgözü, 120
Super Tuscan, 248
Teran, 192
Touriga Nacional, 196
Truffles
Amarone, 212
Barbera, 14
Nebbiolo, 110
Tuna
about: grilled, 116
Cabernet Sauvignon, 30
Nero d'Avola, 116
Pinot Noir, 128
Turkey
Meritage, 232
Öküzgözü, 120

Veal
about: braised, 218; chop smothered in mushrooms, 110; grilled, 56; veal parmigiana, 14; veal piccata, 150
Barbera, 14
Cinsault, 56
Nebbiolo, 110
Petit Verdot, 122
roast, 122
Sangiovese, 150
Xinomavro, 200
Veal, grilled
Vegetables. *See* Grilled vegetables
Vegetarian bean dishes, Touriga Nacional with, 196
Venison
Amarone, 212
Tannat, 180

Wiener schnitzel, Zweigelt with, 208

GENERAL INDEX